MW01096930

"We're The Police"

Stories Of An NYPD Patrolman
Volume One

Written by
Tony DellaValle

Library of Congress Control Number: 2014914743

CreateSpace Independent Publishing Platform, North Charleston, SC

To my wife Karen, for enduring years of endless nights of overtime, missed family events and excessive worry for my safety and well being. Through your strength, you enabled me to compile these stories and enjoy a career in what I truly feel is the world's greatest profession. Thank you for being there for me, my success starts with you.

Table Of Contents

The following stories have been recalled from the author's memory of true events that have occurred in his career. While this is a non-fiction book and the author has tried to represent the stories as they have originally occurred, it is important to note that some of these stories have occurred more than twenty years ago. There is no intent to misrepresent any person or occurrence in this book and any change from the actual occurrence of the original event or person(s) involved in these events is accidental and without malice. All details, dialogues and facts contained in this book are to the best of the author's memories and while it may be impossible to recount events exactly as they have happened, given the time that has passed between these events, the author believes the essence of these events to be both true and accurate.

Author's Note

I suppose people pick the title of their book for all kinds of reasons. Along with my book tittle, I have chosen to title each individual short story in my book as well. You will see that the names of the individual stories don't necessarily tell what is to follow. Sometimes, the name or phrase I chose is just the way I remember that particular occurrence or what triggers my memory so that I am able to recall it. You have to remember that some of these stories happened over twenty years ago.

The title, "We're The Police", actually came from a phrase that I have heard a Captain use countless times. He was assigned to our division and was working in the NYPD at the same time that the majority of the following stories occurred. His name was Captain Terrence Tunnock and the phrase, "We're The Police", was one of the things that I always remembered about him. To me, that phrase also seemed to sum up the job of a police officer as well. So, for me, it seemed like a perfect title.

The job of a police officer is a complex one. It varies wide, as wide as one can imagine and then further than that. To be a good cop you really had to excel in many tasks, very often handling things the common person would walk away from or avoid all together. When you heard Captain Tunnock utter those words, "We're The Police", it was usually in response to just that sort of situation. The truth of the matter is that it was these instances where the degree of difficulty was raised. These were the tasks that were not easy and very often of a sensitive nature. At the very least they were unpopular or made the general public uneasy. It was in these circumstances that we, and by we I mean, of course, with Captain Tunnock by our side, would respond to the masses, "We're The Police." This phrase was used in the same way a parent would tell a child, "Because I said so, that's why." In our case it would be said because, "We're The Police", and thats why! End of story!

This phrase was a definitive stand and an inevitable completion to a job. After those words were spoken, the situation was handled. Outcome liked or not, the job was complete. We did our job. The phrase was not meant to make friends or massage egos. This phrase and the work that developed as a result helped me to understand, even as a rookie, why not everyone liked the police but everyone loves a fireman. Fireman don't make arrests, use force on people or take away their freedom. "We're The Police", we have to do these things. This is part of the job, it is expected. This term was to an extent the thinking behind my book. I wanted to show people just how diverse our job is. How wide it ranges, how strange it can get. How it can go from boring, to comical, to down right unbelievable over the course of a few days or even in an instant. In the end, the phrase is truly appropriate to our work. "We're The Police", we have to handle the job that's in front of us at that moment. To take it for what it's worth, deal with it and then file it away in your own little compartment to either forget about it or draw off it for a future job. While the phrase may seem one-sided with power and benefit slanted solely to the police, in reality it has two edges. The phrase also reminds us, the police, that just as we may have the last word and the inevitable conclusion to a situation, we also can not just walk away from a job like an ordinary citizen if it is unpleasant or challenging. "We're The Police", it's our job, our responsibility.

The stories you will read in this book are written just as I perceived my career. They are a series of jobs with a beginning and an end. Some end quick, some were a little longer but they all inevitably came to an end. Whether it's human nature or by desire, a cop needs to forget about these completed jobs and go on to the next. At least temporarily we need to not take our work home but as the saying goes, "Leave it in your locker", in the hope that it does not affect your home life. This is done to keep the home and the work worlds separate and hopefully your life intact. In the end, the hope of every cop is to come out of the job with a pension and your health. I always looked at the pension a police officer gets as a winning lottery ticket. To win this lottery, you need to do your twenty years and in return the Department pays you a pension for the rest of your life. So, all you need to do is navigate through those years and come out the other side to collect that prize. Sounds easy, doesn't it? It isn't, and in this world not everyone wins that lottery.

Unfortunately, this was the other reason why Captain Tunnock was a source of inspiration for my book. There wasn't a personal connection between us. I didn't know the man in that manner. From all accounts about him from his peers, I have to say I wasn't lucky enough to say I was a friend. I only knew him professionally. I watched him work on countless occasions and admired him for the work he did on the job. The depth of his police knowledge and experience and how he seemed to be extremely well liked and respected by his peers, both bosses and police officers alike both admired and looked to him for guidance. How he went about his job was a marvel to watch and on the occasions when I heard him utter that phrase,

"We're The Police", it reassured us that this job was over. It brought closure to that moment. It was complete and we can move on to the next one.

I know I used the word "unfortunately" earlier in this paragraph when speaking of Captain Tunnock's career. I also mentioned how not all cops come out the other end of their career winning that lottery. They don't all get a pension or retain their health. The deal is not as easy as it sounds and this job can take it's toll on a person. However, "We're The Police", we have to accept what comes with the job. Not everything happens as we want, we have to take the good with the bad. We can't just walk away at the first sign of something unpleasant. Captain Tunnock didn't deserve what happened to him, his family didn't deserve it either. "We're The Police", these things shouldn't happen to us but they do. Captain Tunnock took his life and there is no easy way to break that news. There is no way to sugarcoat that reality. If you research the event you can find out all the particulars surrounding his suicide. The story will tell all the speculation and rumors that surround the case. All the inner politics and turmoil within the NYPD at that time. All the truth the investigating parties will let you know. All that doesn't really matter. What really matters is the reality of the incident and the outcome. Captain Tunnock was a police officer, a protector and a good man and now he is dead. In the end, after helping countless people, he couldn't even help himself. "We're The Police", we should be able to handle this too. Like I said earlier, all stories come to an end. Some good, some bad, but they all inevitably end.

Introduction

Did you ever notice how many movies or television shows, both fiction and reality, are based on cop's lives and the work they do? Not only does the frequency of these shows seem to be higher but they also seem to be among the longest running shows as well.

Ask a little child what he or she wants to be when they grow up and very often the response is, "I want to be a police officer!" The allure of being a police officer is almost forced upon us as young children and grows as we become adults. Symbols and signs of police officers and the work we do is seen everywhere throughout our daily lives, our schooling and our work. There is a definite affinity for the life of a cop in today's world.

Yet, as amazing as it is that so many people are enamored with the life and stories of a police officer, there are many people who equally despise the police and what they stand for. The one common ground between the two diverse groups may still be the interest level both groups hold in the work we do and the lives we lead.

Police work is a hard job. Unlike the entertainment world, it is not always glamorous and it doesn't always appeal to everyone in a positive way. Everyone loves a fireman because a fireman does no wrong in the eye of the public. No one objects to putting out fires, it is always a good thing. Police officers don't have that luxury. We have to arrest people and do things that aren't always popular, appealing to the public or pleasant to hear about. Taking a person's freedom or their life is not as the movies portray it. That officer is not a "star" and doesn't just walk away and continue to work like nothing ever happened after a serious event has occurred.

Yet, regardless of the circumstance, be it good, bad or otherwise, police work is a unique profession. To some people hearing about police work is more of an escape from reality than what it actually is. The following stories are a good mix of what police work is actually like. It is not all glory and it is not always exciting or something you want to repeat. However, I feel it is a great representation of the ups and downs we go through as police officers and shows the realistic side as well as the variations of jobs we handle on a daily basis.

You may not like all the stories that follow but I don't think you will dislike them all either. Just like on a television show some episodes seem better than others or may appeal to one person's particular taste, while perhaps getting the opposite effect from another person from that very same episode. Keep that in mind as you read my book and my hope is that you will find those stories that appeal to you, entertain you or educate you as you read a realistic collection of writing that shows the work of a police officer.

1. Don't Shit Where You Eat

When I was a rookie cop there were not a lot of Asian police officers on the job. It was rare to have one in your precinct and there was always a need for them as translators down in Chinatown or other areas of Asian population. Chinatown in NYC is a heavily populated place, filled with hundreds of businesses of all types. All this is crammed into a relatively small space. While this area is unique in the amount of trade that can occur on a daily basis, it still has the same laws as everywhere else in NYC. Needless to say that along with the hustle and bustle of the area goes the crime attached to it, just like anywhere else in the city. The only difference being that crime here seemed to be in a concentrated form.

When I was a rookie, it seemed that most of the Asians on the job were assigned to work in areas that were populated by Asians. This was purposely done out of necessity for the area and the needs of its population. While using manpower in this way made sense, it still didn't amount to the number of cops the department needed to handle the crimes and service calls of that area. You could imagine the frustration of working in an area where you constantly need another cop, or have to rely on a by-passer to translate for you. It was totally possible if it was a late shift or a holiday that you could actually have a tour of duty where not enough Asian cops were working when needed to handle a job requiring translation of that particular language or dialect. Everyday run of the mill jobs can be usually handled by using the citizens around you to get the story but for real important stuff, like investigations, you really feel more comfortable using a cop. If the local precinct didn't have an Asian cop to handle the translation, the Department would borrow a cop from another precinct to translate and to help out with the investigation.

I worked uptown in Harlem and we had an Asian cop assigned there. He was a Sergeant and he actually lived in Chinatown. The department had a rule that you could not live where you worked. This was done to avoid conflicts of interest and possible corruption. So, the Sergeant could not be assigned to Chinatown and he wound up in Harlem. Supposedly, not only did he live in Chinatown but he owned a good deal of real estate there as well. For him, working in Harlem was great. He could do his job without seeing or coming into contact with any people he lived near while he worked. He seemed happy enough with the arrangement and he was a pretty good boss. Most of the cops never seemed to have any serious problems with him.

While all areas of the city have varying degrees of the same crimes, some areas do have some criminal activities or a way of life that may be unique to that area. In Chinatown there was always a black market, sweat shops and phony or stolen merchandise. If you walked the streets where the bulk of the businesses were, that element was very evident. Tourists flocked to Chinatown and the small shops and street vendors made a lot of money engaging in business with them, both legal and illegal. This type of activity naturally breeds mob or gang mentality and the crimes associated with it. This was probably the reason the Sergeant liked to keep his job out of the area. You can see how working in the area where he lived and owned property could cause him some great conflicts and maybe even jeopardize his career, his safety or the safety of people he knew. The old adage is, "you don't shit where you eat" and that makes sense no matter who you are or where you live or work.

The Sarge was a little guy but he had a big accent. At times it was extremely hard to understand him and of course the cops goofed on him whenever they could. The Sarge didn't help matters either by killing the English language and some well known phrases as he went along. He would often say things like, "You know, shit roll downtown" or "Sometimes you gotta bite a bear and sometimes the bullet bite you". It was hysterical.

One day on the late tour a call came through on the switchboard. The call came from the precinct that covers Chinatown and they said they had a possible gang style, robbery, shooting. Supposedly they had a suspect who seemed to not only be involved in the crime but was part of the underworld shit that went on down there. They even felt he might possibly be a major player in the ranks of these types of people. Needless to say, they told our precinct to get the sarge down there as soon as possible. They needed a translator and felt that this suspect could give some real good information on the area, other criminals and anything else that could help on things going on in Chinatown. Geographically, Chinatown is anywhere from 5 to 10 miles away from Harlem. On the midnight tour, in a police car that does not have to worry about speed limits and lights, you could probably get down there in 10 to 15 minutes or less. We were told later that it took the sarge about two hours before he showed up at the local precinct, where the detectives and all the top brass were waiting for him to start interrogating this perp. Needless to say, the bosses were pissed off. Due to time constraints, the bosses quickly cooled themselves off and united the perp with his soon to be translator.

The following story was related to us from investigators who were in the room and have no reason to make it up. If you know the Sarge and all the particulars surrounding the incident and the Sergeant's life, the obvious conclusion is that this story is absolutely one hundred percent true. All the parties involved are settling in. The investigators, top brass, the Sarge and the perp are all in their places, getting ready to begin. The lead investigator, probably over anxious at this point to get going, says to the Sarge, "Sarge, ask him his name". The Sarge turns to the suspect and says in his usual heavy, thick Chinese accent, "Wots a you nim?" I guess they were trying to give the Sarge the benefit of doubt, or maybe just in shock that he asked the perp the question in broken English. In any case, the chief quickly says, "No, no, Sarge...in Chinese, ask him his name in Chinese". To which the Sarge responded, "Chi-nese, I don spik a chi-nese". We were told the room went silent and after the last person in the room was able to pick their jaw off the floor, the Chief cursed the Sarge, the perp, his wife and anything else he could think of and stormed out of the room. Supposedly, the last thing the Chief said before he stormed out of that room was, "He doesn't speak Chinese, he barely speaks fucking English". The Chief was pulled to the side and explained why the Sarge was reluctant to translate, or even get involved at all. We were told the Chief didn't like it but he had to understand it and accept it as well.

The Sarge was already working in what the Department called a "dumping ground", so they just sent him back to his precinct. The Sarge got what he wanted. He got to go back to Harlem without helping to prosecute a possible gang member from his own neighborhood. I cant say I fault the guy. I went through my entire career without seeing anyone at work from the neighborhood I lived in. Believe me, it's nice to not have any friends or relatives working or living in your precinct, to put you in a possible awkward position. In the end, the Sarge may not have done the right thing in the eyes of the department but he definitely did the right thing for his own personal life and sometimes that matters most.

2. An "EDP" Radio Call

I was working steady midnight tours and although I only had a few years on the job, the midnights was mostly made up of old timers. These guys were great. You could learn a great deal about the job just by watching them work. If you were lucky enough to work with one, you could really learn how to be a cop.

Along with all their experience, these guys were also huge practical jokers and loved to goof on other people. If you fucked up or something strange or funny happened to you, they made sure you knew about it along with the rest of the precinct as well.

It was about 5 AM and my partner and I were just rolling around the streets, listening to the radio. A call comes over the radio for an EDP (emotionally disturbed person). We were actually the backup unit but we got to the location at the same time as the sector that was assigned the job. The job came over as a non-violent EDP but that really didn't matter because the manpower was thin on the late tour and on the job in general, during this time period. To make a long story short, it was the four of us against whatever was going on inside whether it was good, bad or otherwise.

The four of us walk in and head up the stairs. Everything in the precinct is either a walk up or a project with an elevator that is either broke or smells like piss. Every time we got in an elevator, my partner use to joke and say, "The hepatitis is so thick in here, you can cut it with a knife". All things considered, the walk up was the more preferable option.

We get to the floor the job is on and were greeted by the family of the EDP who states what most of the EDP calls state. They tell us the all too familiar story of another EDP who didn't take his/her medication and is talking funny and acting like a nut. Okay, so we head into the apartment and go to the room where the EDP is supposed to be. The EDP is in the bedroom and while he isn't huge, he is not little either.

One thing I should mention about EDP's is their occasional ability to be very strong for their apparent size. Sometimes, they have what cops coldly refer to as "retard strength". Sometimes, they don't even feel pain the same way a normal person does. You might get a small guy, or even a girl, who will be able to push off a few cops and it will take several more to cuff or restrain them in any way. They could get physically hurt and still continue to be combative as well.

Looking at the EDP, you can see he is obviously bugging out and has a sort of paranoid look on his face. He also doesn't seem to be able to or want to communicate with us and is not responding to any questions the other cops are asking him. He kept swinging his head back and forth and looking behind him every so often. He is in a half crouch and standing by the head of the bed. We are by the door and there are no windows, so he is blocked in with nowhere to go. The usual nods and signals are made between the four of us and we are all slowly shifting into position. We all know that while this guy is not doing anything right now, based on the info from the family, he has to go the hospital to get back on his medication. If not, he will definitely be a problem for someone or himself in the near future. It is also apparent to us that because he is not communicative and is unwilling to move from his location by request, we are going to have to force him to come along.

As I said, we were the backup unit. The sector that was assigned the job makes the call on how they want to handle this. It has to be that way because whatever follows is going to be theirs to handle, so the decision is rightfully theirs. If he goes to the psych ward they will babysit him. If he gets hurt, they will have to take him to the hospital. It's their job to handle the situation as they see best. From all indications of signals, nods and eye contact, it is apparent this guy is going for a ride in the "rubber bus" to the psych ward and that it will be a forceful take down. It is apparent the other unit has decided on a sneak attack, jumping him by surprise and taking him down. All at once, the four of us converge on the EDP. I guess this guy had a crash course on secret police eye signals because I swear he jumped at the same time as us moving in on him. What transpired next must have looked like a dolphin show with bodies flipping and twisting in all directions, landing on the bed tangled up in a series of arm and hand locks. At one point, the wrestling match was so confusing that one of the cops was grabbing my arm and not the EDP's. Finally the EDP gets pinned face down on the bed, his arms sort of free but not able to do anything because of the four cops holding him in place. The initial unit was in charge so that meant everything, including the radio transmissions for ordering a bus as well. In the midst of trying to secure this EDP one of the lead officers dropped his radio in order to secure a loose limb, which he was still holding onto with both hands. Unknown to us, the EDP picks up the radio which apparently was on the bed right next to him. He keys the microphone and begins to scream at the top of his lungs right into the radio, "Help me, they're kicking my ass". We weren't kicking his ass but just holding him in place. That didn't really matter because to Central and the rest of the midnight platoon on our division, they hear what sounds like a cop screaming for help. It was not immediately evident to us that he had the radio. We thought he was just screaming for help. All of a sudden you could hear one of the cops say, "Hey, give me that, he got my radio". Now we know the whole platoon is going to come storming over to our location to help what they believe is a 10-13. No sooner as that thought left my mind, you could hear all the radio chatter of Central trying to find out who it is and all the units on the move. They were already heading our way because we were the only ones out on an EDP. We also couldn't respond when they called us to check our status because the nut still has the radio and is intermittently keying the mic which is jamming our transmissions which is probably making the situation seem like a real emergency. The race was on to get that radio out of his hands while still holding him secure and set the record straight on the radio before a cop gets hurt racing over for no reason. Again, we start fumbling around on the bed pulling arms and hands and I'm pretty sure for a second time a cop pulled my arms again thinking I was the EDP. Finally, we get the guy to drop the radio and cuff his hands behind his back. As we are calling over the radio to say everything was okay, we could hear what sounds like a small army storming up the stairs. The EDP was sent to psych and thank God no one got hurt but we all knew the ribbing we would get for this would last for years to come.

Months later, we would be down at court walking in the hall or standing on a foot post at a parade detail and you would hear someone yell, "Help, they're kicking my ass", followed by laughter. Eventually, the laughter becomes your own.

3. First Time Caller, Long Time Listener

My partner was on vacation. When your partner is off, on vacation or out for any reason, you get stuck with all the loose ends that either have no partner or no one wants to work with. Sometimes it's good, sometimes it's bad. If you have some time on like I did, you get "volun-told" to take out a rookie on a guided tour of the streets and show him the job. Well, all that fell into place one day and I got a rookie to take out. Except this was no ordinary rookie. This was like the rookie from misfit island. He fell into the "nobody wanted to work with him" category. He was a young kid, rail thin and a self proclaimed vegetarian. He didn't look a healthy thin either. He was sort of sickly looking with no muscle tone at all. Honestly, he looked like a skeleton with hair. The story on him was that he was known for falling asleep at the drop of a hat, anywhere, at anytime. The kid really looked undernourished and if you spoke with him you really felt his brain matter was being deprived the food he needed to function correctly. I think when he fell asleep, it was because his body was out of gas and was shutting down. It wasn't just me who felt that way. The whole precinct felt he was far from being the sharpest tool in the shed and cops generally avoided working with him. Even the boss who told me to take him out had this grin on his face like he knew he was fucking me over by putting me with him. The boss also knew the kind of cop I was and that I wouldn't cry over it like other cops would.

Resigned to the fact that I was taking this kid out, I also knew there was no fucking way that he was going to drive. I could just imagine him falling asleep at a red light or as we slowly cruised down the street. This means he rides shotgun and becomes what we call the "recorder". Along with other duties, the recorder is the cop in the car who handles the radio.

I have only seen a few people in my entire career kill a radio transmission like he did. I mean he was awful. Wrong radio codes, inconsistent speech, long pauses between transmissions, wrong addresses and keying the mic at the wrong times. Truly painful to watch and hear. You could hear the frustration on the other end from dispatcher as well. Along with that, were the comments from other cops on the air as well. Finally we both had enough so I told him to listen to me handle the radio for a while. I figured if he heard it being done correctly long enough, he would be able to take over again before the day was over. I modeled several radio transmissions for him and explained in between calls the reason behind each transmission. I told him why things are done in a certain manner and gave him great examples of how the radio should sound. I did this for most of the tour until we got to our scheduled meal break. I felt like I had really put in maximum effort to help the kid be better on the radio.

I pulled the car into the rear of the precinct so we could take our meal break. Protocol is that you transmit over the air to dispatch for your meal break. This will officially sign you off the radio for an hour and lets the dispatcher know where you will be in case they need you. The minute we parked the rookie began telling me how much he wanted to handle this transmission. He felt he had heard enough examples and was now ready to handle the radio, as he put it, like a "veteran". So I said, "Okay kid, go ahead and put us out for meal". The kid picks up the radio and with a cocky grin on his face says;

Rookie: "28 Adam to central".

Dispatch: "28 Adam, go ahead".

Rookie: "Show us 63 at the house".

Dispatch: "10-4 Adam, time out 63 is 13:07 hours, enjoy".

With the biggest grin stretching from ear to ear the rookie turns to me and says with his chest puffed out, "How was that? Perfect, huh?".

To which I replied, "That was great kid but we're not 28 Adam, we're 28 Henry". His smile vanished and turned to a frown in an instant. All I could do was laugh and tell him not to give up.

4. Harlem Sunrise

I was a rookie cop assigned to an older cop as his partner for the tour. This cop really looked the part of an old time cop from days past. He was just like the old stereotype of a typical cop from when I grew up. He was the way I remembered the police officers in my neighborhood as a kid. He was a big burly Irish cop, with a red nose and the reputation that accompanies one. It was not uncommon for him to come in slightly drunk or even as cops would say, "three sheets to the wind". Most times though, he would just be hung over from the weekend festivities. The incredible thing about this cop, was that no matter what shape he was in, he was a great guy. Everybody liked him and I was also at the top of his fan list. He was street smart and tough as nails and full of good old police experience. I didn't think there was a job that he couldn't handle. He was especially good at handling physical problems and would never shy away from a confrontation. Still, he was a great guy and fun to be around. He was no problem unless you were a perp, skell or just someone causing his headache to get worse. In that case, if you were one of those types, then you were headed for serious trouble and the wrath of an old time Irish cop.

It was a day tour and we hit the streets at about 7:30am. While that might seem early to some people, it was late for this cop because he was just getting in from an "all-nighter". He had a slight odor of booze, red faced and all he wanted was to sit quietly and go home at the end of the shift with as little interruption as possible. He let me drive (proof that he was fucked up-I only had a year on the job) and the first job right out of the station house was a noise call. Immediately I'm thinking, "Great, the one thing he probably wants least of all-noise." This was no way to start our day.

We pull up to the location and a slimy looking female crackhead is having a three story argument from the front sidewalk with some loser she considers her boyfriend. The argument was about absolute bullshit. This was a Sunday, and in between her and the three floors she was yelling to were people who were trying to sleep. Those were the people who were now calling in the noise complaint. The thing about noise complaints is that until you fix the problem and get rid of the noise, they will keep calling it in over and over. If enough calls come over for the same location, the boss will eventually show up to see what's going on and why it's not being handled. My partner definitely didn't want that.

We get out of the car, and to his credit, he didn't immediately blow his top like I fully expected him to. Instead, he tried to reason with the crackhead as best he could. He then took a deep breath and let me take a crack at handling it. It's hard enough trying to talk sense into someone who is that heated to begin with. Add the effects of crack and you might as well try to talk to the wall. I always said that I wished everyone could experience some of the less glorifying, all too often jobs we handle. I think the public might appreciate us a little more.

A few minutes into my attempt, it obviously appeared that this was going nowhere fast. Interrupting, the veteran cop says in a loud nasty tone, "Dear, shut the fuck up, this is bullshit and it's over and if I have to come back here again for this, it's your ass motherfucker! You've been fucking warned lady, just try me." He turns to me and says, "Let's go kid". The crackhead just stood there, blank faced. I think she was shocked, but in any case, she turned and sheepishly walked away. All I could think was, "They never taught us that in the Academy" and "Damn, this guy is good". Once I got in the car I began thinking of how he had handled that job and how impressed I was. In my mind I'm saying, "It must be the tone he used or maybe the curses." In any case, she knew he was pissed and he got the job done.

We get back in the car and I give the job back to the dispatch with a final code 91, which is condition corrected. We cruise a few blocks away and I park at a spot where hopefully we will have a quiet Sunday with few, if any, jobs for the rest of the day. No sooner as I start going over the job in my head again, thinking of how great he handled the job, dispatch comes over the air giving us the same job again. The dispatcher states that the caller says the same woman is back again at the same location, yelling and screaming. As the call was coming over, I was looking at my partner's face and I swear I could see it going from slight red to bright red right before my eyes. I remember thinking that if he was a cartoon, there would be smoke coming out of his ears with a whistling sound like a tea pot.

In a deep, serious tone he says, "Let's go". It didn't sound good and I was trying to imagine what might happen when we get to the location. As we are pulling up to the front of the location you could see the same crackhead yelling up to the third floor, waving her arms and cursing. There were no cars parked in front of the location so I was able to pull right up along the curb in front of the building right where the lady was standing and shouting. I hadn't really come to a stop yet and I didn't have the car in park yet either. I think the crackhead must have seen that same steam coming out of my partner's ears because she immediately turned and started to walk away from the building with a fearful look on her face. She was right to be scared. My partner was already opening the door with one hand and reaching for his night stick with the other as we were coming to a stop. As he is opening the door and getting out I hear him say, " That's your ass motherfucker!". With that, the crackhead bolts down the street, screaming at the top of her lungs, with the cop hot on her tail. I rode down the street along side them, following them as close as possible. Although I knew it wasn't funny, and this lady was in for a rough morning, it was kind of comical to see. When the two turned the corner it was all over. He had caught up to her and grabbed onto her shirt from behind. After a few strategically placed kicks in the ass and a few whacks with the old cocobolo the crackhead went off screaming and limping into the Harlem sunlight, which was continuing to rise in the distance.

The whole event sort of slowed down and seemed to be unfolding in slow motion right before my eyes. I parked the car and felt compelled to watch what was the weirdest sunrise I ever saw. My partner walked back to the car, slumped back in the seat and said, "Okay, let's go." We never got that call again and I don't remember ever seeing that crackhead on that block again either. Now that's what I call police work!

5. Super Cop?

When you become a cop and get assigned a precinct, you look up to the veteran cops that work there. When I say veteran cops, I mean the ones who actually hit the streets on a daily basis. The cops who have been out there, actually doing the job, years before you get there. You especially look up to the really active street cops that you see bringing in the really good collars. You are in awe of these hard nose, gritty cops who aren't afraid to mix it up or get physical with a perp. These cops are the ones who might come in with a bloody perp or a torn uniform as a result of a hard fought arrest. I'm talking about hard working, real street cops. Not "house mouses", hiding in the precinct and making believe they were cops simply because they had a gun and a badge.

The really good cops weren't sergeant's lap dogs or ass kissers either. If you had any self respect, this was not how you became a successful cop or got ahead on the job. A real cop got what they wanted from consistent hard work over a number of years. The respect came as a result of this body of work. It was a matter of pride in your work.

These cops were rough and tough and had great street smarts. It seemed, at times, that these cops could somehow sense crime on the street. They knew how to hunt for a collar and not just respond to radio calls they were given to handle. These cops routinely brought in drugs, guns and countless other arrests like it was easy. This was how I always envisioned police work. This was how I wanted to be.

There was this one cop who had about 12 years on the street when I was assigned to that precinct as a rookie cop right out of the Academy. He was well respected and thought of as a great street cop by the whole precinct. He could be seen routinely bringing in guns and drugs. All of us would stand there with our mouths open in awe as he booked his perps in for processing. Rookie or not, it was an amazing sight to watch him unload piles of evidence onto the desk in front of the Sergeant. We all dreamed of the day we would be that good and all wondered how cops like him did it. We were eager to learn those skills.

Police work is a series of steps you grow into. You start off with formal academy training. You then hit the street and walk a foot post for quite a while. Later on, after a break-in period, you go on to sector car patrol.

One day, mid morning, my partner and I were on a standard rookie foot post. When you are new, you get a foot post that usually covers a few blocks and a few avenues. Your foot post is usually in a bad area of the precinct where crime is pretty rampant. While crime might be happening all around you, we were placed there mainly for a show of uniform presence to the neighborhood and to respond to any jobs that might occur in that area. While walking these foot posts, we would try to learn everything we could in anticipation of future assignment to sector car patrol. Patrol in a sector car was like a graduation to the next phase of doing police work. In a sector car, patrol gets much more serious. You start getting the heavy, more dangerous jobs that get called into 911.

So, we were standing out there on our foot posts. I imagine we probably looked like tourists, looking around, taking in all the sights. All of a sudden, "super cop" pulls up across the street from us and calls us over. We ran over, just happy that we can talk to this guy. I mean this could be a huge opportunity to learn something.

I generally look at everything as a learning experience. This philosophy was something I was taught by my Academy training Sergeant. I know that from this cop's reputation that any interaction can be an education.

Super Cop looks at me and says, "Yo, kid, we need you two to back us up on this bust!" I might as well have just been told I hit the lottery. I mean this was overwhelmingly great news. We were both as happy as can be. Not only would we get a chance to learn but actually work with this cop on a real bust. My partner and I were rookies but we knew enough to back these guys up without saying anything. We both knew our place and what we were expected to do. Basically, we were just there to watch their backs, do what we were told and only act if the shit hit the fan. We both knew there would be plenty of time for a question and answer period later after the collar was made, especially if we did a good job. In my head I was thinking that if we did good, we would be in with this guy. Also, later on we could critique and dissect the collar and would be able to ask him all the questions that would possibly reveal some secret to his genius level police IQ.

At this point in our career, this guy was like a god to us. We both stood there like soldiers as he got out of the car, popped the trunk and calmly took out a sledgehammer. Police work and life in Harlem, in general, was different back then. Carrying a sledgehammer to a job really wasn't all that strange to us and in fact was quite a common occurrence. Besides, this only made us even more anxious to get this bust rolling. I mean in the head of a rookie the math being computed was: super cop, plus sledgehammer, plus bust with us as backup, equals unbelievable experience. We couldn't wait and it was difficult to contain ourselves. We were sure this could only get better from here.

With sledgehammer in hand, Super Cop leads his partner, with us in tow, towards one of the worst buildings in the precinct. This building was known to be a real broken down shit hole and labeled as a place for heavy drug sales and drug use. We weren't even allowed to do vertical patrols in there alone. In training, we were told by the Sergeant that this building was on the list as a mandatory two man location at all times.

Super Cop and his partner gave us the universal "be quiet" symbol and with that, we all quietly walked up the stairs to the third floor. Our radios are off and we are holding any equipment close to our body that might make noise as we walked and could possibly alert the building to police presence.

The building stunk and there was garbage all over the hallway. The stairs were littered with crack vials and cigar wrappers. It was the winter time and I swear it was colder in that hallway than outside on the foot post. Super Cop goes to one of the doors at the far end of the hall and puts his ear to the door. He stayed in that position for about thirty seconds. The rest of us just stood there motionless, waiting on his lead and course of action, which was unknown to us.

Without any notice or indication at all, he steps back and swings the sledgehammer at the door targeting the peephole. With that one swing, he knocks the peephole right out of the door, into the apartment, creating a nice size hole, which he uses to now look into the apartment.

At this point, I think we were both a little stunned and stood there in disbelief. It was like something that startles you but makes it impossible to look away. We were definitely eagerly awaiting his next move. In an instant, he moves to the peephole and while looking through the spot where the peephole once was, says in a loud and deep, menacing voice, "I see you in there, motherfucker!" He proceeds to slam on the door with the sledgehammer, targeting the top and bottom, where the hinges were located. It couldn't have taken more than four whacks to take the door totally off the hinges. He knew exactly where to hit that door, in order to get maximum damage in a minimal amount of time. It was clear that he had done this before and was now a pro at it. With the final shot, the door became totally unhinged and crashed into the apartment. Splinters of the broken door and dust were flying everywhere. As if he was in continuous motion, he dropped the sledgehammer in the doorway and heads in with his partner right behind him. Right behind his partner were the two of us. Once inside what looked like an abandoned apartment, we catch the tail end of a young black kid, about 19 years old, attempting to scramble out the back window of the apartment. Super Cop and his partner easily drag him back into the apartment and with minimal force. He quickly got cuffed with relative ease right there by the window on the floor.

Even though we were in motion, I think we were still pretty stunned. It was like watching a movie. I mean we really didn't have to do anything but stand there and be backup. Super Cop picks the dude off the floor and hands him over to us saying, "Here, hold this motherfucker." He then walks by us into the other room which we just ran through. There, on a table that we just ran past, was a shitload of crack. I had never seen so many drugs in my life, aside from in the movies. This wasn't the movies and it still seemed pretty unbelievable.

Later on at the precinct, we didn't get a chance to talk to Super Cop about the collar like we hoped. However, we watched him and his partner bring in several more great collars just like that over the course of our 6 months of field training. From time to time, because we had worked with him, he would talk to us and help us with our training. He explained a lot of his collars to us when he had the time to do so. We learned a great deal about police work because of him. When he didn't have time to talk to us, we would watch with amazement at the amount of drugs and guns the two of them brought in to the precinct on a regular basis.

One day we came to work and all that was over. We were told Super Cop had failed a random drug test and was no longer a cop. The rumor was that he tested positive for cocaine and just like that his days of police work were over. We were crushed. I mean this guy was not only a good guy but a great cop. It really shook us as a group to get that news. Of course, the speculation surfaced after that and people would say things like, "Now we know how he made all those great collars!" It was hard for me to believe that. Maybe I was in denial. I really didn't want to believe those rumors and there was no proof to those rumors anyway. I chose to believe what was in front of me. This guy was a great cop with a bad problem. Instead of getting help, he got caught.

Either way, he was gone. I learned in the Academy to make everything a learning experience. I took the good things he had taught us about police work and used it to be a better cop. I put the bad things that were being talked about all over the precinct in the back of my mind as a cautionary tale. Knowing him personally and about what happened to him taught me the importance of taking the positive out of everything and to always make everything a learning experience.

6. Relax, It's Not Your Blood!

My first radio car patrol partner and I were on a routine day tour patrol. When you're in a sector car, you get all the really heavy jobs that come over 911. It was mid-morning and a call came over the air for an EDP near a back loading dock in the rear of a housing complex. We picked up the job and both figured it would be a pretty easy job to handle. Most calls for an EDP end up the same. They usually all end up with a trip to the psych ward for them and a boring day of babysitting the EDP for us. Once they get admitted, we are free to resume patrol. This process can take anywhere from a couple of hours to an all day event.

We arrive at the location and walk down the ramp which leads to the rear of the building and faces the loading dock. The doors to the bay were in the open position outward towards the parking lot side. In the doorway was a rolling cart and on the cart was a man who obviously either had something wrong with him or was high on drugs. He had a weird look on his face. He was definitely a disturbed individual and he was holding a broom stick handle.

At this point in my career, I had quite a few arrests and quite a bit of experience in drugs and their effect on people. In particular, the effect of PCP or angel dust. The area we were in was notorious for dust and from the looks of this guy, I was already leaning towards that as a distinct possibility.

So right off I'm thinking dust and what I was taught and had previously experienced with this type of situation. I start to quickly recall the things about dust I need to remember to handle this job. The thing that is paramount with dust heads is that they can possess tremendous, super human strength. Aside from being extremely strong, they also may not register pain like the usual person does. You are taught in the Academy that you don't want to get too close to these people and never lunge at them. You don't want them to grab onto you or to be able to pull you into their grasp. In these cases, what you want is space, a place to retreat, if necessary and ideally a way of isolating and containing them until the proper type of restraints or necessary manpower is in position to handle the person. With one call to the boss or ESU, we could have all we need to successfully take this EDP down with minimal force and injury to either us or him.

Now this sounds like a lot of information and it is. However, when you are actually working, your mind sort of sifts through all this and calls up what you need and helps you to handle the job. At least I felt that was how my mind processed the jobs I handled. This may seem like a long process but it actual happens very fast and the more time you have on the job the quicker you begin to react.

While I was computing all this in my head, only a few seconds had passed. All of a sudden, the EDP starts spitting at us. The guy is dead center between the two doors and on the cart and not moving at all, just spitting. As he is spitting, I leaned over to the side and closed the door next to me half way to shield me from his spit. This guy was not just nuts, he was gross and who knows if he had any diseases or anything. And even if he didn't have any diseases, who wants spit on them? I mean it's bad enough that we were going to have to touch this guy. We could do without the exchange of bodily fluids. Needless to say, I was thinking time, space and perhaps some of those fancy restraints that ESU keeps on their truck. I assumed my partner was thinking the same.

Well, you know what they say about assumption. I guess my partner had either fell asleep that day in the Academy or didn't process information the same as I did, because he didn't close his side of the door. Instead, he lunged at the EDP and grabbed a hold of him around the chest area on his jacket.

My partner was about 5' 10", 200 pounds. He was a non-smoker, in good physical shape and worked out regularly. The EDP was my size, about 5' 6", 160 pounds but looked wiry. He was the type of guy who appeared thin but probably the type of thin that is muscular with no body fat at all. Under normal circumstances, in a fight, the edge would go to my partner. Wrong. In an instant the EDP took hold of my partner and threw him to the ground like a rag doll with no effort at all. In the time it took me to react, which was a split second, he was already on top of my partner trying to twist his head and putting his fingers inside his mouth.

If I had to think like this EDP, I would say he was trying to see if my partner's head could be unscrewed. That's exactly what it looked like. One person trying to unscrew the other person's head off. My first instinct was to try and pull him off my partner. I wanted to pull him back and give my partner some space to retreat out of that position and away from this nut. In the few seconds while attempting this futile move, the EDP was now trying to wrap the radio microphone cord around my partner's neck. This scene was getting ugly real fast. I mean this whole scenario is getting to the point where in the back of my mind I'm thinking, "Am I gonna have to shoot this fucking guy or what?" I know I wasn't worried about justification for force or shooting this guy because if this kept moving in the direction we were headed, it really was going to be a matter of life and death for my partner. The real problem was that along with the near dire situation, this EDP was on top of my partner. From the position we were all in, shooting my gun safely would have been a difficult thing to do. I mean my partner was directly below the EDP and in the same line of fire. We were quickly coming to the point where you would say we were fucked.

In those days not all cops carried a nightstick. Especially on day tours, most cops either carried the "Harlem Flounder" or four cell flashlight. The four cell flashlight was essentially a steel pipe, with large D cell batteries and a bulb. It was what we called, a dual purpose item. With all options out, I leaned over the top of the EDP and with all my might proceeded to slam this flashlight down on the top of his head. One, two, three, four shots directly to the top of his head, with no effect at all and no movement from the EDP to stop what he was doing to my partner. At this point, my partner was screaming in pain and this guy still seemed intent on unscrewing my partner's head. Shots five through 8 also were ineffective on stopping his actions. However, something physically was definitely happening to this guy's head. I mean superhuman strength, yes. Superhuman flesh and bone, no. Plain and simple, pain or no pain, whether he felt it or not, it's still a human head. From about the ninth shot on, with every blow to the head, this dude was getting opened up. It was like little zippers, installed on his head in several spots, were being opened one at a time each one letting out a trail of blood. Now any doctor will tell you that head wounds bleed a lot. I can honestly tell you this fact is true and this guy was proving it. Along with the amount of cuts to his head and the area it was in, there was also gravity working as well. The EDP was still in that same position, over my partner, and in a few seconds all the blood flowing had traveled downward onto my partner who was still at the bottom of the pile. In a matter of seconds my partner looked just as bad as the EDP.

All of a sudden, out of nowhere, the EDP just lets go of my partner, gets up and bolts into a janitor's room, right next to where we were brawling. I ran after him and saw that he was headed straight towards the back of the room. With a quick scan of the room I could easily see that he was trapped. The room had no other way out and the windows had locked gates on them. I quickly closed the door, looked back at where I had just come from and saw standing in the corner, white as a ghost, was a maintenance man. Apparently, he was there for most of the fight but too scared to move, help, or call the police. I yelled to him and he jumped, like he was snapped back to reality. I told him to watch the door and to let me know if the EDP came back out of the room. I ran back to my partner, who was still on the floor, writhing in pain. At last, I was able to put the location over the radio, stating that we needed help quick and an ambulance as well.

What I now had was a cop down and a barricaded EDP/perp. My partner was battered, bruised and had blood all over his face and neck. He was also dazed and somewhat confused. This whole event happened in a few minutes but felt like an eternity. It must have felt like three eternities to my partner. With one of his hands, he reached up and after feeling around his face saw that he had a handful of blood. At the sight of the blood he gasped and tried to jump up. I quickly placed my hand on his chest to keep him down and said, "Relax, it's not your blood."

A second later, the cavalry came running through the door. All I can say is that when you need help and that help arrives, the sight of those uniforms rushing through the door is the most beautiful sight in the world. At this point, I was pretty wiped out and the sight of backup meant I could relax a little and let them take over from here.

I quickly relayed the story in short form and pointed out the room the EDP was in, being sure to tell them it looked secure. I watched the entire group of cops carefully crack open the door and peer into the room in a tactical manner. Imagine the look on my face when one of them said, "No one's in here!".

I was just about to tell them that I never saw him come out and to double check with the maintenance guy, who was still standing in the same spot watching the room, when the dispatcher came over the radio with an emergency call for our location. The dispatcher stated that she was getting a call for help from inside our location. At that moment, one of the cops noticed the telephone on the desk was pulled down underneath to the floor. The fucking nut was calling 911 from under the desk. The dispatcher was on the phone with our perp and he was asking for the police and help. With that, the crowd of cops went storming into the room and I went back to my partner.

The sounds coming from inside that room was like a small recurring earthquake. All that could be heard was the sound of things breaking with intermittent yells, screams and groans mixed in. To get a full understanding of this guy's strength, you have to realize that this guy was just in a fight with me and my partner where he suffered some serious injuries to his head. To this add the 6 to 8 cops he was now fighting with inside that room. Unbelievably, it took them another 5 to 10 minutes to finally get this guy cuffed. When they finally dragged him out of that room he looked much worse then when he went in.

Back at the precinct, EMS showed up and gave him what we called a "two-eight turban". Basically, he looked like a human Q tip. He was slumped to one side on the bench of the prison cell. It was just a quick patch job, he was definitely in need of further medical attention, stitches and a doctor.

My partner got stitches to his elbow, bruises on his head and neck and several scratches inside his mouth. He also received a tetanus shot and refresher course in dealing with dust heads, that I'm sure he remembered for the rest of his career, probably his life.

I got a felony collar for assault to a police officer, a shit load of overtime and the beginning of a court case with this nut that would last for months. Eventually the case went all the way to trial.

I remember, months later, being on the stand at trial for this case. At one point, the defense attorney asked me, "Officer, how many times would you say you had to strike my client during the struggle?" To that I responded, "15 times sir." The defense attorney said back to me, "15 times officer, why 15 times?" I calmly answered back, "Because he didn't get off my partner the first 14 times." By the look on his face, you could tell that he didn't like that response one bit. Well, fuck him and his client. I really didn't care what he, the judge or the jury thought. In my mind it was a disgrace that we even had to go to trial for this case. As for the defense attorney, all I could think was, don't ask questions you might not like the answers to.

I was told later that year that the same nut got out of jail after doing time on our collar and got arrested again. Supposedly he held a knife to a security guard's throat while he was once again dusted out of his mind. A cop from the precinct who happened to be a black belt in karate showed up and the dude got fucked up again. I was told this time they sent him to the psych ward instead of prison. They deemed him not a criminal but insane.

Last update we heard about him was that the psych hospital quickly found him competent and sent his ass back to jail after he wigged out and damaged thousands of dollars in computer and medical equipment at the hospital. I'll bet they couldn't wait to get rid of him just like us. I'm glad to say, I never heard about him or saw him again after that.

7. The Hard Way Or The Easy Way

When you are a rookie, you sometimes look for an incident or arrest just so you can prove yourself. It's not yourself that you doubt. I think most cops are pretty sure of themselves and their abilities or limitations. When you're a rookie, it's about what other people think of you that seems most important. Proving myself to my co-workers was extremely important at this point in my very young career. I couldn't imagine being thought of as an incompetent cop or looked at in a negative way. By this I don't mean you had to be the best cop in the universe but at the very least you had to be a cop who did his work and did it well on a consistent basis. A Sergeant who I worked for years ago use to say, "No one should ever be a harder judge of you than yourself." I guess if you follow that rule everything else will fall into place.

When you first start out, there are a lot of eyes on you. Not only is the street watching you but your colleagues are watching you as well. In the police department, a cop quickly gets a name. Be it good or bad, you can get a label pretty fast in this line of work. From the very beginning, I always wanted to be known as a hard working, active cop. I wanted the cops I worked with to know that I wasn't afraid to take a collar, regardless of the type. I also wanted to show that I wasn't afraid of the street or the physical aspect that can sometimes accompany it.

One of our steady rookie foot posts had a really nasty subway stop on it. This line was a local train and didn't skip stops like the express train did. Because this train made every stop on the line it took longer to complete its route and as a result, this train didn't arrive at the stops as often. This schedule was common knowledge to everyone so naturally there were less people going to this stop. If you have less train and pedestrian traffic, you get more undesirable people in the area and as a result, more crime. Stations that have more crime don't get looked after as much and this creates more filth and garbage as well. Pretty soon you get a vicious cycle that spirals out of control and what you are left with is a big mess.

This particular subway had spiraled to the bottom. It had become a regular place for crack heads to get high and for skells of all types to hang out and go to the bathroom. Very often, the homeless would be seen sleeping on the benches or camped out on the floor as well. All this and more was going on in this subway. The street above was only slightly better and only because it was in public view. Crack heads, drunks and the homeless freely roamed the area like an army of zombies. On the whole, the area just wreaked of piss and shit and was a place that anyone decent avoided.

It was because of all these reasons that we were placed there. We were supposed to curtail some of that shit and make the area seem a little more like some of the other stops where crime wasn't so bad. I really had no complaints about being there or handling that mess. The way I looked at, this was a great place to learn. There were collars everywhere and the public and the bosses were behind you a hundred percent. It was also a place where no one was going to scream about over zealous cops or make bullshit claims of police brutality either.

There were three of us on that post and it spanned out in opposite directions several blocks with the subway being a common point where the three of us met. Every so often during our tour, we would meet up and do what was called a "subway vertical". A subway vertical was a routine check of the subway, platform and token booth area. It was meant to give some uniform presence to an area where cops don't usually go. The token booth clerks were always happy as shit to see us. In fact, the only time these guys came out of the booth, other than change of personnel, was when we were there. This was before Metrocards and during the years where the public was still using tokens to ride the subway. The clerks would wait for us to come down to the subway before going out to remove the tokens from the turnstiles. It was the only time the workers felt they could safely do that part of their job.

Anytime we would go down to the subway, we would turn down our radios first. We tried to be as stealthy as we could. You never knew what you were going to encounter and you definitely wanted the element of surprise on your side.

This particular time we proceeded down in the same quiet manner. As soon as we turned the stairway corner which led to the platform, standing in the corner, was a crack head. He was beaming up (getting high) right in plain view, with a loaded crack pipe in his hand and several bottles of crack in the other.

This guy knew he was caught red handed, but he did what all criminals do and reacted by throwing the evidence as far across the platform and token booth area as he could. From where he was standing, the evidence could only go so far and would be easy to retrieve. His little act didn't change anything and he was about to be a nice little collar in an area where the bosses wanted that kind of arrest. We moved in and cornered him right where he was standing. He didn't try to run because he was in a bad spot, there were three of us and there was no where for him to go. I was thinking this was going to be easy but at the same time, I could also tell that he definitely had already smoked a bunch of that shit before we got there.

The dude was about 5' 10", but with a lean muscular build to him. He probably was much heavier before he got hooked on crack but lost some weight as a result of his addiction. However, I've noticed that crackheads do seem to keep a lot of muscle even with the weight loss and the addiction. He had the crackheads version of one of those supplements you see in a health food store. All muscle with no fat. He was what people in the gym would refer to as "cut up".

The dude looks at the three of us with a cloudy, strange type of look on his face. Obviously, the crack he had already smoked was beginning to affect him. I really didn't think he was going to say anything and then he said, "I can't go to jail man". On the inside I'm thinking, then don't smoke crack asshole. Those thoughts were only internal though. I had enough time on on the job dealing with crack heads to know that a five minute encounter is not going to rehabilitate this guy no matter what I said. This guy needed professional help to be cured of his addiction. This, of course, would have to come after he gets arrested and sent to Central Booking.

I was the one that was standing in front of him. On either side of me were the other cops I was with. I thought I would try a hard nosed bluff. The thinking was that maybe some tough talk, coupled with the fact that we outnumbered him three to one might be enough to take this guy in without any incident.

I slowly took out my cuffs and held them up a little so they were obvious for him to see. In a calm but serious tone, I looked him dead in the eye and said, "Yo man, you got caught, you gotta go. Now we can do this the hard way or we can do this the easy way. What's it gonna be?"

The response I was expecting would be something along the lines of, "Okay man, I ain't looking for no hassle, let's go." With that, he would turn around and get cuffed and it's off to the stoney lonesome for arrest processing.

Instead he looked at the three of us going from one to the other, than back to me and said, "Well fuck it then, I'll go the hard way" As soon as he finished that sentence you could see his whole body start to tense up.

To be honest, I did not expect that at all. I don't think any of us did. Anyway, I have always been a pretty good improvisor and I knew this was the kind of arrest that could get us noticed as workers. It would show that we do the job we were given and if this got physical, it would also show we weren't afraid to get down and dirty if the situation called for it.

In my mind this situation called for use of physical force. The statement he made clearly rung the bell and the fight was going to be on. That being said and remembering being told that nine times out of ten the guy who swings first wins the fight, I swung the cuffs I was holding and cracked him right in the face as hard as I could. The other cops had no way of knowing that I was going to do this. I think my actions shocked everyone, including the perp, and he was momentarily put back on his heels for a second. He did a slight bounce off the wall, back out towards all of us, and after that the four of us just went at it. I must say that for a guy who was trying to fight off three cops, he held his own pretty good. I'm sure the crack helped him a great deal, as it always seems to give them extra strength and durability. The fight lasted a good five minutes but in the end the numbers were in our favor and he inevitably lost the fight. When it was all over, the perp was not only lumped up but maced as well.

All over the ground in the area of the brawl was scattered police equipment that was either dropped or used in the fight. It looked like a mini battlefield. The four of us were all coughing a little bit from the mace being sprayed in a closed in area, but none worse than the perp. He definitely got the worst of everything in that encounter. Later on, as we always did, we got together and talked about the incident. We would always try to talk about what happened and what we would do the same or different, if we could do it all over again.

In the end, it all it turned out okay. We made a pretty good arrest in a fucked up area. No one got badly hurt and and we actually got some praise from some of the older cops and bosses, who heard about our scuffle and arrest. However, now when I think back about the incident I don't think I ever used that line on a perp again.

8. Hairy Situation

One day we got a call directing us to the local pharmacy. The call stated that we should see the pharmacist in regards to a woman who was trying fill stolen prescriptions. There was always big money in drugs of all types. However, at this particular time in NYC, the prescription drugs being moved on the street was at a high. All kinds of scripts were out there. The most common were, of course, the pain killers and psych medications.

This particular pharmacy had a real bad ass as far as pharmacists go. I mean he thought he was the Charles Bronson of pharmacists. He seemed to take everything dealing with drug addicts personally. It was like his own little war on drugs. This particular time he seemed extra annoyed with the situation. Not only was he not going to fill the scripts but he was obviously not going to give them back to this lady either. A lot of other pharmacists would give them back to the junkies not wanting any trouble. Those pharmacists would just tell the junkies to go somewhere else and that would usually be the end of the whole ordeal.

In the eyes of the lady trying to scam the pills, this was a double loss. Not only did she not score her pills but she couldn't even try to score somewhere else. Her bogus scripts were gone and she was pissed. This lady started to argue with the pharmacist and I guess one of the other workers called it in to 911. This is the part where we come in, right in the middle of a heated dispute between a junkie and a pharmacist vigilante.

We enter the location and the place was actually really nice, considering the area it was in and the climate of the city in general. It was a squeaky clean, totally legit place. The store had really nice glass display cases which had nice gadgets and gifts set up all over the store. The owner was a decent guy and was actually just trying to do the right thing and run a nice business.

We got the gist of the story and realized that this could go down one of two ways. This could either be a simple dispute and we could send the lady on her way, without her bogus scripts or it could be a collar for trying to pass a phony, stolen prescription. I had encountered these situations before and it was hard to prove the scripts were stolen. The prescription pads were usually not reported when they went missing and the DA's office were pussy's about prosecuting these sort of cases. Weighing the options, it would actually make more sense to send this lady packing instead of making the arrest. Besides, she lost her scripts and was going to have to start over somewhere else from scratch.

The lady looked a little kooky and the owner seemed happy to just confiscate the scripts and really didn't want to press charges. With this information, it seemed reasonable to mediate this argument and just move this lady on down the road. Unfortunately, this lady was a real dumb bitch and she wasn't going for that plan. She was adamant about getting her scripts back and she was intent on staying in the store until she got what she wanted. Imagine the nerve of this junkie asshole. She actually felt like she had a right to these stolen prescription pads. It's amazing how a junkies mind works.

Plain and simple, we couldn't give her phony scripts back to her and we couldn't wait around all day for her to leave either. We had other jobs to handle and had to move this along one way or another. At this point, neither side was budging and it was becoming obvious that we would have to make a decision for both parties. We tried one more time explaining the situation to this lady. We even tried bluffing her with the possibility of arrest, hoping she would realize how lucky she would be to just walk away. The problem with bluffs are that if the bluff gets called you are all out of options and have to take the next step, regardless of the outcome. We were out of options, she refused to budge and reluctantly, we knew she would have to be arrested.

We told the lady she was now under arrest for attempting to pass stolen prescriptions and she had to turn around and place her hands behind her back to be handcuffed. She immediately changed her tune and said, "Okay, I'm going." With that she attempted to head for the door.

This was in the afternoon, around one p.m. and the store was pretty crowded. The lady's antics to this point had drawn a little bit of a crowd and it was now to the point where we really couldn't go reverse on our actions. We already told her she was under arrest and other curious patrons heard this as well. It definitely wouldn't look right to let her just walk out of there at this point. Besides, this bitch had been given ample opportunities to leave before getting to this point. If we let her go now, it would make us look like we were punks or lazy to the general public that was around us. Besides that, we regularly patrolled that sector and word spreads fast on the street. We definitely didn't want the locals to hear that we let some junkie dictate to us how to handle the situation. I mean we were the police, we are in charge, not her. We made a stand and we're going to have to stick to it, no matter what.

Well, she was intent on attempting to walk on by us to the door. I guess in her mind it was settled and she was leaving. Well, she was wrong and we both grabbed hold of her arms to restrain her and stop her from moving. She was a little fat lady, with a big overcoat, medium length hair and glasses. She looked about forty years old, was about 5' 2" and had a real tight skinned, mean face.

The moment we applied resistance to her stride, she went wild. She started swinging her arms and kicking her legs like an animal. I immediately went for her wrist with a handcuff in an attempt to try and get her under control. This action caused her to get distracted from my partner and focus on me. My partner seized this opportunity and gave her a hard palm strike upwards to the bottom of her chin. With this shot she went backwards into the glass display case behind her, smashing it. The crash sent the case and its contents to the ground breaking all around the three of us. I tried an old reliable move from days past and grabbed her hair and gave a good tug to one side as hard as I could. Her hair came clean off in one swoop. It was a fucking wig. She was bald as an eagle and that thing was just sitting on her head. I remember being surprised that it was a wig and thinking that without her hair, she looked like a real short Marvin Hagler. The funny thing about the wig coming off was that, until that time, the scuffle was moving along at its own pace. Once the wig came off, it was like someone hit freeze frame and we all stopped for a split second and looked at each other. A second later, after it sunk in, the three of us were back in motion again, going at it. With a few more pushes, pulls and several more broken display cases, we dragged that lady down face first amidst all the broken store property and managed to rear cuff her on the floor. We forcibly helped her to her feet and pushed her though the store. Once outside, we gave her the necessary assistance to get her to our car. At this point, she was screaming and complaining. The crowd, which easily doubled by now, was looking on in amazement. We shoved her, face first, into the back seat of the car and my partner tossed her wig back there as well. I remember him saying as he threw it at her, "Here's your fucking wig!" With that, we were off to the Precinct to book this lady for arrest processing. Naturally, she would now have a few more charges to go along with with the original charge of stolen prescriptions.

My partner told me later that when he went back to the store to get the pharmacists information, the store was a total mess. Several display cases and their contents were totally destroyed. He told me that not only was the store a complete mess but the owner was very upset. After that incident, I don't remember getting another call from that location. I imagine he must have realized that its not worth it to get that involved with these junkies. After that, he must have fell into the same routine as the rest of the owners in the area. If you're a simple, civilian store owner, that kind of incident is sure to change the way you look at things or proceed in the future with similar incidents.

Back at the precinct, the perp didn't give us any trouble. She really didn't seem to be concerned about being arrested or the charges at all. Her only real complaint and concern was not having her wig and having to sit there in the cell with a bald head. Since we had her wig and she was behaving herself, we asked the Sarge if she could have it back. He didn't care one way or another so we gave it back to her. She was pretty grateful for that and was good from then on without any complaints for the rest of her time with us. She had her wig and she was ready for jail.

9. Disorder In The Court

Traffic court is very often referred to by cops as a "Kangaroo" court. This is with good reason. The way cases are tried is just plain idiotic. It is definitely a flawed system, yet a marvel to watch. If you ever get the chance to sit in and watch a session, I encourage you to do it. If you could break down the entire process to look at all that goes into making it work, you can really see what a waste of money it is. Not to mention the waste of manpower, both civilian and police, which could be doing much more productive things. This is after all NYC and it's not like the police department doesn't have anything else better to do. Equally amazing, was the actual number of cops who spend a significant portion of their day at this crappy court. Most of the time only to come out with below average results.

The majority of judges who work in traffic court have the attitude that they are the end-all of administrative law. You would think they were handling murder cases the way some of them act. I think it's because their authority rules over driving, which is a privilege and not an absolute right, such as something afforded by the Constitution. I think it is in that notion that their arrogant manner of ruling is born. You can see a great deal of them straining themselves to act important and impose their will on what always appears to be the hard working middle class. Some of these judges have to strain themselves to act intelligent as well. One session with the majority of these judges will tell you all you need to know about why they are not trying criminal cases. I have seen all types of judges in my time as a cop. Truthfully, they are not all bad. It's true for all professions that there is good and bad and this crowd was not spared that truth either. Just as there are good cops and bad cops, the same goes for judges as well. Unfortunately for them, the plain fact is that they are a smaller group and that makes the bad ones stand out that much more.

In my twenty years of policing I must have gone to traffic court over a thousand times. Usually, when I went, I would be there for twenty or more cases for one session. On this particular day, I went to court for the violation of disobeying a traffic sign. Specifically, it was a "no left turn" sign violation.

So that you fully understand the violation, I will describe the sign that this motorist failed to obey. It is a large white sign which is four feet by four feet in size. It has on it a big black arrow which faces to the left and has a bold red circle around it and going though the center of it as well. I mean, do we really need a Judge for this? This violation is not open to interpretation like some other violations. It's not a debate as to whether a light was red or yellow. We don't have to argue if the motorist actually stopped for a sign or merely slowed down. This was a sign, plain and simple. It says: no left turn. If you go left you're fucking wrong, end of story. Not in New York. In New York City, everyone fights everything. Why shouldn't they? Most of them find a way to get off either not guilty or at least get the fine reduced, in the rare instances where they are actually found guilty.

So there I am again, thinking to myself, "What's the fucking point anyway?". Here I am again in this kangaroo court playing this idiotic game. It would be so easy to just shut down and do the amnesia routine that so many cops do by saying, "I don't recall.", to every case. However, my entire career I have always held myself to one rule. That rule is, no matter what task I performed, I always tried my best. In this instance, I tried to win every case. Naturally, I didn't win every case but I still tried my best for every case I had. Even if I was having a bad day and was frustrated with the Judge, I still tried my best. This I did for me and no one else. It became a matter of pride. Actually, I had a very good record in traffic court. Proof of this was seen by how much the attorneys who worked there for the motorists hated me. You could see the disgust on their face when I fought them tooth and nail and got a conviction where most cops would give up and take the loss. It's truly like a game. After a while, you can almost perfect your testimony and after years of success in traffic court, I was asked to help train rookies so they would do better in court as well.

I began going through my long winded, robotic speech for this offense. It usually takes about five minutes for me to state this obvious violation. The reason it takes so long is because you have to state key phrases and descriptions of the violation or the case gets tossed and the motorist is found not guilty. You can imagine after doing this hundreds of times it becomes very routine, almost like "sleep talking". When I begin my testimony I am usually looking at some notes in front of me. I don't really need them because the whole testimony is pretty much memorized but just in case I get interrupted or lose my train of thought, I have them in front of me.

I never look at the motorist fighting the summons. The majority of these people are jackasses anyway, looking for a problem. Nothing good comes out of a staring match and it can get me worked up and I'll forget what I'm there for. The worst ones are the motorists who stand there next to you and make sound effects while you testify. Some of them will suck their teeth in disbelief, huff and puff, or even say, "what?" out loud even though they know they are guilty as sin. It's quite an Oscar worthy performance. They should sell tickets at the door. I always try to talk and look straight toward the Judge because the Judge is the one who needs to hear the facts, not the motorist.

On this occasion as I was talking I swore I could smell booze. Not like an open bottle of booze but like heavy booze on a person's breath. I could tell it was booze breath because it comes in waves, just like someone breathing. Strong, then not so strong. Like a drunk Darth Vader, heavy smell then faint smell over and over in a rhythmic manner. I myself don't drink, and as a result, I became quite exceptional at smelling booze on people's breath. I could even determine how drunk someone actually was just by the smell of booze on their breath. The other cops in my precinct would frequently call me to car stops to see what I thought about the driver they had stopped for suspicion of DUI. I would go talk to the driver, ask him/her some random questions and then give my analysis of their sobriety. From talking to them for a few minutes I would be able to tell if they were over the limit and going to be a DUI arrest. The other cops called me a human breathalyzer due to my success.

So there I am testifying my heart out and I'm smelling vodka, real heavy. Now I know people say that you can't smell vodka, it's an odorless alcohol. I personally think that's just something drunks say to convince themselves that they haven't had too much to drink. In my mind and nose, it has a distinct smell and it was definitely coming from the dude next to me who was there to fight this violation. I tried my best to ignore the odor and continue to testify. I concentrated on not looking at him even though I had the urge to check this guy out.

Finally, I finished my testimony and without a doubt, I nailed it. My testimony was damn near perfect from start to finish. Even this guy's booze breath didn't sway me from doing a great job. In my estimation, without exaggerating, this performance was worthy of training material for rookies. This was a closed case for sure. All that remained was for this guy to give whatever lame excuse or bullshit lie he could think of and I would be on my way with another victory. As long as the judge wasn't sleeping during my speech, it's a clear cut and easy conviction.

The motorist started to talk, explaining why he made the left turn. His excuse for making the illegal turn was that he didn't see the sign. He went on to explain that the reason why he didn't see the sign was because he wasn't wearing his glasses while he was driving.

Right after that statement, I began to hear some muffled laughter coming from other cops in the court room who were waiting their turn for their cases to be called. When I think back, I remembered that they were doing that while I was testifying as well. When I stopped talking, I guess it finally registered in my head what was happening. I tried to think of why they could be laughing and figured they also thought the motorist's excuse was pretty lame. I had actually heard much worse excuses than that but figured that everyone finds humor in different things. In any case, I felt we were all in agreement that this guy was guilty and the excuse he gave was not going to save him.

The motorist continued to talk and the laughter continued from the crowd of cops. At times it would get almost to the point where I really felt the Judge was going to say something. Before long, I began to get self conscious and thought maybe they were laughing at me. Stupid things were going through my mind. Did I have a split in my pants? Did I have bird poop on my back? I knew they couldn't smell the booze where they were seated, it was too far. I took a quick glance at myself and quickly checked myself out. Everything looked okay, then I took a quick glance at the motorist. With that glance it became clear why the cops were laughing. This clown was standing there testifying while wearing a pair of gag phony eyeglasses.

I am sure everyone has seen gag glasses like these somewhere before. People usually wear them on Halloween as part of a costume or perhaps on April Fools Day. They have thick black frames and the lenses are like the thickness of the bottom of old time Coca Cola bottles. When you look at the person straight on, the glasses make your eyes look like they are bugging out of your head or that your eyes are three times bigger than they actually are. One thing for sure, these glasses were obviously fake. Obvious to everyone but the Judge. This Judge was not laughing, smiling or even grinning. The
Judge begins to engage this guy in a serious conversation and starts asking him if he thought it was a good idea to drive without his glasses. She proceeds with more follow up questions like, "Are they prescription?, "Is that a restriction of your license?" and on and on she went. Here you

have a guy who was making a mockery of the Court and treating the whole event as a big joke and the Judge is dead serious. Now, like the other cops, I was struggling to hold back my laughter. The cops who were still in the courtroom looked like they were busting at the seams. A few cops left the room because they couldn't control themselves. You could hear the cops laughing in the hall outside the court room door.

After a few more questions the motorist just started agreeing with everything the Judge said. The whole time he was doing this he was making weird faces and gestures with both his face and head. The Judge continued her process as serious as a heart attack. At last, the bizarre conversation came to an end. The case was over and thankfully the Judge found him guilty of the violation. As all judges do, she checked his driving record to assess a fine and found that this guy's license was already suspended. I'm thinking to myself, "There's a fucking surprise!". The motorist agrees totally that his license is suspended, gets his fine and he leaves the court room. As he leaves the room he turns to the entire audience in the room, smiled and waved to the entire crowd. In a clownish and exaggerated manner he says, "Bye bye". Everyone in the court laughed, except the judge. All she did was shrug her shoulders.

After the session was over, all the cops meet up in the sign out room. They were all rolling in the aisles with laughter at the whole absurd event. They couldn't believe that this guy did that, in Court, in front of a Judge. The fact that the Judge took the whole thing serious and didn't realize that this motorist was making a mockery of her was really unbelievable. All they kept saying was how clueless this Judge was. I guess justice really is blind.

10. Shoot Or Don't Shoot?

No cop ever wants to kill anyone. No matter how cool they make it look in the movies or how glamorous the special effects make it happen. For any person, especially a cop, to think that way would tell you there must be something seriously wrong with them. In any walk of life, anyone who has had this unfortunate occurrence will almost always say it has changed their life in someway forever.

If you get through your entire career without ever having to shoot someone, they say you had a good career. If you are active and aggressive on the street and you achieve this, I would say you had a great career. Thankfully, in over twenty years of policing, I never had to shoot anyone. I was an aggressive and active cop with a lot of arrests but I never had to shoot at anyone. I had that great career I mentioned earlier.

I worked in a busy precinct and over the years, I have pulled my gun out of its holster too many times to count and for numerous reasons. In some years, when crime was at an all time high, it became just one more thing I did during the course of a usual days work.

However, unlike the majority of times when I did draw my gun on somebody, there was one instance where I came the closest to actually shooting that person as I ever did in my entire career. Strangely enough, it happened at the start of my career when I was a rookie and doing steady midnights.

This particular instance was a domestic call. It came over the radio as a fight between a mother and daughter. Any cop will tell you that domestic calls can be the most dangerous calls you ever get. They usually take place indoors in either the victim or perp's home. Right off this gives them the upper hand as they are the ones on familiar ground. Additionally, emotions are always running high because these arguments have usually been boiling for days or weeks before you get there. When these arguments reach their limit, they usually explode in rage. To all this you have to add all the unknown variables. The worst one being the unknown number of people actually involved. This is one of the many things you won't know until you get there and by then it could be too late.

My partner and I arrive at the location and you could hear the yelling from the lobby. It sounded like only two people screaming at each other but you are always taught to be cautious and prepare for the worst. We walk up the stairs and we are as quiet as possible. You want to use the walk time up to the location to listen to the argument that you will soon be in the middle of. This is the only time you are relatively safe and in a great position to learn about what you could be walking into. Any extra information here can literally be the difference between life and death. The sort of information you listen for to help you could be anything. Do you hear dogs barking? Does it sound like a physical fight or just verbal? Do you hear threats, sounds of breaking furniture or items being thrown? You just take it all in until you get up there.

When you get there, you don't just go right in either. Now you listen for a second time, but you do it outside the door. This gives you more time to gather information as well as get ready to go in. In our case, we walked up but if we had ran up, this would be the time to catch your breath. You don't want to go into a fight tired or out of breath. Always think preparation for the job at hand.

From all the sounds and conversation, it sounded heated but not violent at this point. However, you learn all that can change in an instant, so we would always err on the cautious side. The yelling sounded faint. We both figured this to mean they were probably in the rear of the apartment, furthest from the door. This gave us a reason to believe that the argument wouldn't all of a sudden spill out into the hall without giving us some kind of notice first. In most cases, space is a good thing. Space allows you the time and the ability to plan your action, rather than rely on reaction.

The door was closed but when I quietly tested the door knob, it was clearly unlocked. The unlocked door is actually quite common. Sometimes, a complainant or caller will do that to allow the police to get in on their own. Particularly if they are frightened of possible assault, or think they may need to either get out fast or get help to them in a hurry.

When I opened the door and slowly pushed it totally open, we were able to scan everything in front of us. My view was a long hallway that went straight to the back of the apartment. The apartment had several rooms off either side of the hallway. It was probably four or five rooms total and the furthest room appeared to be where the argument was happening. That room appeared to be the living room and looked to have the lights on. The rest of the apartment and hallway were dimly lit, at best. The closest room and door was to our immediate left, only about five feet away and it was the kitchen.

As we stood there listening, we could hear cursing and we were able to tell it was definitely two women arguing. My partner was behind me, which made sense tactically because he was taller and could see over my shoulder. In this set up, we both had a clear view down the hall to the back room of the apartment.

In the distance, in that rear room, we could see the two women appear and then disappear, moving further into the room and out of view as they continued to yell. This went on for a few minutes and the last time they came into view, one woman had the other woman by the shirt and was holding a large kitchen knife to her throat. At this point they had stopped moving but continued to yell at each other. The one woman with the knife was holding the blade right up to the other woman's throat.

At the sight of that knife, I pulled out my gun as fast as I could. Afterward, I remember thinking that the reaction of pulling out your gun really is a reflex reaction. It's definitely not something you think about, you just get to that point without noticing it. In any case, there I was, gun out and pointed down the hallway, directly at the two women. I gave several quick, very loud commands to drop the knife. I didn't want any confusion about who we were and what I wanted. When people are in that state of argument, with that much rage, all they see is red. They can get tunnel vision really fast and it could take more than a bit of urging to snap them out of their rage.

I stayed in the frame of the doorway with my gun pointed and my partner over my shoulder. The woman with the knife looked down the hall at us and let go of the other woman. However, she didn't drop the knife. Instead, she turned toward us and started walking down the hall in our direction. I yelled again, "Drop the knife!", with my gun still pointed at her. The hallway was about thirty feet long but the distance between us shrunk to about fifteen feet in no time. She continued toward us and she still had the knife in her hands.

In every shooting involving weapons other than a gun, you have a safe range before you have to act. With every inch less than that safe range, you run the risk of serious injury or death depending on the circumstances. This lady was getting ready to break that range of safety for me and my partner.

The apartment was dark. I could see her shape but once she stepped out of that light from the room she was in, I couldn't see her face. I could see the shape of it but not the expression. I could plainly see that the knife was still in her hand and it was about waist high with the blade pointed up. She was still walking toward me and I still couldn't tell if she had just zoned out forgetting about the knife in her hand or if she had some kind of death wish and was thinking of taking me or the both of us out.

The third time I yelled, "Drop the knife!", she was about ten feet away. At this point she was already too close and past that safe range for me and my partner. From here, if she charged at us I would be able to get a shot off and most likely hit her but she probably would be able to stab me as well. In these situations, with the person's adrenaline all pumped up, she would have more than enough rage to carry her through extra space even if she did get hit with a round.

I know I had my finger on the trigger and I remember holding it tight, tighter than ever. The pressure that I had on the trigger was probably the most I could apply without actually pulling the trigger back and firing a shot. I remember moving into position, in a shooter crouch and aiming my gun at her chest. I don't know how I remember this, but I distinctly remember my partner over my shoulder say, "Cool.". For him, it was like he was watching a movie or something. I guess the way we were set up, there was nothing for him to do but watch at that moment, as the scene unfolded. It was still a little weird, but he was a little weird too, so maybe it all fit.

The lady continued her slow, almost methodical walk toward me and just as she got about five feet away in what was the last second before I was going to shoot, she took a hard right turn into the kitchen. In one motion, she threw the knife to the counter and sat on a stool, put her head in her hands and cried.

As quick as I could, I holstered my gun and put her in handcuffs. She didn't resist and was easily cuffed as she sat there continuing to cry. There was no need for physical force at all. She was totally compliant but extremely upset. She cried the whole way to the precinct and in the holding cell for quite a while.

Later on, in the precinct, I took a few minutes to be alone before I started the arrest process. I sat in the quiet for a few minutes and just relaxed. In the end, this was really just going to be a bullshit, domestic violence arrest. In fact, if the other woman didn't press charges or show up at Court, the case would get tossed out all together just like it never happened.

That was their reality. They could just forget about the whole thing. This definitely wasn't the first time, or the last, these two women had been through this. For now, It was over and they could ignore what happened until their next argument. For me, it wasn't that easy right at that moment.

Sure, by the next day I could easily forget about the seriousness of that moment. That's what cops do. Right now, it was still fresh in my mind. The reality of that moment was right there in front of me to think about.

For a brief moment in time-a few seconds-there was a period where a life changing event could have taken place. A lot of things could have and almost did happen. Right there, on the third floor, standing in a doorway. Things that could have altered the course of a lot of lives. Thank God it went the way it did but you can't help but think, "What if things went differently?". How would that have changed the future?

Police work has been described by experts as hours of boredom and seconds of panic. I agree.

11. The "Usual" Suspect

When I began working steady midnights I found two things to be absolutely true. The first was that you were always doing your best to get accepted by the cops who were already working that tour. The midnight crew was very close-knit and different from the rest of the Precinct. They looked different and they acted different. The nature of the time of day we worked and the necessity for "having your co-workers back" made it that way. There were less cops and the work was more dangerous. You absolutely needed each other and the bond on that tour was clearly evident.

The other thing apparent about this tour was that while this tour had some of the best cops in the Precinct working it, it also was a group that had the biggest practical jokers. These guys loved a good laugh. It was the way they let off steam and dealt with pressure. If you fucked up on this tour, they let you know it along with everyone else who would listen in the entire Precinct.

The tour had just begun and my partner and I just got out of roll call. The entire night was in front of us and we were already talking about making collars. The midnights were all about making arrests and overtime. The cops on this tour used the phrase "collars for dollars". Obviously, Court wasn't open and as a result, it was a great tour for overtime. By the time the DA's got in at nine or ten o'clock and had their breakfast, cases were piled up waiting for them from the night before. You were guaranteed overtime just waiting for them to get to you, aside from actually drawing up your actual case.

If a collar did come up tonight, I would be first to get it. My partner had the last arrest the night before and we always went back and forth taking arrests. It was a fair way of sharing the collars and the overtime. As we walked out of the muster room, the clerk who takes the walk-in complaints calls us over. She motions to a woman standing in the complaint room and says, "Hey, you guys looking? Maybe you guys can help this lady.".

We made a bee line to the lady in the complaint room to find out what's going on. In short form, she tells us that her live-in boyfriend assaulted her and she wants him locked up. I'm thinking, "Great, a collar right off the start of the tour.". While I'm thinking that, I'm also looking her over while she said she was assaulted. She wasn't beat up or bloody. So the obvious question running through my mind is, "Where is the assault?". My partner, thinking the same thing, asks her, "What did he do?". With that, right there in the complaint room, she drops her jeans to the floor in front of a very crowded area full of cops, civilians and other complainants. She says to us, "Look at this!". She points to her inside upper thigh area. The wound wasn't bleeding too bad but you could see two perfectly marked sets of teeth embedded into the skin on her thigh. It was swollen and red and looked real painful.

At this point, I'm thinking, "Well that was a little unexpected.". However, it is evidence of an assault none the less and who knows, maybe after some more questioning we can bump this charge up to a felony or add some additional charges to make the case stronger.

I looked at her and said, "You want him locked up?" She snapped back, "Hell yes!" I appreciated her conviction in this matter. However, just because I have a willing complainant and evidence of an assault, that doesn't mean I'm going to just run over there to grab this guy without asking the necessary questions. By necessary questions, I mean the ones I need to make the arrest, while keeping me and my partner safe.

I show the complainant where to sit and begin to fill out the complaint report. The information for this report will give me all need to know about the incident, as well as the location we are headed to.

I began with the usual questions. Is he a drug user? Does he have any weapons in the house? Is he usually violent? Is he drunk? Do you think he is still there and is he alone? I might have asked a few more questions to get the whole picture but I ended it with the same question I ask all my complainants. I said to her, "Is there anything we should know that you haven't told us already?". She answered pretty quickly, "No, I don't think so.".

Feeling pretty good about the impending arrest and all the information we had, we headed out to grab this guy. On the way out we let the sarge know what we had. He said, "Sounds pretty easy, let me know if you need me. If not just bring him in.".

We take the lady outside, she hopped into our car and we headed over to her apartment building. She lead us up to the fourth floor and to her apartment door. As we are getting close to the door, she said, "That's it, right there.", as she is pointing at the door. I gave her the "be quiet sign" and both my partner and I stood there and listened to the door for any sounds. It was totally quiet. Not a peep from the apartment. Most times this means the dude left to avoid being arrested. However, he could be in there asleep or just sitting there, doing God knows what. I told the complainant to open the door and she told us that she didn't have the key and that she ran out without it. Of course, this means that we would have to knock and give up our edge for a silent, surprise entry.

I told the lady to move down the hall, out of harms way. Besides, It would be better if this guy didn't see her right away. We didn't want her anger fucking up what could be an easy collar. I knocked on the door and announced ourselves in a loud, clear voice. "Sir, this is the NYPD, can you open the door?".

In what seemed like a few seconds, we could heard scurrying from behind the door. It sounded like boxes or maybe drawers, opening and closing. It kind of sounded like someone hiding something or perhaps searching for something. Then we heard that distinctive noise of the peephole being opened. This of course was followed by silence that told us he was now checking us out. After he saw what he wanted, we heard the peep hole close. Then more sounds again like hiding or searching for something.

You can't help but think the worst in this situation. He knows what he did and knows that if the cops are here, he's going to jail. The sounds we heard were not comforting. If he was hiding something, then what has he got in there that he didn't want cops to see?If he was searching for something, then what was he looking for, with cops at his door about to lock his ass up? In my head I'm thinking, "This guy just assaulted a woman, so he is violent. He knows the cops are here and that he is probably going to jail.". The quick math in this scenario tells me guns, drugs or God knows what. In any case, we are both thinking the worst. At this point, that door should have been open. Too much time has passed and the possibility of getting set up for a violent confrontation is getting very real.

I saw in my partners face, that I wasn't the only one getting pumped up by the unfolding situation. We quickly put on our skell gloves and got ready to do battle. With the elapsed time, the thought of a weapon is still in my mind. However, it could also be a nine foot tall dude, the size of a gorilla looking for a brawl. We wanted to be ready in either case.

In what seemed like slow motion, the door locks could be heard coming off one by one. After that, we could hear and see the door knob turn. Next, the door began to slowly pull away from the frame and open up, with a dim light coming from inside the apartment. I don't know about my partner but I'm thinking, "Here it comes.". I started to unlock my gun from its holster and I'm as ready as I'm going to be, no matter what happens.

When the door opened, standing in front of us was a one armed midget with one leg longer than the other. It was obvious that this condition seriously affected the way he stood and would walk. Yet there he was staring up at us like a kid in a candy store with his mouth wide open. This is the part where if you were there, you would hear the unique sound of two NYPD cops jaws hitting the ground. Also, we now knew what the noises behind the door were. The dude wasn't hiding anything or getting a weapon. He was moving a wooden crate over to the door to stand on so he could look out the fucking peep hole. His limp and the fact that he had one arm accounted for the elongated time it took to complete this task.

At the sight of this guy the lady says, "That's him, I told you not to fuck with me.". "I want him arrested.".

I looked at my partner and he looked back at me and we were both thinking the same thing. Now what? In reality, we both knew what we had to do. It was simple really. We had to take a one armed midget with a limp to jail for assaulting his girlfriend. Well, his situation aside, he did assault his girlfriend and she wanted to press charges. With that, we told him he was under arrest.

I cuffed his one arm to his pants belt and helped this dude down the stairs and out of the building. Once he was in the back seat, I closed the door and asked the complainant, "When I asked you if there was anything else about this guy that we needed to know, nothing crossed your mind?". She replied, "Like what?". To which, I plainly said, "Like, he's a one armed midget with a limp.". Believe it or not, she said, "Oh, that.". That was enough for me. I said good night and told her that the District Attorney would call her in the morning for her statement and to get some more information.

As we drove toward the Precinct, it felt like the ride of a lifetime. The sad thing was that we actually were only about three blocks from the Precinct. It was the thought of bringing this guy in to the Precinct and in front of the Desk Sergeant that was making my stomach turn. I knew I was in for it. This was my collar and I already got my fair share of ribbing because I wasn't exactly the tallest cop in the precinct, not by a long shot. Yet, next to this guy, I was like a freak of nature as far as height goes. I could already imagine the jokes in my head. The best jokes came from the Desk Sergeant who said, "Hey kid, you finally got one shorter than you!". The Lieutenant also said, "What do you got kid, armed robbery?".

Anyway, I took my collar and my abuse along with a lot of overtime to process this guy. The next day, as I liked to do with all my perps, I checked his criminal history to see what else he has been arrested for in the past.

His records showed nothing for the past several years because he was in jail for manslaughter during that time. I could hardly believe my eyes. Evidently, he took a plea deal and did seven years in an upstate prison for killing a man. From the brief narrative on the arrest report, it seemed that this one armed midget with a limp used that one good arm to shoot a man dead.

I printed out the report to show the rest of the guys on the tour that night. It's a real lesson learned to come across something like this. It was a reminder for me, for years to come, that this job is real dangerous. You can't take anyone, anything or any job for granted. The old saying, "Don't judge a book by its cover." and "Assumption is the mother of all fuck ups.", immediately came to mind. Thinking back on the job from beginning to end, I know we handled that job the right way. Although I may have got some ribbing over it, we came out okay in the end. It proved anyone can be a bad dude, you just never know.

12. Source Of Information

There was a building that we knew dealt weed. It wasn't only known to us but to pot heads from around the city. Evidently, word got out that this guy had good shit. That's how it works. Word gets out where you can buy good smoke and then it spreads from locals to their friends. Before long, you have a conga line of customers throughout the hall, waiting to buy weed. On the weekends, it gets even busier. Customers can be seen going in and out all night long.

You are probably saying, "It's only weed, so what!". This thought is not unique and a lot of people feel the same way. In fact, some people don't even view this as a criminal offense. They feel it's harmless or it's a victimless crime. Well, ask those same people if they would want this sort of thing going on in the building where their children and family live and watch them change their attitude. Bottom line, this is a thriving, criminal business that brings criminals into places where good people have to live and raise a family. The weed itself may not be so bad but the crowd that comes with it always carries the potential for a problem and a risk of violence.

This particular dealer had a really great set up. The way he ran his spot made it almost impossible for the average street cop to arrest him. To get this guy required the services of an undercover operation and a search warrant for the location. If all that was set in motion and worked, you could still run into trouble with prosecution because of the way he dealt his weed. First of all, it was an inside location on the third floor of a building that was a little run down. The dealer only dealt through the keyhole of the door to his apartment. The keyhole was a fake and it pushed out from the inside like a tiny drawer. The buyer would knock on the door and the dealer would take the money through this keyhole. He would then push out the weed to the buyer and the deal was done. No words were said by the dealer and you never saw his face. He was like a human marijuana vending machine. You can see the legal obstacles this set up might pose for prosecution. Like I said, a really great set up.

My partner and I were beat cops who walked the street in uniform, handling various complaints. Among those complaints were trespassing, drug use and drug sales in the various buildings on our beats. This building had been called into our office as a problem for the few good people who still resided there.

Through talking to enough complainants and perps we would bust in the area, we were led to the spot pretty easily. With minimal street surveillance and a few off the record conversations with some of the pot head customers, we had the whole set up pretty much laid out for us. Yet, with all that information there was no way we could get this guy. He was relatively safe behind his door. His clients, however were a different story. The way we figured it, if we targeted his clientele, we could kill his business. Just as word spreads of a good weed spot, we hoped word would also spread that the building was hot with police presence. After enough time and arrests, word would get out and the business would dry up. Hopefully the dealer would move on and the complaint would be handled. Not exactly the way we wanted it but it would be taken care of without the need for outside resources.

The first thing we did was to get the building signed up in a trespass program the City had initiated at that time. It took some doing to track down the owner. These landlords were sometimes shifty, slum lord types and were hard to locate. When you did get a hold of them, they were reluctant to help you because they didn't want to get involved with court cases. To them it was a business and as long as they got their rent they were satisfied. After all, they didn't have to live there so they didn't care what was going on in the building. After some strong police persuasion, we convinced him it was in his best interest to get on board with this service we were offering.

Once we had the building signed into this program, we had the right to enter the building anytime we wanted and to stop and question all traffic coming and going in the building. The affidavit we received from the owner stated that the building was for tenants and guests only. It also stated that anyone else was subject to arrest for trespass. This wasn't a heavy charge by any means, but it was enough to make the arrest. We would then recover any drugs and begin to get the word out that we were watching that building. With every arrest not only did we gain more information on the spot but were legally allowed to search these people and recover the marijuana as well.

These pot heads were easy prey for us the minute they stepped into that building. Once they passed through the doorway, they were ours. They weren't residents or guests so they went to jail. No one in that building was going to vouch for them especially not the person whose door they came from.

In some cases, it became comical when we grabbed a pot head and would ask them questions as to why they were in the building. We would usually start by asking them if they lived in the building. Once they said no, we asked who they were visiting. To this they were usually dumbfounded, with no response. From there, it just got worse. Sometimes, they couldn't even tell you the building number, the apt number or even the street they were on. Most of the buyers went to the building by direction of what the building looked like, its shape or physical location. Even if we got an occasional buyer who actually knew the address, it still didn't matter. They still needed someone to say they were legitimately visiting them. That wasn't possible. What would they do? Walk with the police to the dealer's apartment and knock on his door for a reference?

Once we played that little charade, it was off to the Precinct and then a trip downtown. The charges may be minor but we never saw a person return after getting locked up. Once was enough for these people. Besides, there were tons of other places to buy weed where the police weren't busting people. These buyers were not crack heads. Some of these people were decent looking people with suits and nice cars. Most of them were picking up some smoke for their weekend parties. They weren't looking to get hassled or begin racking up a criminal record. These people who don't come back are the ones who spread the word that the spot is burned and that will kill the business.

We did this for weeks, taking body after body for trespass and the weed possession. We made dozens of arrests in a relatively short time. We would grab these perps in the lobby and sometime even right in front of the dealer's door, right after they bought their weed. Busted red handed and in full view of the dealer behind the door. We were sure that the guy behind the door could hear and see what we were doing. We did this to piss him off and let him know it was us that was fucking with him and killing his business.

One day, we found out that our street narcotics sergeant and his team were gearing up to hit this spot at the end of the month. The story was that one of his team's arrests flipped on the dealer and was going to swear out a warrant so the sergeant and his guys could take it down.

Because we had been so active in that building we asked the Sergeant about it and he confirmed the information we had was true. Even though it was our beat, we asked him if he wanted us to stay clear of the building. He assured us that it was okay to continue making visits like normal. He felt that if we just stopped making visits all of a sudden, the dude might get spooked. We felt that made sense and told the Sergeant we would continue our visits. We also asked him for some intelligence on the spot and the supposed dealer. All we really wanted was to know what type of criminal this guy was in case we ran into him in the building. The Sergeant assured us he was just a low level weed man. Nothing to be concerned about at all.

I have to say, my partner and I never really liked that Sergeant very much to begin with. He had a sneaky, wormy look about him and a reputation that alluded to him having major integrity issues. I had even heard rumors that before he got promoted, he was a crooked cop who never got caught. Needless to say, we always steered clear of him and dealt with him and his team only when absolutely necessary.

We kept doing our normal building checks and paying visits to the front of the dealer's apartment door. We would continue to grab pot heads for a few more weeks, making our petty collars and fucking with the dealer's business.

One day we went to that building and found that the spot was boarded up and padlocked. The sergeant and his team evidently executed his warrant and closed him down. Naturally, we were curious on the amount of weed and who or how many perps got taken out of there on that warrant. We went in to the Precinct to check the arrest paperwork on the warrant for that building.

Imagine the look on our faces when we saw the paperwork for that apartment and the subsequent arrests made inside. It showed that along with the perp they took three fully loaded hand guns out of that apartment. Not only did this Sergeant neglect to tell us this but we found out that all that information was given to him and his team when he signed up the informant and got the warrant paperwork rolling. When we asked him about the spot, he already knew there were guns in there and chose to keep that information to himself. When we confronted him on it, he made up a lame excuse and then let it out that he was worried about losing the collar to us if we came across this guy on a visit.

In the meantime, he put me and my partner in serious danger by keeping that information from us. There were numerous days when we were in that building alone and in front of this guy's door. Meanwhile, this guy was packing some serious fire power just on the other side of his door. All that separated us from those guns was a cheap wood door.

My partner, who had a lot of time on the job, had it out with the Sarge in public. As for me, I just did a number on his reputation, talking bad about the guy to anyone who would listen hoping he would confront me. He never did. However, I did run into him after he retired and we had a bit of a heated discussion. It ended with me telling him that I had always heard that he was more crooked than some of the streets in Harlem. He didn't like that so I told him to go fuck himself.

After that incident I never really trusted anyone at work just because they were a cop. I only had a few years on the job at that time and that incident really educated me and taught me a great lesson. It proved that there is good and bad in every job, regardless of the occupation. It also taught me to question everything on the street, no matter who or where the information comes from. That might sound like a shitty way to work and live but in the end that's what it's about, living and survival.

13. The Beginning Of The Beat and "Ace"

Being a beat cop is like being the sheriff of a small town. Taking care of a beat was like stepping back in time to the way I imagined police work used to be. It was the old way the Department worked in the early days of policing before they used cars for patrol. Being a beat cop meant being out there on foot, walking the neighborhood and getting to know everyone in your assigned area or beat.

Your assigned beat was made up of a grid of blocks, usually about six streets by three avenues. You were expected to know that beat, it's problems and everyone on it inside and out. Actually, expectations of the Police Department aside, it really was in your best interest to know everything and everyone out there.

Being a beat cop was what community policing was all about. It was the only unit left in the Department where you actually had the time to know a part of the precinct thoroughly. Unlike regular patrol cops, you could stop and visit with residents, business owners and even keep tabs on the criminals who reside in your area. The harder you worked, the more information you would have. As your beat IQ grew, it became easier to handle your beat as well as the daily complaints that came in.

When working a beat you aren't just reacting to the radio calls like in a patrol car. On the beat you have to identify the cause of a problem and come up with a solution to fix it. These problems can be just about anything. They can vary from hard acts of criminal violence to mundane quality of life violations. In most cases they are the sort of complaints that are not a quick fix. They are very often the ones that linger around and attack the community on a daily basis.

For a good portion of the week, the beat cop works alone and usually on foot. If you are lucky you get an adjoining beat cop to work with for at least part of the week. Ultimately, you will be out there by yourself, handling business without immediate backup. For this reason it was important to make your rounds, be seen and introduce yourself to the general public. You had to let people know you were in charge, running the show and would do what ever you had to in order to get the job done.

Knowing that you would eventually be out there alone made you handle things different from the usual two man sector patrol car. You had to rely on your strengths, know your weakness or limitations and be ready to handle what ever comes your way. You had to constantly send out messages to the regulars that you were confident and strong minded. Every action became a statement. You must be fair but tough. Kindness is often mistaken for weakness and lack of action can be mistaken for cowardice.

If someone gets in your face out there you have to deal with it quickly and accordingly. If you don't make a stand, your reputation can be built in a negative way. Before you know it, every asshole on your beat could be testing you. That kind of problem can get you hurt or even killed. On a beat, how you act and react can literally save your life, not just at that moment but in the future as well.

When I inherited this beat it was in real bad shape. The previous beat cop had been promoted and transferred. As a result, the beat went unmanned for a few years without the regular everyday presence it needed. There was no one to stake a claim and take ownership in the area. No one to stand up and enforce the laws to keep the area from slipping into a degenerative state. Very quickly, the beat went down hill and the regulars who hung out on the various corners got used to doing whatever they wanted. They began to act in a free and easy manner without worrying about consequences. This lack of police presence, combined with a few years of a rising crime rate, took its toll on that area. Several corners became hang outs for the neighborhood degenerates. There were drug sales, drug use and an overall lack of respect and unruly behavior. The unruly behavior included all kinds of quality of life violations and this was where a great deal of our complaints would come from. Ideally, you would like to solve these problems without force. Reason is a great weapon. However, I quickly learned that reason is lost with most criminals, especially drug dealers and drug users. Reasoning is not a skill these types of individuals practice. It's not practical to think that a drug dealer making a ton of money for doing very little can be talked into moving on or change his ways. Likewise, the corner bum or local crackhead can't be rehabilitated in a short conversation or be expected to spontaneously start a new life. Most of these junkies and bums were just occupying space and killing time until they died.

In either case and needing to deal with both circumstances, I realized that if I was going to make an impact and actually clean this area up, I was going to have to make a statement. That statement would have to be followed up with relentless enforcement in the days that followed. It was going to have to be good old fashioned police work, one skell at a time. If I couldn't get what I wanted with reason, I would use action and rely on word of mouth to spread the news of change coming to the area. What I wanted was for these skells to begin to feel uneasy on the street. These bums should be looking over their shoulder to see if I was coming and not doing as they pleased. They should move on at the mere sight of me and not wait for me to ask them to leave. We're the police, we make the rules. If we don't get respect, how in the world is the little old lady going to the corner store going to get it?

A plan like this is like getting a big stone to roll down hill. In the beginning it will take a great deal of effort. Once enough force and hard work is used and it gets rolling, things will start to happen on their own. Once I establish myself and get known, it will be easier for me as well. Take out a known dealer and the replacement guy will most likely not be so good. Lock up a few bums and junkies and the drug business will slow down. Make it known that some new tough bastard cop is out there busting balls and the area will benefit. In return, punks won't test me and I will get the respect I need to work safely and to start a change on the beat.

When I was offered the beat I only had five years on the job but I had already made a name for myself as an active cop with a lot of arrests. It was a huge undertaking but true to my nature, I enjoyed a challenge and proving myself.

The beat was truly a shamble and that was a known fact to all the other beat cops. I remember when I was offered the beat, there were a couple of older cops standing behind the boss giving me hand signals, prompting me to turn it down. I immediately accepted the bosses offer and took the assignment. Those veteran cops looked at it as too much work to correct the problem. I looked at it as a turning point in my career. A chance to learn a new style of policing and hone my skills for future endeavors. The way I saw it was that if I could be successful at this, I could handle anything that came my way the rest of my career.

My initial game plan to correct this mess was to do nothing. I intended to sit back and take it all in. By doing this, I could take note of the various hot spots and the regulars who hung out there causing trouble. Additionally, my quiet presence alone would confuse these assholes and get them thinking. These guys weren't accustomed to police presence and they definitely weren't ready for an extreme change like I was planning.

Day 1 on the beat. I walked out there and found a good safe spot to stand. I put my back against a wall and just stared at everything in front of me, making mental notes at each location. Right from the start it was obvious that the crowd of usual characters were uneasy about my presence. They would be laughing one minute and then all of a sudden be very quiet, like they suddenly remembered I was there. On some of the corners they acted like a pack of wild animals that noticed a new animal on their turf. Just like animals in the wild, they were checking me out trying to figure out what was safe and what boundaries were being formed. I was doing the same thing to them.

I decided I would do this for an entire week before I acted. In that week I discovered a great deal about the daily routines of several regulars and the corners they occupied. I was able to figure out who looked important to the corner and who was just a follower. I could also tell who looked like they were going to be trouble and who had to go first.

By the end of that first week it was evident that on one particular corner, the worst one, the crowd was getting use to me and yet were nervous at the same time. A few of the followers of the groups were sent over to feel me out and even tried to engage me in conversation. I would quickly skirt any conversation and say the bare minimum, if that much. This only further confused these guys.

The one guy on that corner who I pegged for a problem from the first time I saw him seemed to be the loudmouth of the group. He would very often talk loud to his fellow bums so that I could hear his tough talk. He could be heard bragging about what he might have done in the past and showboating how tough he was. Obviously, he was doing this because I was there. He was trying to send me a message as well as posturing for the rest of the knuckleheads. He was the one I wanted. It would start with him. He didn't know it yet but he was going to be my statement collar. The more he flapped his gums the more I zeroed in on him and sized him up. I was going to have to break that son of a bitch if I was going to do anything out there at all.

After asking around and talking to a few of the store owners, I found out his name was Ace. Naturally, that wasn't his God given name but that's what everybody in that area knew him by. It was clear after a few conversations with the locals that Ace had done more than his fair share of terrorizing the community. The tales of woe were revealed to me and they were all the same. He was a cancer in the area, constantly drinking or drunk. He would carry on and do whatever he wanted and was seen smoking weed and urinating in public regularly. If anyone protested, he would get violent and damage property. A lot of the decent folks were afraid of him because of his reputation and his unpredictable nature.

Ace was a tall, skinny, black guy. He was about six feet tall but his body was alcoholic thin. He probably weighed about one seventy or so. He was clearly a boozer and that was evident in the red glow on his face. It was like my partner used to say, "When you see a black guy with a red face, you know he's heavy drinker.". Ace was just that and more. The rest of the story on Ace was that he would supplement his booze high with weed and crack. He was pretty scary looking as well. He had no teeth in the top front part of his mouth except for the ones on the sides. When he scowled, he sort of looked like Dracula because those teeth became exposed and were very prominent. They seemed almost longer than they should be. His attitude matched his looks, as he had a "I don't give a fuck" attitude and could be heard cursing with every other word that he said.

There was absolutely no doubt about it. If I was going to make a name for myself on this corner, I had to start with Ace. It didn't really matter what I arrested him for or how long he was in for. I wasn't looking for the collar of the year, that wasn't the idea. As long as he went to jail and it either went down in front of the rest of the crowd or the word got spread around the area. It just had to be done. After that, I would continue with whomever was dumb enough to take Ace's place. I had to show that the party was over and when I'm here you better get in line and act like a normal citizen. If you don't, your going for a ride downtown as well, plain and simple. They also had to know that when they got out, things were different. I was still going to be here and their little trip earned them shit. If they came back out and acted the same, repeating their asshole antics, they were going right back to the Precinct and downtown again. I wanted to be known as relentless, a real pain in the ass. Unwavering and constant.

Because I knew what time the corner started to get hot, I made sure I got there first. I found a nice little hiding spot just across the street in a lobby where I could see without being seen. Like clockwork, the corner started to fill up with all the regulars. One by one they showed up on the corner like they were reporting to work.

Then, "He" showed up. Disheveled, loud, yelling and cursing, Ace came strolling onto the corner in all his glory. I'm sure the sight of me not there made him feel even more ballsy than he already was. Patiently I waited and watched the crowd and within a few minutes Ace pulled out a nice size bottle of what looked like good old fashioned bum wine. He proceeded to guzzle it down right there in public view, on the corner, without a care in the world. I watched him recap the bottle and put it back in his pocket and continue to socialize on the corner. He obviously was settling in for the day. I put my black leather skell gloves on and slowly emerged from the lobby. I calmly strolled across the street and onto the corner which was full of regular losers.

I walked right through the small crowd, parting the group in two. I walked right up to Ace and made it known by my gait that at this moment he was the intended target. This was done for the benefit of both Ace and the group who would be watching our entire interaction. I started off civil but stern. We exchanged a few words, most to his obvious displeasure but during that brief conversation I did get him to hand over his identification. If nothing else I now had his real name and address and he knew that I was directing my attention at him. I began to sense he was going to blow off this conversation. So, I told him that drinking in public is against the law. To a boozed up loser, this statement is funny. It was also funny to some of the clowns who were standing there watching our interaction.

The laughter turned to silence when I told Ace to put his hands on the wall. I wish I had a picture of the shocked and confused look he had on his face. This dude had been unchecked and living a life of unruly behavior for quite a while. What just happened to him was like a spoiled child getting disciplined for the first time. Ace went from party time to giving up his identification and being told what to do in an instant. Ace was confused, as was the crowd, and that gave me the advantage. Ace complied but while facing the wall he started to complain and was slowly getting louder and louder. I knew he was posturing for the crowd and trying to save face and reputation. I thought to myself, "what a coincidence", so was I. At this point, I had one hand on his shoulder and could sense he was going to turn around to face me. If that happened, most likely all of the advantage I had with both position and state of shock would be lost. We would be on even ground and with a crowd behind me I didn't want that at all.

What I wanted here was a quick and swift action with no mixed messages. Take control, take charge and let the perp know he fucked up. End the interaction as quick as possible. Just like shock, surprise is a great weapon. A familiar quote was again ringing in my head, "Nine times out of ten, the person who throws the first punch usually wins the fight". In police terms that means you can't give a perp time to think because all that he will think of is how to run or how he can hurt you.

With a quick, hard push I shoved Ace face first into the brick wall in front of him. He only had one hand on that wall so he couldn't push himself off or brace himself as his face crashed into the bricks in front of him. From there I dragged him to the pavement in a hard and forceful manner. As the confusion went through his booze soaked brain and the pain struck him, I did my best job of speed cuffing him face first on the concrete. I was taking full advantage of the situation. I think that particular incident was my all time best for speed cuffing as it seemed that in a blur Ace was lying on the concrete, cuffed and bleeding from the nose and mouth. For dramatic effect and the benefit of the rest of the mutts out there, I pulled out the bottle of booze from his back pocket and let it be seen to the crowd. The clear message was being sent to the entire group. The message was simple. Yeah, it's a petty bullshit violation and I am not afraid to do it now or in the future. It also said that I wasn't afraid to get physical. Ace was living proof of that for all to see. More shock value.

The crowd that was once loud and laughing was now quiet and shocked. The smarter ones in the group, or the ones that wanted to avoid police contact, started to immediately walk off on their own without me having to utter a single word. The rest left when I told them to get the fuck out of there or I would be back for their ass next.

With the corner set straight and dispersed, the only thing left to do was to take Ace in for arrest processing. So I called radio for a transport and off we went to the Precinct. This would mark the beginning of what would be a rough few years out there for me as I tried to get a grasp on that beat. It would also mark the start of a very odd and tenuous relationship between me and Ace for years to come.

Oddly enough, although Ace was older than me, he was born on the same day as I was. Unfortunately I made the mistake of saying that out loud during the arrest process we spent together. Incredibly, no matter how bad our relationship would get in the years to come, Ace would always look for me to remind me and to wish me a happy birthday.

14. Shit Happens!

It's funny what you can remember over the course of a twenty year career. I don't remember every arrest I ever made. I can't even remember the names of some cops I worked with. However, as if it just happened yesterday, I can remember the first two people I ever saw take a shit in the street.

The first time happened when I was a newly appointed police officer, fresh out of the Academy. I had only been assigned to my Precinct for about two weeks but I knew the area was pretty run down. I was on my way to work and the street I took to get to the Precinct had one of those traffic lights that takes a little longer than others to change. As a result, it would build up a row about ten cars long and then only let about half the amount through before it changed to red again. You would usually get stuck for two complete light cycles before you made it through.

This particular day I was going through that street and I noticed her from a distance. When I came to a stop for the traffic in front of me she was about two car lengths or so away from me. She was in the street, just off the curb and on the same side as my driver's side window. She was obviously a crack head or some sort of addict. She looked like she weighed about ninety pounds at most. Her hair was a wreck and her clothes were ripped and dirty. She was between two parked cars and she had about four to five feet of space so she was not hidden by the vehicles at all. She had her pants down around her ankles and I didn't see any panties at all. She was in a bent, sort of crouching position. She looked like a baseball catcher in a crouch that was a little higher than normal and pushed back to the rear a little more as well.

The light changed but for some reason the traffic only let though a few cars before it changed again. This left me even with her, in full view with no obstructions whatsoever. I looked over to her and there she was in all her glory. I really didn't want to look but it was so odd to see that I couldn't look away.

I swear the first thing I thought of when I saw her was that it looked like a whiffle ball bat was partially hanging out of her ass. This turd was so long that it was bent and part was on the ground and part still stuck in her ass. Thank God it was a cool day so I could keep the windows closed. The sight was nasty enough that I didn't want the smell I can only imagine that went along with it. It was nasty. As nasty as she was, she went one step further and shook her ass a little to get the whole log out. It fell to the street and she pulled up her pants and waddled away.

The second one I saw was from a bona fide heroin addict. This guy was complete with missing teeth, sunken eyes and sores readily visible on his skin. This guy decided to be a little more discreet and used the stairwell of a closed entrance to the subway. It was closed for repairs but people could exit through that side but could not enter. This subway exit had what we called an "iron maiden" or a floor to ceiling turnstile type of gate. So, he was in public view but in a recessed sort of way.

This guy also had his pants down but was a little more classy. He had underwear. His underwear were around his ankles and he was bent over and very close to the tile wall behind him. This guy was not just shitting but spraying diarrhea all over the wall behind him. The best way to describe it would be to imagine a flame thrower and how it shoots out in burst. Now, imagine one that works with diarrhea instead of flames. This dude was forcefully spraying shit out his ass and he had sound effects to go along with the show. Slowly but surely he was covering the wall behind him and his diarrhea was running down the tile wall to the floor as well. I did not wait for him to finish. I called down to him and got his attention. When he looked up, I called him a fucking slob and quickly left to go on a coffee break.

15. A Nice Little Old Church Lady?

Sometimes the Department would give us overtime for a particular violation they wanted to go after and enforce. This time it was seatbelt enforcement overtime. It's amazing that no matter how many tickets you give out for an offense, you can always find more. The Department doesn't give you a quota on how many they want for the overtime but they let you know whether your performance was good or not. In any case, I knew I had a certain amount I needed to get in order to be done. I knew that I wasn't planning on giving too many breaks because I was trying to get done as soon as possible. The more breaks I give, the longer I will have to be out on the street looking for violations. In the police department we use a term, "get 'em and forget 'em.".

So, right out of the chute I'm banging every driver I see with no seatbelt and giving them a summons. I'm thinking be merciless and get this done so I can move on to some other stuff I needed to do out there as well. Besides, towards the end you start to get tired of doing the same thing over and over and just want to get finished.

After getting a nice little rhythm going, I managed to get almost all the summons I needed for the day. The Sergeant came by and saw that I was doing a good job and really hustling to get him his "numbers" for the tour. He was really satisfied with what I got and he told me to just get one more and then take a nice break before going back to my regular assignment. After hearing that I was feeling pretty good. All I needed was to get one more and I would be done. The next driver I saw with no seatbelt would absolutely get a summons. Not a chance in hell of getting a break, no matter who it was.

No sooner had I said that, I see a large white Cadillac slowly rolling down the street towards me. The driver can just barely be seen behind the wheel but it's clear the driver has no seatbelt on. The seat belt buckle can be seen hanging in its retracted position shining over the driver's left shoulder, clearly unattached. The sight of this made me real happy. I'm thinking, "This is it, I'm done.". I quickly reminded myself, "No break here, just write the ticket, move on, and be as quick as possible.".

I motioned for the car to pull over to the curb. The driver complied and pulled over in the same slow manner it had been driving in the whole time. I walk up to the car and looked in the window and saw the typical little old church lady. She was short and a little chubby with big frame glasses, about five feet tall at most. She was older, probably close to seventy years old and dressed in her Sunday best. The outfit was complete with white gloves, a fancy hat and her hair was neatly done under it. The dress she had on was frilly but conservative and looked like a updated version of a nun's habit. She had a big friendly face and was wearing an even bigger smile.

I said, "Hello.", and quickly asked her, "Ma'am, why aren't you wearing your seatbelt?". She glanced at the belt, which was hanging there, and told me she was on her way to church and that it must have slipped her mind to put it on.

Besides this being the last summons I needed, it was also the summer and close to midday. It was already hot and getting hotter by the minute. I had been working all morning and really needed that break. I hated to do it but this nice little old church lady was going to have to get the ticket.

I told her that I understood why she didn't have it on and asked if I could see her driver's license. She replied, "Why, sure Dear.". She handed me her license and the other papers for the car as well. I thanked her and told her I would be right back. I walked back to my parked police car and began to write the ticket for not wearing a seatbelt. I wrote as fast as I could. I was beginning to feel the heat. I was tired and just wanted to get out of there. I quickly hopped out of my car and went back to the lady who was listening to what sounded like gospel music on her radio.

I said, "Okay ma'am, here is all your paperwork back and here is your summons for not wearing you seatbelt.". I quickly continued talking and ran through what she needed to do with the summons as far as paying it or fighting the ticket in Court. The whole time I was talking she had the ticket and paperwork in her hand and a puzzled look on her face. She was quiet the entire time I spoke to her and when I stopped talking, she said, "You wrote me a summons for not wearing my seatbelt?". I replied in a apologetic tone, "Yes ma'am, you need to have your seatbelt on at all times, it's the law.". She looked up at me and said, "You motherfucker!". With that, she pulled the car away from me, actually squeaking the tires a little bit and leaving some dust at my feet.

All I could do was stand there and laugh as she rode off down the street in a pretty hasty manner for an old lady. I was amazed at how this driver went from a nice little old church lady to a truck driver in an instant. The whole thing was comical and the way she acted towards me actually took some of the guilty feeling away from me. I always felt better about giving a summons to someone when they were nasty or cursed me out. In any case, I was done and going on my break.

16. You Can Check In...

The best way to observe a drug operation that takes place on the street is to find a location where you can watch from an angle and where you are preferably elevated. You need to try to get a spot that is a half of a block to a block away at most, with some good powerful binoculars. If you score a spot like that and use the type of binoculars that are available today, you are going to make some good collars. From that distance and under those conditions, you can see a vial of crack in a junkie's hand.

It's the junkie who helps you figure out what's actually going on out there. Junkies can't wait to see the merchandise they just bought. Dealers will tell them not to smoke around the "set" and to wait until they are some place out of view. This much they can do. Even the really fucked up crack heads know enough not to piss off a dealer and get their ass kicked. However, after you have dealt with enough crackheads, you realize these people are under a spell. The drug has them in a trance. To them, getting crack is like the holy grail. They absolutely can not wait to smoke. The next best thing to smoking is the anticipation of smoking it. They do this by looking at it as they walk away. The crack dictates their actions. They absolutely cannot resist.

A drug transaction is real fast. From beginning to end, it is all of a matter of seconds. Even with binoculars trained on the hand area of the dealer or buyer, it is going to look like an exchange of money for a small object. To some people it may even look like an exchange of money for nothing at all. You have to be patient and wait for it. You have to forget the dealer after the exchange and follow the crack head as he or she walks off. Keep your nocs trained on the junkies hands and before long, maybe within a few steps from the dealer, they will instinctively open their hand and look at the goods. There have been times when I have even seen some crack heads smile at the sight of the crack in their hands. They don't even know they're doing it. These people are gone.

Sometimes to get one of these premium spots you need to do a little trekking through the back lots of the buildings. To get to your destination you will cross other buildings, alleyways and several fences or other obstacles. Some of these roof tops are high and the climb up is sometimes shaky at best. However, if the information is good, it's well worth the work of getting up to one of these spots.

One day my unit got their hands on some real good information on a street dealer who was supposed to be making a killing dealing right out in front of a building. The building was situated in a way that this guy could see the cops coming from a mile away. With the view he had he was always able to stop dealing and hide his shit without even coming close to being seen. To get this guy we would have to scope him from a distance and then run up and grab him when he thinks he's safe later on.

We had what looked like a perfect spot to watch this guy from. It was across the street and up the block a little bit. On top of that, most of the apartments were vacant which meant less chance of being spotted sneaking around. To get to this spot we would have to gain access through the rear of the building by crossing through the lots that connect from the next street over.

We were probably ten buildings away when we started out on our little expedition to our observation post. We crossed several vacant lots, jumped a few fences and climbed up the fire escape of an abandoned building to the roof. Once up on that roof, we had to cross over several roofs to get to the one that we wanted. Some of the buildings we crossed over were burned out and you had to be real careful about where you stepped. A few of the roofs were in bad shape and you had to walk like you were stepping through a mine field in order to cross safely. I can remember this one roof in particular where I was walking across slowly while listening for the sound of cracking wood.

Finally, we were able to see the building we wanted to get into. The last few obstacles were a fire escape to climb down, a few wide ledges to cross and a climb up a drain pipe. That path would lead us right into the open window of a vacant apartment that hopefully had the view we needed. One by one, the three of us managed to climb up and into the apartment. However, the last cop was a little bigger than me and the other cop so he struggled a bit at the very end. As a result, he broke the drain we had just used as a ladder to get in. This apartment was three floors up and although we got in okay, none of us felt really safe about going back down that way. The pipe just didn't look like it would hold up. It was obvious we couldn't exit the building that way if we were going to take part in the actual bust. In any case, we were in and happy with that. We were all feeling pretty good and figured we would just use the door to exit. The building was far enough away that we could sneak out the front door when no one was looking so as to not burn the spot for future use.

We were finally set up and ready to begin making out observations on our dealer. The spot was great. The view let us see everything and there was no way we could be seen from the street. The apartment we were in looked like it had been recently vacated. When the tenants left, they left the shades on the windows. We quickly cut a few small holes to look through and had a comfortable place to see all the deals go down. All we needed now was a little time and patience and we would be set.

We couldn't have been in there more than a half hour when the dealing began. Once this guy got rolling, it was like a free for all. This guy was dealing like mad out there. It was like watching a sale at a department store. Crackheads were coming to him from every angle and he served them all with speed. We watched this guy do business for a good fifteen minutes, hitting off crackheads left and right. Our field team was running around like crazy trying to pick up as many crackheads as possible. These junkies would get arrested for simple possession. It was a misdemeanor that we could use to corroborate our observations against the dealer.

All of a sudden the dude stops dealing. He was working so fast he actually ran out of crack. While we were debating whether or not to move in and grab him before he quits for the day, a second dude walks up to him and starts handing him bundles of crack right there in plain view on the street. Our dealer took some and shoved it into his jacket and placed the rest in the garbage can that was in front of him. We knew we wouldn't get another chance like this so we radioed our team and told them to move in and pick this guy up.

The wait is the worst part. You can't help but get nervous about losing this guy and coming away with nothing. You start to think about all the things that could go wrong down there in the street. In reality, we weren't that far away and knew we could get there way before the team did. On top of that, we knew who we wanted. The team was only following our description. We decided it would be better if we climbed down to the street and got involved in the actual arrest. At the very least we could be backup for the field team or be on the ground close by in case the dude ran.

Remembering that we couldn't use the drain pipe to get to the lot below, we made our way to the front door of the apartment to exit the building from the front. Imagine our surprise when we found out that the front door to the apartment was not just locked but nailed shut from both sides. Basically, we were trapped inside the apartment with no way out.

Two things were motivating us to get out. First, we wanted that guy real bad. This was going to be a decent street bust with some good drugs. Second, who the fuck wanted to have to call for backup to come and get us out of that apartment? Not only would it be embarrassing but the other cops would give us shit about it for weeks to come. I started to kick on the door as hard as possible. The door sounded like it was weak and might actually give way. With that, the three of us took turns kicking on the door and then tried kicking it together, two at a time. Before long, the wall around the door started cracking and sounded like they were coming from both the door and the frame as well. With a few more kicks, the door gave way and crashed into the hallway, taking the frame around it. Pieces of plaster and wood from both sides went flying everywhere. When it hit the floor it sounded like a small bomb had gone off, echoing in throughout the nearly vacant building. The hall was filled with a big cloud of dust and dirt and you could hear debris tumbling down into the stairwell.

When the smoke cleared a little bit, one of the last remaining tenants in this shit hole of a building was standing there with her mouth open, just staring at us. My partners didn't want any part of explaining what was going on or why we just destroyed a door and wall in her building. They quickly walked around her and headed down the stairs for the front door. I looked at her, quickly pulled out my badge and said, "Hey lady, did you see a guy run through here?". It was all I could think to say. It confused her for a moment, yet long enough for me to go around her and run down the stairs behind my partners. I could hear that old lady yelling at us the whole way down and even in the lobby below.

We quickly exited the building and ran around the corner. It was perfect timing. Just as we were coming onto the set our dealer was looking the other way watching our team slowly pull up in the other direction. He was busy checking out our police van and never saw us exit the building or run up on him. We took him down quick and hard and without any further incident. Before he knew what hit him, his ass was in cuffs and laying on the ground. A few crackheads who were nearby went running off down the street. That's always a funny sight.

Between what he had on him and his stash from the garbage can, we had about two hundred vials of crack and a shit load of money. Back at the Precinct we also had a bunch of crackheads under arrest for possession from his earlier sales. Altogether we had a pretty good collar and a nice case for court and some good overtime, which is always good. As far as street narcotics goes this was a good collar. After we got our paperwork done, we took a little break and all laughed about that old lady from the building. The look on her face and the way she yelled at us was worth all the work we put in to get that collar.

17. Walk Lightly

When you are a rookie cop, the Department say's you are full of "piss and vinegar!". You want to save the world and believe that you really can. It's not until later in your career that you realize all the arrests you made are like shoveling shit against the tide. At best you are holding things at the same level, no better, no worse. If you get some time under your belt and still think you will eradicate all crime in a big city like New York, you need serious help.

As you get older you get wiser and generally have more to lose. In turn, you are not as quick to do the things you did as a naive rookie. You still do the job but you learn to do things more carefully and more thought out instead of being reckless or impulsive. Hopefully as you mature on the job and in life in general, you will be less apt to do things that can cause you harm or even get you killed. After going through this maturation process, you would think that when it comes to doing something unsafe, history would not repeat itself. Not so for several occasions in my career but one in particular that I will always remember.

A great deal of what you learn is from other cops who have been down the road that you are headed. It's the experience of doing something and the success or failure of that experience that makes you grow. In the first few years of police work you are listening to other cops, watching them work and experimenting with the job when the opportunity arises.

I learned a lot of strategies and tactics over the years from paying attention to older more experienced cops. When possible, I would improve on that education by altering what I learned to fit my needs. Not all the stuff you learn is something you should repeat. It might have worked but some shit is just too crazy to do. The education I received from a couple of older cops was just that type. It would have been best to hear it, enjoy it and then leave it alone. Like I said earlier though, it's that "piss and vinegar" that makes you do things. You get bent about a perp who thinks he's smarter than you and you get obsessed with getting the guy. You will do almost anything to get him dirty and lock him up.

The funny thing about this idea that I heard about from two older cops was that although it sounded crazy it also sounded exciting and like it would actually work. As reckless as it may seem to some people, it was a way to combat some of these drug operations that seem to have the perfect setup. I only did this once but I thought about it afterwards dozens of times. I would never do it again and absolutely do not recommend anyone else try it at all.

The dealer we were targeting was a dust dealer on 116th Street who had a really good set up to sell his crap. He would simply sit on the lobby stairs which led up into the building. From where he sat he was able to look right out onto the street, through two sets of locked glass doors separated by about 10 feet between them. He was an additional 20 feet or so from the second inner locked door. Basically, he could see who was coming a mile away before they even got near the two locked doors. He was long gone at the sight of anything he didn't know or trust. Plain and simple, if he thought it was a cop he took off up the stairs to an unknown apartment. After he felt comfortable enough he would return later and start up again. This dude was so far and secure in his spot that we couldn't even get a good look at him, let alone arrest him.

After weighing our options, we realized that the only way to get this dude would be to get him from behind. We would have to come down from inside the building and drop down to the part where he was going to run to, not run from. A nice quiet approach from the roof down to the lobby.

First, what we needed was some good old fashioned recon. On a day when the dude wasn't working a few well chosen cops and I went into the building and went up to take a look at the roof. The building where the dealer worked was a free standing building. The building next to it was identical but they were not attached. They had a small space between them which looked like it was full of garbage at the bottom. The space was about eight to ten feet wide and the building was eight flights tall. Looking down from the roof you could see it was a good sized building for that area. Looking over, we knew the only way to cross was the same as I heard about from the last cops that did it. It was crazy but it was the only way. No guts, no glory.

We headed over to the local construction yard and talked the foreman into giving up a premium piece of lumber they used for ceiling construction. This wood was in fresh cut shape. It was strong as metal and long enough to reach across the space on the roof. Before carrying it over to the building we tested it a few times for strength purposes. I guess it was partly to convince ourselves that it was going to be okay. In any case, the wood checked out as advertised and was perfect for the job.

In civilian clothes and disguised as construction workers, we made our way to the adjoining building. We carried this lumber into the building and right up to the roof. We picked the right time of the day because both buildings were like ghost towns. Once we were on the roof we stashed our wood safely against the roof wall and exited the building with ease. All we needed now was for the spot to start working.

We tell if a spot is working by the clients who go into the building. Each type of junkie has his or her special traits and look about them. Crackheads, dusters and heroin addicts all tend to look and act a certain way. Additionally, the type of drug very often dictates what type of junkie you will encounter. This will give you a good indication of what is being sold in that area or building.

In this particular instance, we were working on a building that was known for selling dust. During this time, Harlem was still predominantly Black. However, the majority of the junkies coming to buy dust were white. For the most part that's how the traffic ran. Dust heads were White, crack heads were Black and heroin addicts were a mix with Hispanics added as well. Needless to say, the White dusters stuck out like a sore thumb as they walked through the streets and into the building. Dusters also had a kind of dumb or spacey look on their face. Once you have them stopped and begin asking questions, the cat was out of the bag. Aside from the fact that they obviously didn't live in Harlem, they weren't smart enough to lie quickly or correctly. The minute they opened their mouths they sounded like they were still high. I guess if you fry enough brain cells that's the price you pay. Lastly, If you talked to them long enough you could actually smell the dust on them.

Dust, or PCP as it is also known, has a unique smell. It's hard to describe the smell but once you smell it, you never forget it. The best way I can describe it is as a mix between a mint smell and a chemical smell. The smell is so strong that the odor can get on you and stay there for some time, especially on your skin. Very often we would smell the junkies fingers and check if he was smoking or handling it recently. If he or she had just rolled a joint with dust in it, you could easily smell it on his or her fingers. When I gave a suspected junkie a pat down I would listen carefully as I squeezed and patted their pockets. If I heard the sound of crumpling cellophane or plastic, like they use to package Chinese fortune cookies, it was a good chance that was a pack of dust. They use that type of air tight sealing to package dust to keep the odor down and make it less obvious. Besides the fact that it is such a strong drug. I have seen cops handle it without gloves during processing and get sick from the contact high it can give a person.

Aside from trying to detect some of these junkies and the drugs that are out there, you will also encounter regulars you have arrested before. Sometimes ones that you have arrested numerous times. They can't resist the area or the shit that a particular dealer is selling. Sometimes you can follow these regulars for blocks and they will lead you right to the spot they buy from. Numerous times I have used regular junkies I know to lead me to a spot then follow them away from the area and question them on the whole set up. Once you get them alone, all you have to do is threaten them with jail and they sing like birds. In no time you got the whole layout of the spot down to the last detail. Its easy, you just have to know how to ask.

Before long we could see the parade of White junkies coming and going into our target building. The time a junkie spends in the building is important as well. A quick in and out visit that lasts a few minutes could mean the dealer is right in the lobby. It may also mean that the buyer did not score. A longer trip could mean the deal is a few flights up and away from the door. In any case, you take what ever information you can and add it all up to get as much of an edge as you can.

In our case it was quick hits and he was, as we expected, selling in the lobby from the stairs. The junkies we stopped gave us all we needed down to the detail of the dealer's clothes and facial features. Armed with our intel, all signs pointed to the spot being up and running and doing a good business. It was time to take a chance and see if we could get this guy.

Dressed in civilian clothes, another cop and I set out through dozens of back lots to get to the rear of the building next to the intended target. We carefully and quietly started up the rear fire escape, stopping at each floor to make sure the windows were clear of unwanted eyes. The last thing we wanted was a 911 call for two burglars on the fire escape. A parade of uniform cops would definitely have fucked up our plan.

The fire escape was eight flights up plus the last ladder at the top which went up and over the roof ledge. Even at our slow and careful pace we got up there pretty quick. Once we reached the roof we took a few minutes to gain our composure and get ready for our next move. After taking a good look at the board to make sure it was still okay, we carefully moved it into position. All that was left was to cross over to the other roof.

The original cops who did this just quickly went across in one motion. That crazy, I am not. We brought along an additional item the original cops didn't use in their operation. We added a rope to our adventure. The whole thing was still risky but we felt a little safer doing it this way. We tied a rope to the elevator room which is basically a brick enclosed room on the roof. Once it was secure, I tied the other end around my waist and without hesitation I went across from one roof to the other. The trick was not looking down and to keep moving. Once I was across, my partner untied the rope and tied it on to himself just like I had done earlier. Next, I tied my end of the rope to the elevator room on the roof I was on. In the same manner, my partner came over to my roof and it was done. We had made it across safely and whether or not we got this guy, we had succeeded in completing the hard part. We untied the rope and took the board down from its spot. All things considered, it really wasn't that bad. Would I do it again? Hell no and I would never encourage or advise anyone else to do it either. It was a stupid thing to try and the only way I would do something like that again would be for life and death situations only.

However, what's done is done, right? As stupid as it was, it was over and we now needed to focus on getting the dealer. With both of us still hoping the dealer was still working the lobby, we quietly entered the roof landing and closed the door behind us. Stepping on each stair as if it were made of egg shells, we made our way down the stairs. The whole time we slowly descend to the lobby below I'm listening for any sounds. In this case, any sound can be a clue to what you are about to encounter. Maybe you can discern how many different voices you hear which could tip you off the fact that you might be outnumbered. For the immediate future, it was just the two of us in that building. Backup was nowhere near us and wouldn't start rolling to our location until we cued them to move in. It was just us against whatever was down below.

Once we got within two floors of the lobby, I keyed the mic which told backup to move in to the front door. We did it this way for two reasons. First, we needed to make sure that the front door would be secure. We didn't want our dealer going out and we sure as hell didn't need anyone else coming in while we took the dealer down. Second, in case we dropped in on a real mess and got into some heavy shit, at least backup was on its way to us.

We made our turn to the last set of stairs going down and there he was, just sitting exactly where we were told he would be. He was sitting on the next to last step looking out into the lobby. Next to him was a small paper bag that was propped open. I could tell he was watching out the front door intently. Within a few seconds we heard the chirp of the police siren from outside the building. That was our cue which told us that our backup was out front and headed for the front door. The dealer looked like he was trying to figure out whether or not the cops were going to try and get in. With all of the dealers attention toward the door we made our move. In one quick motion, my partner stuck his gun right in the guys ear as I grabbed onto his arm with both hands. My partner said, "Don't move, don't fucking move!". I wish I had a camera. The dude looked like he was going to shit his pants. I already had my cuffs out and cuffed the dude as fast as I could. He let us cuff him without incident. Next to him in the bag was a shit load of dust and money. In several of his pockets was even more of the same. It was a good bust considering the challenges we faced to get the guy.

Later on, while talking with the dealer during the arrest process, we found out that when he realized we were cops he said he was actually relieved. He told us that at first he thought he was getting robbed and figured we were going to kill him for his cash and drugs. What a way to live. He lost his shit, all his money and the drugs were gone. He was now going to jail and yet he was happy it was the cops who got him.

Later that same week we saw him out on the street walking in a different section of the neighborhood. Some dusters whom we stopped told us he was already set up again and working a new spot selling dust in another building.

The cycle started again. We again started gathering intel for the new spot. It never stops and neither did we. In any case, you can be sure we weren't walking across any more fucking boards to get him or anyone else for that matter. That's for sure.

18. Smoky Perception

It's funny how some people perceive their problems. Do they think what they are doing is wrong or bad for them? Do they wonder if they even have a problem at all? Drug users are the absolute kings in this area of fucked up thinking. Most times I think they talk to convince themselves more than anyone else. They see the world and their addictions in their own warped way. Some of them will argue with you or tell you how they believe the events are taking place to the point where you will get a splitting headache. If you try to reason with them they just keep arguing from their perspective. It becomes comical, sad or just a waste of time.

A prime example of this happened one night while me and my partner were checking out a weed spot we got tons of complaints on. In the process of visiting the location we grabbed this guy for a simple possession of marijuana arrest. Not the crime of the century by a long shot but still illegal and something we had received numerous complaints for. Because we had so many complaints, we had to make the arrest to show we were addressing the problem and actually visiting the location.

We didn't mind making the arrest. They are super easy to process and most of the time pot heads are really not bad people. For the most part, they dress normal and lead normal lives. They don't give you a hard time and a lot of them give you good information in order to get a break or a summons instead of going to central booking for the night. Some of these pot heads will even give you good information just for being straight with them and treating them with respect. Besides that, we always stand to make some overtime off arrests, which never hurts. All things considered, nice work if you can get it.

So this guy had a few bags of weed on him and we were going to give him a summons for the violation and cut him loose. He seemed like an alright guy. He wasn't nasty to us, so we figured we could let him slide a little and avoid the trip to central booking. He was happy to be going home in a few hours and we were just talking during the arrest process. I always tried to engage my perps in conversation during the finger print part of the process. This part of the arrest process is where a good cop can turn one collar into another or learn all the facets of criminal behavior. All you need to do is talk to the experts you have just brought in. Perps love to talk. If you get them started and ask the right questions they will tell you all you need to know about street life and criminal behavior. I think this part of policing is dying fast.

It seems like the new cops who were hired at the end of my career don't do this. They seem to feel that the arrest ends these events and they just want to get done as fast as possible and go home. They clearly don't learn as much, if anything, from arrests more than the initial incident allows them to.

Anyway, we were moving along with the arrest process trying to get the guy out of the Precinct in decent time. My partner was doing the paperwork while I was fingerprinting him. My partner asked him for his age and he responded, "Forty three.". With that response, I stopped for a moment and said to him, "Forty three and you're still smoking weed?". He replied, "I'm not hooked on that shit, I could go eight or nine hours without it if I had to.". He wasn't joking. He was dead serious. He actually had a tone of conviction, pride or accomplishment in his voice. The look on his face was as if he was telling us about a great feat he had accomplished. I replied back, "A whole eight hours, huh, wow!". He was unfazed and the remark went right over his head. That was pretty much the end of the small talk between us. It did however give us a glimpse into the minds of people with addictions and how they slowly change into a new person with a new life style. Denial is heavy with these people and it will eventually take them over. It's like they can't change, so they change their life to accommodate their activities.

Whenever I hear someone say, "Marijuana is not a drug, it doesn't make a person into an addict or change their life.", I begin to laugh on the inside. When I hear anything along those lines in an attempt to justify any type of drug use I can't help but think back to this incident. That guy's statement and how he now perceives himself tells me all I need to know about marijuana or any drug. You have to be on drugs to think otherwise!

19. Running For My Life

Inspiration is truly all around you. However, sometimes you have to look for it or at the very least be willing to see it. In police work you need to keep a fresh perspective on life and be willing to accept that some things are put in front of you for a reason. These events, if you let them, can change your life. When that happens, be grateful, because very often you can use these moments over and over in all areas of your life.

Cops don't just do patrol and look for bad guys. Part of the job of a police officer is to handle what we call "details". These details can be any kind of assignment outside of routine patrol and very often outside your assigned Precinct. Some examples of these which I have handled time and time again are; street fairs, parades, protest demonstrations and large city events like the NYC Marathon.

My partner and I worked the New York City Marathon for years. It's a long day and sometimes cold and rainy but the overtime was always good. In our minds we looked at it as a good day to make some extra cash. Although we worked the detail year after year, we never really paid any great amount of attention to the actual race itself. This was strictly a money deal for us. Thinking back I can't even remember how many years went by at that event, working crowd control, directing traffic, or standing in front of a police barrier without actually realizing what a great accomplishment finishing a marathon is.

When I was a rookie, the partner I was working with always told me he was going to run a marathon. Every time I heard him say that I would always laugh at him thinking to myself, that's impossible. In my mind it was too hard. The distance was too long and he was too old to start training for a marathon. You have to think about it. It's 26.2 miles! Some people get tired driving that far let alone walking or actually running it.

Those thoughts were from a rookie straight out of the Academy. Along with being young on the job I was also young in life, being only twenty years old when I became a cop. I had my whole career ahead of me and tons of things to learn. What I needed to learn was not just limited to police work but life as well.

Flash forward 7 years and now I am a 27 year old cop. As usual, the New York City Marathon detail came up and again, the allure of the overtime made me sign up to work it. At this point, I had a new partner and we had been working together for a few years. He was older than me, had more time on the job and had a much more mature outlook on life. To me, the marathon was always memorable because it always occurs just before or after my birthday. A few times it actually fell right on my birthday and I worked it anyway. Like I said, it was overtime. Nothing more, nothing less.

I guess the years that had passed changed my views a little and I had grown some what in those years. Once again, I was headed to the marathon detail with my partner. We went for breakfast before the marathon and this time we had decided we would actually check out some of the race this time, rather than count the hours as they passed. For the first time, we were going to look at what kind of people actually run this race. We were actually curious as to who would want to put their bodies through this torture and run a marathon.

The first thing we watched was the small pack of front runners or elite runners, as they are often referred to by the media. These guys were miles ahead of the rest of the pack of regular runners. These runners ran together in a tight pack at an incredible pace. It was amazing to see these runners go by our post at the twenty mile marker as if they had just started the race. They didn't even look tired and I know that if I chased after them at that point, I would never be able to keep up with their pace or run better than them across the remaining 6.2 miles. Amazing, right? It truly was an amazing sight to see but it was far from the only amazing thing we saw that day.

What followed next was the pack of runners who were good runners but not elite. These people were not in the shape of the front runners and had the look of most people who run to keep in shape. This pack of runners, which looked like it would never end, was made up of old people, young people, skinny people, heavy people, people in costumes having fun, soldiers in full uniforms wearing boots, people who were dedicating runs to deceased loved ones, or fighting cancer and even cancer survivors themselves. They just kept coming down the street. The more we looked the more diverse the group became. Some runners were smiling. Some were in agony. We saw one runner fall and get back up. We saw some stop to drink water or take care of a cramp. We saw some who were bloody and one guy who looked like he had an accident and his bowels let loose all down his legs. I didn't see anyone give up and they all kept going. It was an amazing sight and we actually clapped for several people who were struggling or stood out from the pack a little bit. For the first time after working the marathon for years, I appreciated the accomplishment that was unfolding before me and I was amazed.

Up until now, what I saw at the Marathon was truly amazing. What came next can only be described as a moving inspiration at its best. It was the type of feeling you only get a few times in your life. Those times and moments are usually reserved for something personal or family related. This sight, although not linked to me personally, moved me.

It was the sight of a runner coming down the street amidst the pack and passing me at the twenty mile marker with no legs. This man was a double amputee. Right after his knee, where his legs should be, were the beginning of metal strips. These strips continued to the ground and had some sort of sneaker type bottom which appeared to be a permanent fixture. That permanent fixture, which appeared to provide traction, was curved at the bottom and seemed to give some spring or shock action as he strode with each step. I imagine that slight motion helped to absorb the shock of the pounding effect of running with prosthetics. He was running at a great pace and he was running in the meat of the pack and was headed for a great time. From the way he moved and the look on his face, I knew he was going to finish that race. This must have been obvious to anyone who saw him that day. I thought back to when I had said that the marathon was impossible or just too hard. At that point I was 20 years old and had made my assessment from the point of view of two able bodied young men. Up until now, all the other runners who had passed me impressed me but this one really hit home and woke me up.

I was determined from that day on to train and complete my own marathon. So, at the age of 27 I began training and worked hard through out the entire year. I read all sorts of training books, put myself on a schedule for running and stuck to it. I even trained when on vacation and out of state. I ran in the heat, the cold, the rain and even in the snow. When I struggled I thought of that inspiring runner and how much harder his training must have been. After that I would always feel better. I would think of how lucky I am and continue my training. Not only did the training seem easier but it was hard to complain.

Later that year, just before my 28th birthday, I was at the starting line for the 1998 NYC Marathon. I had made it through the entire year of hard training and was now ready to start my own marathon. I admit I was nervous. I looked around, wondering if anyone else was nervous as I was and then I saw a shirt that read, "The miracle wasn't that I finished but that I had the courage to start.". That shirt immediately brought my mind back to the sight of that courageous double amputee runner and all that he must have went through to train and run a marathon. After that I wasn't nervous anymore. I was just ready to run.

I ran my race. Just as I found inspiration to decide to run a marathon, to train and to actually take my first step, I also found inspiration along the way. That inspiration came by running thorough the very Precinct where I worked and by seeing friends and fellow cops standing at the very posts I had been at for years. When they saw me, they cheered me on. It was a huge lift mentally and physically. I remember one cop who was at a post about two miles from the finish line, recognizing me and giving me a high five saying, "Way to go, Tony D!". That lifted me and gave me exactly what I needed to carry me right through to the finish line.

I often wondered and hoped I inspired a few of those cops I passed to do something for themselves that they might not have normally tried to do. Maybe not a marathon but something that they had doubted they could do, before seeing me. They say inspiration can be contagious. It was for me.

I finished the the 1998 NYC Marathon with a respectable time of 4:13:34. It was extremely hard but I did it and it felt great to finish what I had set out to do a year earlier. Just to show you differing perspectives, I remember watching the news later that night and seeing an interview with the winner of the marathon. This man had finished in just about half the time I finished. He felt people like me had it tough because we had to run for 4 or 5 hours while he could do it in 2 hours and go home to rest.

Although I never ran another marathon since, I have kept up running consistently, making it a part of my life. When ever things get tough, I challenge myself with different running paths and I always think back to that same runner who started it all. I have often recalled that runner's image through my years as a police officer and in my personal life as well.

I truly believe it's people like that unknown runner who have helped me to succeed on the job and deal with problems in life. As the father of a child with autism, that runner made me realize that while I don't have it as easy as some, I don't have it as hard as others as well. When I get upset with the hand I was dealt in life I think about a child in a wheelchair. A child who has cancer or that runner with no legs. It helps to cut down my own complaints and be grateful for what I have. Life can always be worse and it certainly is for a lot of people.

20. Plain Old Good Advice

Every so often you either get advice from a really good boss or a quote from an old timer that really hits home or just makes good sense. This kind of advice stays with you forever. Usually it's the kind of advice that when your career is over, you can still look back and remember the line and think of a bunch of ways that it helped you. When you really think about it you also realize the advice not only helped you at work but in parts of your home life as well. When that happens, consider it proof that you have received solid, good advice or worthwhile information and not just a random quote.

I have had the privilege of working with hundreds of people who I consider to be masters of their craft. All of these people rubbed off on me in some way, shape, or form in a positive light. After a while you begin to take a little bit from each of those people you see as a positive role model. What you take from them is what you perceive as the reason that person is respected or successful. After years of doing this and adding your own traits, you become a new person. You have become all these people rolled into one with yourself as the final addition and you become that much better.

Two particular pieces of information stand out in my mind. To only tell two pieces of advice from among the countless people I have met over my twenty years as a police officer, I am doing a great injustice to all those who have made me what I am and have helped me to succeed in my job.

Regrettably, I can't detail every little piece of advice I feel has molded me to the person I am. That's not possible. However, I can speak about two pieces of advice which stand out the most. I remember these quotes as if they were told to me yesterday, when in reality, I was given this advice over twenty years ago. I can say without hesitation that the two statements helped me time and time again. I can credit them to success and an overall positive way to work and act when you are in a position of authority, such as that of a police officer. Even more than success with police work is being able to retire in one piece without the need of a cane or worse in order to get around. Believe me, a lot of guys don't make it out in nearly the same shape or even close to the way they came in. Some who were less lucky than that never got to retire at all.

Going back to when I was fresh out of the Academy and newly assigned to the Precinct, I can recall that most old timers wouldn't talk to you or even say hello. This was customary and a way that rookies paid their dues. After a few years they would begin to warm up to you. Some would even talk to you. I remember this one old timer who talked to me right from the start. He was way past his time to retire and I think he had changed his outlook on life towards the end of his career. In any case, during my first week as a police officer, he saw me in the locker room and called me over to where he was sitting. I walked to his end of the locker room in a sheepish kind of way and stood in front of him not knowing what to expect. He looked at me with a real serious look and he said, "Kid, always treat people with respect, even your perps. If you are hard on them, they will always respect you and the job you do if you treat them right. They might not like you but they will respect you. You show them it's not personal, it's just a job. You tell them that all we did was cross paths. Let's give each other as little trouble as possible and go on with our lives.". He went on to say, "Cops who treat people with respect don't get tested in the street half as much as the cop who is nasty or does things to people in a bad way without reason, just to be abusive. Remember Kid, always do the right thing out there. In the end, believe me it will pay off.".

That's a lot of information to take in, especially for a rookie. Oddly enough, it stuck with me. It was the kind of advice that on the surface seemed simple. The finer points can be taken out with ease. Treat people with respect. It's okay to be tough but be fair and be humane. It's a job. Don't take it personal. Respect is a two way street. You get back what you give out. Always do the right thing out there. All easy to understand and all pretty simple. The meaning behind these words and how they can help you beyond its face value is much more complex.

As easy as those statements were to extract and understand, the impact was very much to the contrary. Below the surface, this kind of advice and approach was generally a good way to be a cop and it probably saved my life and saved me from a lot of pain too many times to know or to imagine. I could play ignorant and say the advice did nothing but I know better than that. The fact is, this advice started my career on the right foot and started to lead me into a certain way of thinking and a certain way of acting. I'm not usually a big proponent for playing the "what if" game, but it does make you wonder.

What if instead of that old timer, I would have met a cop who was the total opposite in his or her views? Someone who said plain and simple, "Fuck these people!". I would like to think I would be smart enough to know right from wrong. Smart enough to be able to dismiss it as bad advice. However, still I would have been subjected to the bad advice, whether I believed it to be true or not. Even if I didn't follow though with those negative thoughts, I still would not have had the benefit of the early planting of good ideals and values. Without those words from that old timer, it might have taken me longer to evolve into what I know was the correct approach to policing. In that time frame who knows what could have transpired. Who knows what could have happened as a result.

From time to time I have worked with cops who were just nasty, miserable people. I often wondered if these people were naturally like this or were they given that bad start that I mentioned earlier? Would alternative thinking or good advice have mattered to them? There were so many variables to consider. It's easy to sit and reflect on it at the end of your career. To be able to take the time to analyze it. Unfortunately, police work doesn't allow you time to sit and analyze everything at great length and detail. A lot of police work is reactionary and that can be dangerous, especially to the individual who starts off on the wrong foot.

I considered myself lucky. Because of that luck I benefited to the point where I was able to look back on a situation and say, "That happened because I treated that guy with respect. I did the right thing there.". For as many times as I can say that I came out of a bad situation okay because of my approach, I also can only imagine all the times a perp didn't try to kill me or seriously hurt me because of the way in which I treated him. You have to realize how vulnerable you are out there. Just like a big target. These incidents are the ones you never know about, they just happen. I know some people will say, "Maybe that's paranoia or maybe no one would have ever tried to do something bad to you.". That sounds like fantasy thinking to me. I have seen cops get hurt. I have seen the hate in a perp's eyes directed at a cop. I have been the subject of threats myself. This is police work in the city. It's real and it's tough. I would rather believe that with all that going on I helped my own cause because of my values and profited from them both in work and life.

Going hand in hand with this was advice I received from a great boss who I worked for early in my career. He was the sort of boss who would never ask you to do anything he wasn't prepared to do himself. Often he would walk the beat with us or even climb countless stairs, right behind us, to check out a problem building. Most bosses would wait in the car and it's their right to do so. However, when you see a boss do what he doesn't have to do, it makes you think differently about him and about the job and about yourself. It sure as hell makes it difficult to complain about the job you have to do when you have a person setting that type of example. I Immediately admired that characteristic. It was a desirable trait and something I wanted to emulate. Although I never became a supervisor, I always tried to show other cops that a good work ethic is something everyone should strive for. The by-product of this work ethic was a great reputation amongst my peers and supervisors. All good things eventually pay some type of dividend.

One day, that Sgt. said to me, "No one should ever be a harder judge of you than yourself.". I Immediately thought it was a great statement and a great way to approach life. The obvious meaning being to hold yourself to a high standard higher than anyone will ask of you. If you succeed, you're probably going to be way out of the range of what everyone around you expects. If you fail, you know you did your best and people will notice that as well. As long as you act in that same manner with every task given to you and do it consistently, even the failures will look better than the average person's approach to work.

This approach to work and what comes from it will show everyone what type of person you are. After a while consistently using this work ethic people will begin to notice. Again, just as with the previous bit of good advice from that old timer, you will reap the benefits during and after your career is over. When your career is over and it's time to retire, you can hold your head high knowing you did your best at the job you swore to do.

I know plenty of cops will read this and say, "Who cares about what others think, I'm doing what's good for me.". Thats fine if you don't have a conscience, self respect or took the job solely for a paycheck or the benefits and not because you had a desire to be a cop. That wouldn't work for me. I didn't just take the job because it was available. I had a desire to be a cop. I went into the Academy just as I turned 20 years old. Being a cop was my only dream. When I became a cop I told myself I would work as hard as I could during my career and when it's time to retire, I knew I would be able to do so with no regrets and a feeling of fulfillment.

The advice I received early in my career only served to reinforce my work ethic, my way of treating people and the manner in which I served as a police officer. It would be impossible for me to write down all the incidents, both on and off the job, where these two particular pieces of advice helped me. However, I can say without hesitation, that it must have been in the thousands. After acting in this manner and with those thoughts in my mind, it eventually became instinctual and a way of life. I found myself always wanting to perform at a higher level than the majority of cops I worked with. It became normal for me to feel embarrassed if I didn't do my best. I didn't necessarily have to succeed all the time. Although I did strive to succeed at almost any cost, it became important that the effort had to be there each and every time. Before long you get a reputation on the street as a tough but fair cop who always tries to do his job. Inside the Precinct you become known as a competent, hard worker who people go to for help and to get the job done. You are respected by your peers and supervisors and although it makes you work harder, it also feels good.

In the end, I know that there were times when a situation ended well for me although it could have easily gone very wrong. I'm sure situations similar to my own have gone horribly wrong for other cops throughout the city. I have often thought and realized how lucky I had been. That it's not a coincidence to be on the street all those years, constantly making arrests and never had a bad incident. Never seriously hurt or even jammed up. The advice I received definitely helped me down the road, from beginning to end, and into retirement. Retirement is every cop's goal and I am grateful for the advice and I will never forget it.

21. You Never Know Who You Are Dealing With

There was a gas station in my precinct located a very busy intersection. Because there are so few gas stations in Manhattan, the ones that were there got a lot of business. In fact because the gas station was the only one in the area it became so busy that at times they had too many cars in their garage. To accommodate all their business they parked the cars waiting for service on the sidewalk until they had the time or room to get to them.

Manhattan is a unique place. Even in the areas of Manhattan where the crime is high or the area is run down, you will always have residents who either have money or the ear of a local politician. Some have both and use them to get things done.

In this instance, someone who lived nearby felt the cars on the sidewalk either didn't look good or were blocking enough of the sidewalk to create an inconvenience to pedestrians. In either case, this problem now became a formal complaint. Such complaints travel up and down the political chain until they land at the lowest man on the totem pole, the local beat cop.

The boss at that time called me into his office regarding this complaint. I sat there while he explained what I already knew and told me to handle it. He also told me to make it happen right away. There already was a paper trail and numerous influential local officials awaiting results to quiet the complaints. To me it was a job but to the boss it was a way of kissing ass to the brass above him. Those bosses were in a position to get him promoted at a later date. All he wanted to do was accumulate as many brownie points to get him looked at favorably and get his promotion. After the rank of Captain, it's all about getting promoted and worrying about your own career. He could care less about the complaint or who was making it. He wasn't going to do what it took to get the job done. Most of the bosses wouldn't know what to do out in the street if they had to go out there and do police work. In any case, he was going to make sure it got done. I didn't need him to prod me to do my job. No matter what it was, even a bullshit complaint like this one. I knew how the system worked and quite frankly I didn't care. If the boss benefited off my work, more power to him. I had a job to do and would do it regardless of who benefited from it. This particular job wasn't exactly the assignment of a lifetime but it gave me something to do on my down days and I could probably get some numbers for my activity reports out of it as well. And, once I corrected the situation, I'm sure the boss would be happy and at the very least leave me alone so I could get back to doing enforcement.

I headed on down to the location. Just as reported there were cars parked all over the place. Every inch of sidewalk had a car parked on it. It even looked like some were being worked on where they were parked, with their hoods open or tools spread out next to the cars. To be honest, they were blocking the sidewalk pretty bad and it did look a little messy. That part of the Precinct actually wasn't as run down as the northern end. There were some nice buildings that overlooked Central Park. If there was any money in the Precinct, it was there on that street.

When addressing non-criminal complaints like this I always started at the lowest level of handling a problem and then let the problem dictate where I went from there. Some people don't realize their actions are a hindrance to others and some will correct the situation as soon as it is pointed out to them. In other words, I tried to start with a simple warning, explanation of my presence and what has to be done to correct the situation to have me go away. In this case I did just that.

Evidently this had no effect. Within a few days I was back in the boss's office looking at another stack of complaints and phone calls about the same situation. Obviously, the people running the gas station either didn't take my presence and advice seriously or they figured that they would continue right on with what they were doing without consequence.

It was clear I would have to escalate my authority a little bit. Step two would be to ticket every car in violation and show the gas station that the Police Department means what they say. This simple act would let the station know that I am not out there for my health and they should have taken the warning seriously. In other words, if you don't care about the neighborhood or the people who live there that's your choice. However, you damn well better show me some respect and correct the situation. Now they forced my hand and would have to deal with the summonses for their customers cars as well as correct the original situation. This means the business must put this problem first on their list and deal with it. I was absolutely not going to get called into the boss's office a third time without, at the very least, a fistful of summonses to show that I was in fact working on the problem. I easily had that with that first visit. All I needed to do now was to wait a day or so and make a return trip and summons all the cars again if possible. I was totally prepared to do this every day if I needed to until they kept that sidewalk clear. But in all honesty, it was an easy fix for the gas station and it really should have ended after the first time I wrote all those summonses.

At this point in my career, I had been assigned to uniformed mountain bike patrol. Not only was it a great way to get around but you could really move in on something or somebody before anyone was able to see you coming. I found out quickly that a cop on a bike can be a perp's worst nightmare. It's small, fast, quiet and can go places patrol cars couldn't go.

Quietly and quickly I zipped onto the sidewalk at the gas station and started banging out summonses to every car on the sidewalk as fast as I could. I wasn't looking around. I was just writing as fast as I could. I finished one then went right on to the next. Without fail, after about two or three cars, one of the workers would come running out to start moving the cars I had not gotten to yet. In a comical way, a race ensues. Me doing my best imitation of a meter maid and the station worker playing the part of a valet service on speed.

We both continued our jobs and then finally he got to the car I had already started writing a ticket for. At this point, I told him plain and simple, "Too late. I already started and this one gets a ticket too.". With that, the dude got into the car and started it up intending to move it away from me. In a clear and serious tone, I told him, "Sir, do not move the car until I'm finished.". He ignored me like I never said a word and moved the car along the sidewalk to pull it into his lot where it would be out of the public area. While he did this he had the drivers side door wide open and bumped me and the bike I was straddling as he drove off the sidewalk past me.

Now, I didn't get hurt at all but I will admit he got me aggravated with that maneuver and I could feel myself beginning to boil. I gave this guy clear instructions to do something and he basically said, "Fuck that, I'm going to to do what I want.". This basically showed me he had no respect for me. This also explained why my initial warning to move the cars was disregarded. It was becoming obvious that the people who ran this station didn't care about the public, complaints, the police or anything but their business. Unfortunately, I was going to have to ratchet up my actions to the next level.

I followed the worker, who was now the operator of a motor vehicle, into the lot where he was parking the car. I tried as calmly as possible to tell him that now not only is the car getting the summons for parking on the sidewalk but I wanted his drivers license as well. When he asked why I needed his license, I told him, "You were driving on the sidewalk, you're getting a moving violation.".

He stared at me with his mouth open and then refused to give me his license. I was anticipating and hoping he would take that stand. I was already pissed off and by refusing to give me his license, he gave me the green light to lock his ass up. Legally, I had all I needed to take this guy in. He was escalating the situation and himself right into jail and a free trip to central booking. I was more than happy to help him get there.

In a split second we were going at it right there on the hood of the car he had just moved. We were pushing and pulling each other and he was doing his best to keep me from cuffing his arms. He was bigger and heavier than me but he was also a little older and nowhere near the shape I was in. I could feel him start to tire and struggle to keep his arms away from me. In another few minutes I had one cuff on his wrist. Once you get one handcuff on, it's all over. They teach you in the Academy that once you get one cuff on the person's wrist, all you need to do is either tighten that cuff or bend the cuff one way or the other on the person's wrist. Either is effective in causing pain as it either tightens or puts pressure on the person's wrist. That pain will either force the person to comply or cause them to lose concentration and allow you to get the other hand cuffed as well. In any case, it worked nicely here and I now had this guy cuffed and pushed face first on the hood of the car.

I called the Sergeant over to the scene, explained what happened, and off to the Precinct we went to process this arrest. At this point, this guy went from a parking summons on a stranger's car, to a moving violation, to a misdemeanor arrest for failure to produce a license and resisting arrest.

Once we got to the Precinct, I booked him in for the bullshit misdemeanors and started to do what every cop does-a search of the perp's clothes. Basically, you go through all their pockets and take everything out. Any valuables or money would get logged in and safeguarded until the prisoner gets out of central booking. I started with his pants pocket, taking everything out and placing it on the desk in front of the supervisor. The first pocket had money, keys, miscellaneous papers and two rounds ammunition for a .22 caliber handgun. With that I'm thinking to myself, that's an odd thing for a mechanic to be carrying around. I knew I had done a quick pat down at the location for a weapon and didn't find any gun on him but a .22 caliber handgun can be extremely small. Needless to say, I was concerned. So I placed the ammo on the desk and continued my search. In the other pocket he had some loose candy, more paperwork, money and what appeared to be a tire pressure gauge.

Upon looking at this item closer, I realized it wasn't a tire pressure gage at all. It was what we refer to in the street as a "zip" gun or a home-made gun. It's made with parts you can buy at a hardware store or machine shop and it is capable of firing one round at a time and can be just as lethal as a regular gun.

To understand what this zip gun looked like, imagine a slide bolt used to secure a front door from the inside. The bolt part is fitted into the cylinder and has a spring or tension rod that works against it when pulled all the way back. Once it's all the way back you slide the bolt lever so it locks in place. You then insert the round of ammunition down what is now the barrel of the gun. You would aim it in the area of your target and then flick the bolt upward, releasing it so that the spring will slam the bolt tip forward into the round causing the round to fire and send the bullet off just like a real gun. By no means is this the most accurate of weapons and it really is just an up close and personal last ditch effort sort of gun. However, if used close to the target, especially from behind, it could be effective and even lethal when used with a small round such as a .22. The .22 caliber round is best known for the damage it does inside the body as it very often will ricochet off the victim's bones and cut through several organs before becoming lodged or finding an exit area.

This weapon was also lethal to my perp's freedom as well. I looked at the gun and then at my perp. The look of surprise on his face was immediate. He immediately shook his head and said, "Oh man, I forgot that was there.". Later on, the perp told me that it wasn't his and that he was holding it as collateral for a an old timer who owed him money. He told me if he had remembered that it was in his pocket he never would have put himself in a position to get in trouble, let alone arrested.

Well, they say hindsight is 20-20. At the present, he was as blind as a bat and fucked. Not only was he fucked but now he was going to be booked for possession of a loaded firearm and probably looking at doing some time as well.

This whole event, which really was 100% avoidable, went from a bullshit parking summons to a misdemeanor arrest and then to a felony arrest in a matter of minutes. I tell this story to rookie cops all the time. I try to tell them how a bullshit collar could end up as something much more substantial. I try to prove to them that sometimes the best collars come from bullshit.

More importantly, you never know who you are dealing with on the street and things can get out of hand really fast. You have to always be prepared for anything and anybody. Never take any person or situation for granted because you just don't know what could happen.

Needless to say, the parking situation was never a problem again after that incident. My boss was thrilled with the whole thing from beginning to end and I'm sure he used it to his advantage with the big bosses. The complaint was taken care of and I was left alone to go back to my regular routine of enforcement. In the end, I came out of that whole incident looking pretty good. Although I imagined afterwards how easily I could have gotten hurt, I had to be happy with the results for now and remember what happened for use in the future.

22. The doctor is in...sort of

When I was a field training officer, one of my rookies and the patrol Lieutenant got into a nasty wrestling match inside an ambulance with an EDP. If you have ever been in the back of an ambulance you would know there really isn't a whole lot of room in there. Between the bed, the bench and all the equipment, it's pretty tight. When you add an EMS tech and three more full grown men, you are definitely rubbing asses and elbows with every move. Now picture all those people in there wrestling with each other.

When you're in the Academy, one of the courses they give you is on the proper use of mace. Mace, when used properly and under the right conditions, does work very well. I personally have used it dozens of times and it almost always worked great for me. I have also seen it used improperly and have also been on the receiving end of a poor decision by a cop to use it when the circumstances really didn't allow for its use in an optimal manner. One of the worst times to use mace is in really tight quarters. Another time not to use mace is when a bunch of cops are too close to the intended target. If you add poor ventilation as another time not to use mace, you would have three in total and this rookie touched on all of those by using it that night in the back of that ambulance.

I guess this rookie must have been out the day they went over that in the Academy. In a small ambulance with no ventilation, all four of them were tangled up and he used his mace. So, he didn't just mace the EDP. He maced everyone in the ambulance. As a result the tech, the Lieutenant and the rookie all had to go to the hospital for treatment.

The only treatment you can get for the effects of mace is eye irrigation. Basically flushing your eyes with water until the mace is washed out. When it's cleaned out, you're going to have red bloodshot eyes that are hurt and are irritated for a day or so. Until you get that treatment, it's incredibly difficult to open your eyes. The lids of your eyes are shut, your eyes are tearing and your nose runs as well. The feeling is somewhere between very uncomfortable and a painful feeling. It's pretty strong stuff and you even taste it in your mouth and feel it slightly burning your throat. All these effects are what you want your intended target to go through, not you. It distracts them from whatever action they are engaged in and keeps them temporarily blinded so you can take care of business and restrain them.

The Lieutenant I was working with told me what happened and said, "Let's go to the hospital to see how they are doing.". We headed up to the hospital and went to the ER where they had them separated in two different examining rooms awaiting treatment. At this point they were just getting set up to be questioned and treated. This is the part where they would get their vitals checked, give their information for administration and get prepped to flush the mace out of their eyes.

We saw our rookie cop first and he really wasn't so bad, just embarrassed. We gave him the business pretty bad as cops do to each other. Humor is one way cops deal with stress and the rigors of police work. We continued to tease him about macing the lieutenant, himself and everyone else as well. Like I said, that's what cops do. Aside from the levity that the joking provides, it also serves as a tool for teaching. When you mess up you're going to get teased and taunted for days or even weeks to come. This good hearted fun helps to make you stronger and to learn from your mistakes. We could all be sure that after tonight we knew this cop would always use his mace under optimal conditions.

We moved over to the next room where the Lieutenant was waiting to be treated. He was laying on a stretcher, his eyes were plastered shut, puffy and red. We could see tears streaming from the corners of both eyes. He was in certain discomfort and blind as a bat. He appeared to be doing his best to deal with his condition and relax while he waited to be seen by the doctor. Within a few seconds the Hospital Administrator walked in and started to get his information for his chart. As quick as she came in, she left. We could tell that he was hoping that treatment was coming quickly. A minute later, a technician came in, asked him a few more questions and also left. The Lieutenant was still answering a question to the second technician when a third came in and picked up right where the last left off. At this point it was obvious to us that the Lieutenant had no fucking idea who he was talking to. He couldn't open his eyes yet and was talking as if he was conversing with the same person the whole time. It could be anyone talking to him and he wouldn't have had a clue who it was.

I quickly gave some signals to my boss and the small group of cops who were standing around to move in and check out what I was going to do. The crowd of cops moved in closer and I started my prank on the poor Lieutenant laying in the bed. The following is the conversation between myself and the lieutenant. Keep in mind that I had this conversation using an extremely heavy, German accent:

ME:	"Yes, hello officer, how are you doing? I am Dr. Schwitzer."
LIEUTENANT:	"Oh, okay doc."
ME:	"So, tell me vat happened to you"
LIEUTENANT:	"Well, I got maced..."

The Lieutenant recants the whole story with his eyes closed shut, tears streaming down his face. The entire time the room was filled with cops who are trying their best to hold in their laughter. Some of the cops were turning red, busting at the seams. Some had to walk away to keep from giving away the prank.

Finally, the Lieutenant finishes his tale of woe and pauses for me, as the doctor, to respond.

ME:	"Ok, ok officer, just relax, nurse, nurse vere are you? Come here. Ve are going to do some procedure on you to help you feel better... take off your pants!"

With that his head and upper body shoots up and you can see him straining to open his red, blood shot, crusty eyes in the worst way. He had this look of worry and panic rolled into one. His mouth was open and he said, "What, huh, what, what are you going to do?"

At that point everybody just lost it and burst out in laughter. The lieutenant figured out it was us fucking with him and he just crashed back down to the bed and laid there motionless, shaking his head. The cops were laughing so hard that one of the nurses came over to quiet us down.

I can remember cops approaching me weeks later, patting me on the back, saying what a great prank that was. The littlest things make cops happy. They all love a good joke or prank. I think the joking is definitely a coping mechanism. Some cops use it to deal with a bad situation and some use it to help others deal with that same bad situation. In any case, it's part of the life of a cop and even the ones who don't joke like to see others play jokes and find the humor in it as well.

That Lieutenant was a good sport about the whole thing. I think it may have even helped him to realize he was going to be fine and in reality he was lucky because it could have been much worse. In the end, not only was everyone fine but I think everyone learned something from the incident as well.

23. Musical Interlude Times Two

I locked up a crack head from south for a petty crime. He was like a real hillbilly, complete with a southern accent and missing teeth. Here he was, busted in NYC, a long way from home and it definitely showed. Most people leave NY to go South. Here he is doing it the other way around and now he's getting arrested. Looking at him, I just had to ask him why in the world he would leave the South to come to NYC. I mean, there were at least ten cops in the room and you just knew they were all thinking the same thing but didn't want to ask. He looked at me with a serious look on his face and said, "This is New York, I figure if I can make it here, I can make it anywhere.".

With that there was stone cold silence from the entire room. You could see the cop's brains actually working, saying to themselves, "Did this guy really just say that?". I quickly snapped the room back to reality as I bursted out in song to one of Frank Sinatra's most famous tunes singing, "It's up to you, New, York, Neeewww Yooorrrkkk.". The entire room including the perp started cracking up. Afterwards, several cops said they were thinking the same thing but didn't have the guts to do it.

****

Another time we arrested a vendor who was selling bootlegged music. When we brought him in we had to bring in all his property. His property consisted of a huge boom box radio from the 1980's and a shit load of music. All that crap had to be inventoried and vouchered for arrest evidence in case this bullshit collar ever made it to Court. It was a busy part of the day and although it was quiet, the complaint area, as well as the room in front of the Desk Sergeant, was full. Several civilians and police officers were occupying the area, working or waiting for one thing or another. Reluctantly, I began to wade through all the music so that it could be properly logged in to evidence.

As I was going through the loads of music, I came across a bootlegged CD of James Brown. I looked up and noticed the room was still packed with people but as quiet as church. Looking at everybody moping around, I thought to myself, "What a bunch of stiffs.". These people really needed to lighten up . Even the Desk Sergeant had his head buried in the blotter and he looked like he had the weight of the world on his shoulders. I quietly walked over to the boom box and cranked the volume to maximum. I put the James Brown CD in and cued up the track I was looking for. I pressed play and stood up so I could get a good view of the entire room, including the Desk Sergeant, and waited for the music to start. All at once, breaking the silence of the room at a deafening level, James Brown bellowed, "Owwww, I feel good...". The Desk Sergeant nearly jumped out of his chair and the dozen or so civilians and cops in the area all straightened up in shock. It was funny as shit to see them all jump. All those reactions of shock were immediately followed by laughter as James Brown continued to sing one of his biggest and best known hits. The Desk Sergeant just shook his head and went back to work as the rest of the people in the room laughed and continued what they were doing as well. It definitely loosened the mood in the station house and the laughter made my job more bearable.

24. In The Beginning

The first time you head out the precinct door by yourself in full uniform to a foot post is special. Finally, you are a cop and going out to learn and explore your new career. You have hope and optimism and tons of energy. You get that funny feeling in your stomach, like everything is perfect. Then you meet a cranky, old time, hair bag and all those good feelings can disappear, if you let it.

I was doing just that, going out on my first foot post as a rookie in my newly assigned Precinct. My uniform was crisp and clean and I had a big smile from ear to ear. I was looking forward to starting my new career in Harlem and actually doing police work. Up until now, I just learned abut it for six months during Police Academy training. Now the time had come to put what I learned into action and actually see what type of cop I could be and what the job was really like.

I had just left the Precinct and was no more than ten feet from the front door when I heard a voice say, "Yo, kid, come over here.". I looked around and realized it was coming from the double parked patrol car in front of the Precinct. The motor was running but no one was behind the wheel. In the passenger side was a cop who looked like he had been around a while, to say the least.

He half waved at me, motioning for me to come over to the car. Most of the old timers don't ever talk to rookies so I was actually happy to be having some kind of interaction with a veteran cop who was obviously on the streets doing what I was about to do.

I walked over to the car and could see he was smoking. The majority of cops did at that time. He also had a cup of coffee on the dashboard and an open bag of some kind of chips, or something, between the front seats. During this time on the job the city cops were still wearing light blue shirts. His was littered with stains all across the front and those stains had a matching set on his dark navy tie. Whatever he was eating was laying in crumbs on his pants. Both his pants zipper and shirt buttons were doing their finest to stay together under the stress of a few too many pounds challenging an old pair of clothes. This uniform was obviously from when he was in better shape. He looked to be about fifty years old but I knew he was younger than that. He had a big wiry mustache and was partially bald. This look did not help with his aged appearance at all. He was a real "Hair Bag!".

He looked at me and said, "Rookie, huh? You going out to your foot post kid?". I told him I was and he could probably sense I was excited to get to work. However, he did not appear to share in my enthusiasm as he continued to say, "Let me give you some advice kid. When you are out there walking down the street don't say hello or good morning to anyone you see unless they say it first.". He must have read the puzzled look on my face because he continued to say, "They ain't gonna say it back to you and you are gonna feel stupid. These fucking people don't give a shit about much, no less a cop saying good morning so don't bother trying to be nice out there.".

With that he took a sip of coffee, a puff out his cigarette and looked away from me. At that point his partner came out of the Precinct, looked at me like I had three heads, said nothing and jumped in the car and pulled away. I wish I had a photo of the way I must have looked after that exchange.

I stood there for a good couple of minutes thinking about that advice and quickly decided I definitely needed to put that to the test and see for myself if this cop was right or not. I was wondering if this could really be true. Is this really how bad the relationship is between the public and the police? No better time than the present to test it out since I was heading out to my foot post and sure to pass a bunch of people on the way out there.

My foot post was about ten blocks away so I walked in a sort of zig zag pattern to take in as much of the Precinct on the way out as I could.

I was about a block away from the Precinct when I saw an older man walking towards me. I thought this would make for a good test of the cop's advice. The man was about sixty or so and didn't look angry or moody, just walking along the sidewalk. I got about five feet from him and I said in a loud clear voice, "Good morning sir.". It was like I wasn't even there. He just walked right by me with no reaction at all. I half turned, as he went past, to see if he looked back at me and he didn't even flinch. He just kept going down the street, turned the corner and was gone.

Could this cop actually be right? Is this what I had to look forward to out there on my post dealing with the public on a daily basis? I thought to myself, to be fair, one time would not be enough. I mean, what if the guy was deaf or something? I kept walking and about another block or so away, I saw a woman and a little boy coming towards me. I thought to myself, "Perfect, let's try this again and see what happens.". Again, I waited until I was about five feet away and I said, "Hello ma'am, how are you?". This time I got a reaction. A nasty type of grin with no response at all. Again, I half turned to see if she looked back as she continued down the sidewalk. She didn't turn but the little boy did and was quickly tugged back around by the woman and away they went down the street, out of sight.

To say the least, It was a depressing start to my first foot post and my career. However, I had always prided myself on being a person who was persistent and wouldn't go along with something just because someone says so. I always liked to try my own way of handling things first, then, if I was proved wrong, so be it. At least I made the attempt. This was no different. I wasn't about to be discouraged by the words of an "over the hill, long in the tooth, hair bag" or a few civilians who chose to act a certain way. I knew this couldn't be right and I wasn't about to write off a whole city and career at this early stage in my career. Especially given the limited interaction I had to this point.

Eventually after hitting the streets over and over again and being in the same post numerous times, I began to see some familiar faces. People on the street began to recognize me and became familiar with me and my personality. I was able to interact a little more with the public and some on repeat occasions. Slowly, some of the walls that were up began to come down. Some people would respond nicely to those "Hello"s and "Good morning"s. Some wouldn't and that was okay too.

I wasn't trying to change the world and it's foolish to think that everyone will like you or respond to you favorably, especially being a cop. The lesson I took out of this was two fold. First, being my own person and not blindly taking advice was absolutely the right move. Second, don't give up so easy on what you are trying to accomplish, things don't always come easy.

I still believe it is a good idea to seek out and listen to older, more experienced cops. On the whole, what they know and the experience they have is worth its weight in gold. However, you do need to put your own filter on the end of those exchanges. You just can't accept all advice blindly or go against what you feel is right just because of who you get the advice from. I think in police work being yourself, an individual, will always be the better choice.

As for the second part, not giving up is something that will work anywhere and in any facet of life. Even more so in this line of work where success and failure can result in life and death. Although this particular event was not remotely related to a dangerous or life threatening incident, it does help to show the need for persistence is ever present.

Only the job and the outcome should change, the approach should remain constant. Once you get in that frame of mind, keep it there and approach everything in that manner. After a while, you will get what some people call "muscle memory" and that's when you switch from thinking about performing a certain way to working in a certain way for life, or as a matter of instinct. This change will help free your mind to concentrate on the task at hand and not the process to get to it or through it.

In the end, I honestly feel that although the benefit from an incident like this may not be instantly seen, the positive effect it had is very real. It's the sort of thing that you may have to stop and really think about but once you do that, you will see how it has helped you and your approach to work.

25. These choppers?

Crack heads are unique and amazing creatures. It's mind boggling to see the abuse they put their bodies through and yet they continue to survive. One of my partners used to say, "I"ll bet if we had a nuclear disaster the only thing to survive would be cockroaches and crackheads. Everything else would be fucking dead.". He might be right. I saw and dealt with crackheads on a daily basis. When we saw a particularly really bad one we would joke, saying, "That dude's living on borrowed time!". Then a few weeks or a month would go by and you would still see them walking around. A few months later they are still walking the streets. This would go on for long stretches of time and yet they would continue. How they did it, I don't know. Whenever I saw them all I could think of is how hard it is to get up sometimes and come to work being a healthy person with no smoking, drinking, drugs or night life. Just work alone is enough. Sometimes just working made me feel beat up. How the fuck can these junkies go on with the constant abuse and stress they put their body and mind through? It's a medical marvel and a testament to what the human body can withstand.

Now, don't misunderstand me, I don't mean to say that all crackheads live forever regardless of their habit and lifestyle. I mean, eventually they all take a path. Whether it's death or jail or the rare one or two who actually get cleaned up. Eventually, they all have to end up somewhere. The amazing part is the process that gets them there.

Through all the years of abuse, they go through a slow metamorphosis. If you arrest a crackhead at the start of their decent, before they are in to the lifestyle really deep and they remain in your Precinct, you can see the change in their life and their general appearance as well. If you see one take the journey from the beginning to the end or at least years later, the change is like night and day. In some cases they become almost unrecognizable from when you first saw them.

When you see a crackhead craving for more, they are on a mission and will do anything to get what their body wants. They will support their habit through any type of scheme to get money from people who may not be very street smart or are unaware they are dealing with a crackhead and not an everyday normal person.

A scheming crackhead will commonly try to get themselves into a position or situation that can be corrected or bargained out of through a monetary agreement with an unsuspecting party. Usually crackheads will prey on the elderly, the overly nice person or a foreigner who may not yet have encountered this kind of person or element.

The crackhead has to work quick and get the money before the cops show up. A cop on the scene will put an end to their charade and in some instances can result in an arrest which is really a disaster for them. Considering how fucked up they are, they are clever and will try to make themselves look like the victim, settling for a few quick bucks and leaving the scene appearing to be unhappy. This makes the other person feel like they got the better deal and made the right choice.

I remember this one crackhead who started an argument with a store clerk in a bodega on my beat. The store was run by foreigners from Yemen and they were practically off the boat. It was a fairly new store and although the workers did speak English, it wasn't very good. Even with their limited command of the language, they definitely weren't used to or even aware this type of person existed in life. It was obvious their experiences in this country and dealing with undesirables was extremely limited.

In this case what the crackhead did was start and push an argument to the point that it got good and heated. The idea was to get to the point right before it would get physical. The louder the better, as this would attract attention and witnesses in the immediate area. When the crackhead sensed the breaking point was near, he or she would get real close to the intended target and give a slight bump to that person. If the clerk even flinched back towards the crackhead, he or she would hit the floor writhing and complaining of pain, screaming about how they were assaulted and were the victim of an unprovoked attack.

From this point, the Oscar winning performance would really get going at full blast.   The crackhead would go into some type of instinctive action, such as flopping on the floor like a fish, rolling around on the floor or writhing in imaginary pain and playing it up in grand style, for the ever growing crowd of onlookers. Inevitably, someone always calls an ambulance for an assault victim and that would prompt the police to be dispatched as well.

For the crackhead, the clock is now ticking. They know that eventually the cops are going to show up and they want this little scheme wrapped up and on their way before that happens. While the units are responding, the crackhead will work feverishly to get a few bucks out of the clerk and beat it out of there. If the crackhead can get any money at all they will usually leave prior to the police showing up. In rare cases, like this one, the crackhead will stick around and insist on pressing bogus charges as a way of either getting even for not scoring any money or just to fuck with the guy. Of course the crackhead is hoping the clerk will eventually give in and pay him off. It's a lousy scare tactic on a guy who just wants to work his store and make a living.

If the crackhead is lucky enough to get a rookie cop or a lazy cop who wants to avoid any arrests or work in general, they will usually give in to the crackhead's plea. At the very least, their goal is something for nothing. A free lunch or drink or some other type of compensation. The store clerk will usually jump in somewhere during the mediation and say, "Okay, here is your "whatever", take it and go.". With that, both parties will go their separate ways.

Unfortunately for this crackhead, it was me and two other cops who were just like me doing our usual bike patrol. We had a lot of time on the job, especially in dealing with crackheads just like this one. When we pulled up he was sitting on the back step of the ambulance telling the driver his bullshit story about how he was assaulted by the clerk and injured in the process. With raised eyebrows we asked the dude, "So, what happened?". He gladly retold the story to the three of us. He could barely keep his eyes steady and his head was moving all over the place. The effects of crack were obvious to all of us.

When he came to a pause I asked him, "So, your injured, huh?". He replied, "Fuck yeah, I'm injured and I want that motherfucker locked up.". With a leery feeling I asked, "What's your injury?". He snapped back, "My teeth man, he fucked up my teeth!". The obvious next question was, "Can we see the injury?".

With that he opened his mouth for all the world to see. What we saw were the remains of just a handful of teeth. The teeth still in there were in terrible shape and looked like they were like that for years. They were crooked, cracked, black, green and yellow. We couldn't help but laugh. It was the sort of laugh that once you get going you can't stop.

It was now painfully obvious to the crackhead that his ruse was up. To his credit he put on his best victim's face and said, "What, you don't believe me?". I couldn't help myself and I responded by saying, "Yo dude, those choppers don't look like they were in too good a shape to begin with.". With that he said, "Which? These choppers?". He then spit the whole set of teeth right into his hand. They were actually a set of the most fucked up pair of false teeth any of us had ever seen, including the ambulance driver and his technician.

We all busted out laughing harder than before and with no end in sight. The crackhead jumped up from the bumper and shuffled away down the street as we all continued to laugh our asses off.

Unfortunately, as we were laughing, this piece of shit was probably already plotting the next store and unsuspecting clerk to try this scam on. It's one of those things that is both funny and sad at the same time. Although he didn't succeed this time with us handling the job, we couldn't help but wonder how many times that scam had worked and the problems it caused. Things like this were a usual occurrence for us and a reason why most cops look at everything with one eyebrow raised and are suspicious of everyone. If you do this work long enough after a while you think everyone is full of shit.

26. Two Wheels Beats Two Heels

For almost seven years of my career I did uniform bicycle patrol. It was a lot of fun and a great way to supplement my running workouts outside the job. The department equipped us with mountain bikes that were pretty nice and very durable. They were painted blue and white, equipped with headlights, a tail bag for your gear and even had the precinct number on the side. They were great for getting around the city and for patrolling your beat. They were fast, quiet and the majority of the perps out there never thought to keep a look out for a cop on a bike. Before they could ever recognize you, you were right on top of them and they were busted. If they tried to run they had better get off the street to a place where the bike couldn't follow, as fast as possible. You absolutely can not outrun a bike and the effort you exert on foot attempting to do so is ten times harder than that of a person on a bike. We used to call bike patrol "the great equalizer". I remember tracking down several guys who were big, strong, muscle bound men. In a regular street fight I would definitely have a problem with these guys. However, after running a few blocks trying to get away from me, all their stamina was gone. Meanwhile, I'm on the bike right behind them and when I catch them they are pretty easy to manhandle and handcuff.

I even used the stealth of the bike for getting summonses. I would swoop in, write the ticket and be out of there before anyone knew what happened. This was beneficial in cutting down the inevitable argument you would get from irate motorists. I didn't want to hear them vent and curse. I would rather just get out of there and move on to the next car. I remember times where I rode off looking back over my shoulder at a motorist who was staring at the summons, trying to figure out how they got a ticket so fast and unable to see any cop in sight. You could see them looking all around for a foot cop who just wasn't there.

One day, on a day tour in the mid morning, I was doing some of that stealth ticket enforcement in a busy area of the precinct. It was early and I had to get my numbers so I figured I would spend half the day doing tickets and the other half hunting for a collar.

I was making my rounds and was at the intersection of a pretty raunchy block when I heard the dispatcher put over a call for a gunpoint robbery, a block away from where I was riding my bike. I came to a stop and was just about to turn the bike around towards that location when a car pulled up to me with two people inside. There was a female in the passenger seat, who was white as a ghost, and a male driver who looked pissed. The driver immediately said, "Yo, this guy just pulled a big ass gun out on me, stuck it in my car at my face and he took off. He got my chain and my new sneakers and he ran down here somewhere."

I quickly let the dispatcher know that I had the complainant from the robbery with me and that I needed the assigned sector to respond to take the victim for a canvass of the area to look for this perp. I told the dispatcher that I would meet the sector car at the next corner with the victim and standby for them. I slowly rode my bike along side the victim's car as we made our way to the corner. As we rode together north towards the corner, the sector assigned to the job came south towards that same corner to meet us. As we pulled closer to meeting the other unit, the vicim said, "There he is". He points to a muscular, black male standing in front of a Starbucks right on the corner, diagonally across from us. This perp was standing there, wearing the complainants chain around his neck and holding a shoebox in his hand. He was scanning the immediate area and looked nervous.

Just as the complainant points this dude out the marked patrol car came to a stop about twenty feet from the perp and spooked him into flight. Like a bolt of lightning, this guy takes off down the street away from everyone.

I was already on my bike and in motion and able to track him with ease. As he ran from the location I could see him holding his waist, where he could very well be concealing a handgun. In the other hand, he was still holding the victim's shoebox.

I had to keep one eye on him, where he was running and one eye on the traffic, which I was riding against. I had to grow a third eye and watch his hand at his waistline in case he decided to draw his gun at me. At this point I can't draw my weapon because I am still in motion and want to keep up the pursuit. Basically, I can't stop riding unless this guy tries to shoot at me. It was a long double length block we went across to get to the next avenue. From behind I could hear the sirens but could also tell that traffic was keeping them back. I could also tell that the cops who were running on the sidewalk were starting to fall off as they were probably losing their stamina trying to keep up with us.

Meanwhile, this guy wasn't breaking any speed records but was still going at a steady pace. The fact was that if it were all just cops on foot chasing him that day, he would have got away. Unfortunately for him, I was in the right place at the right time and on that bike. While I felt fresh as a daisy, I could tell he was starting to slow down a bit. We got to the next avenue and he made a left, going north against the flow of traffic. The danger here is that when we turned the corner, we left the view of the trailing officers. Making things worse, going against traffic would almost ensure that no police car would be able to make it through as well. The idea of backup was getting dim to say the least. We traveled two more blocks north and he turned left again into that street, again going against the direction of traffic. I quickly glanced back and although I could hear the sirens I saw no cops behind me. My immediate thought was that this could get ugly quick if it came down to just me and him. I had to start thinking and acting on how to take this guy down.

No sooner had that thought crossed my mind, the perp crossed the street and made a bee line for the nearest building. This was going from ugly to disaster. If he made it into the building, I could definitely lose this guy. If I managed to get in that building after him, I would be dealing with him out of the public area, which is ten times more dangerous. There was no way I wanted to lose this guy or deal with him inside an unknown building. I had to make a move.

The building's entrance was deep set and was hidden by the building on both sides once you exited the sidewalk area. After about forty feet, there was one step with a four foot landing and then an outer glass door. After that, a small inner lobby and a second glass door. Once he exited the sidewalk, into that walkway area, he was totally out of sight from the street. I was in constant motion right behind him and there was no way to stop and radio where I was, where I was headed or what was going on. I proceeded after him and he went up that first step and opened the first glass door to enter into the building's outer lobby area. The only thing stopping him from entering the building now was that second glass door. I couldn't wait to see if it was locked or not nor could I give him a chance to push it open or kick in the glass. In one continued motion I rode my bike up the landing step, through the open door and slammed myself and my bike as hard as I could into the perp and into the second, still closed, glass door.

The glass door gave way, cracking but didn't open. The perp, the bike and I crashed to the floor in a twisted mess. The perp dropped the shoe box he was holding and out fell what looked and sounded like a very large handgun. It turned out the gun he used in the robbery was not in his waist but actually in the shoe box he was carrying the whole time. I couldn't tell where the gun landed but there wasn't a whole lot of space in that outer area. I immediately started punching this guy anywhere I could. He was in total defense mode since he was pretty winded and seemed to be doing his best to cover up from the shots I was landing. As I was punching him, I was also trying my best to crush him with my bike which was wedged between us. After a few seconds I noticed that after every other punch I threw at him someone else's fist was punching him as well. When I realized this was happening I started to think, "Who the hell is behind me throwing punches at this guy?". I knew it wasn't a cop. It turns out it was the complainant. The complainant had followed me with his car, got out on foot and followed us the short distance right into the lobby after we crashed into the door. The two of us continued to punch this dude relentlessly to ensure he didn't go for his gun, which was lying on the floor somewhere beneath us. Within the next minute or so, I got out my cuffs and with some help from the victim the two of us easily cuffed this dude up.

Naturally, after it was all over the cavalry arrived. A dozen or more cops came storming in to help remove this dude. There was more than enough cops to take it from there, leaving me and the complainant to take a breather. The responding cops picked up the perp and drove him to the station house. I had retrieved the gun and gave the gun and shoe box to the unit that had the job. I might have done the bulk of the work, but it was their job and their collar. That's how it goes. Of course, I did tell them that if they didn't want it I was more than glad to take it off their hands. Of course, they took the collar. Who would pass up a collar like that, especially one gift wrapped for you with all the heavy work already done?

At the Precinct the perp was brought before the Desk Sergeant and was still wearing the complainant's chain around his neck. The arresting officer put the gun on the desk in front of the Sergeant for everyone to see. The gun was a huge .45 semi-auto pistol with a full clip of hollow point bullets. The victim's sneakers were still in the box as well. This perp was fucked.

He was still on the line in front of the Dest Sergeant getting booked when his mother walked in the front door of the Precinct and started asking him what he did this time to get in trouble. The guy started crying and saying "goodbye" to his mom right there, handcuffed at the desk, saying how he was going away for life because of a crime he was already on parole for. It turns out he was out on parole for another armed robbery and had several prior convictions in the past. Evidently he was told that if he got in trouble like this again he was going away for a long time. This was a stupid criminal. He obviously doesn't listen and is a danger to society. He definitely needed to go away for a long time. Hopefully the next time he gets out, if at all, he will be too old to rob anybody.

When I think of the crazy chain of events I can't help but think how lucky a person can sometimes be. When I replay the incident in my head and think of all the things that could have gone wrong and how lucky I was that it ended that way, it's pretty amazing. I guess what's meant to be is meant to be.

I stuck with bike patrol for as long as I could. I made a bunch of collars of varying degrees in the years I had with the bike. It was a unique weapon to use against the perps and a lot of fun as well.

27. Ask Not What Your Country Can Do For You...

I have said before that most cops all have a really good sense of humor. It's definitely a way of coping with things that may seem unpleasant to the rest of the world. Cops also have a tendency toward anger and aggressiveness. This comes as a result of dealing with those unpleasant things no one else wants to deal with. If a cop doesn't have these traits when they come on the job, they most likely will get them as they go. Sometimes if you step back and study the old timers you can see how the years manifest themselves and create this odd combination. It's a weird combination when you mix anger, a bad temper and the ability to seeing the world's ugliest scenarios in a comedic way. Unfortunately, this combination is not always a good blend and the concoction can be a little frightening to the outside world.

When I was a rookie cop, somewhere between just out of the Academy and five years on the job, I was working with a lot of cops who had some serious time on the job. These "old timers" could teach you things just by watching them work. By example, they showed you both what to do and what not to do.

For a brief time in the early nineties, JFK's son was working in the Manhattan DA's office as an assistant District Attorney. I was never one for politics but everybody alive knew who his dad, President John F. Kennedy was and the history surrounding him, his presidency and of course, his assassination.

From most accounts, people generally seemed to like President Kennedy, felt he did a good job as President and were saddened by his untimely death. The rumblings and rumors about his son were the opposite, especially in the conversations of the police officers who had dealt with him. The talk about JFK Jr., if you chose to believe it, was that he wasn't nearly as bright as his dad. There were even rumors that he failed the Bar exam a few times before finally passing. I was just a rookie but I heard older cops refer to him as arrogant, unfriendly and with no sense of humor. I absolutely don't know if any of that was true. I didn't know the man outside of the workplace and barely knew him from dealing with him on this case. In his defense I can attest that many people act differently at work then they do at home. I also know that very often people, and especially cops, tend to judge a person based on one particular occurrence that may have not went favorably. With some of these older experienced cops, if just one occurrence goes bad, the person is written off in their book without any shot at redemption for life. Later, in my own career, I saw myself becoming this way as well. I think it goes with the territory of being a cop.

The rumors fly fast and furious in the Police Department and it is extremely hard to get rid of a bad reputation, warranted or not, once you get one pinned on you. I certainly was in no position to judge the man. As I said, I didn't know how he was in his personal home life and this was the first and only time I was actually in his office to see him and get involved in a case with him as an assistant DA. Up until then, I had only been in his office to see other Assistants or merely walked by him in the halls of the courtroom building and recognized him as he passed by.

Even this time, the arrest was not mine. I don't even remember why I was even brought down to Court for this collar. Whatever the reason was, it was minor and dealing with him in person was more memorable than the arrest itself. To tell the truth, I wasn't really even interested in the case and just stayed in the background of the office meeting, kept quiet and let the heavy hitters and JFK Jr. do all the talking. I was merely an observer at this point.

I can tell you that I remember the conversation between the three of them was not good. The kind of conversation where there is a lot of loud explanations, eye rolling and that gasping sound when a person is frustrated. Somewhere along the line, the dialogue went pretty sour and it was abundantly clear that the arresting officers and JFK Jr. were not going to see eye to eye on this case. Every time the cops spoke you could hear the frustration in their voices. One thing about old time cops is they don't hide their emotions and if they thought they were right, which was most of the time, they would not let up, budge or give in without a hell of a fight. This back and forth conversation went on for quite a while and then JFK Jr. told the cops to hang out a minute. He was going to discuss the case with his supervisor. It was a well needed pause to let everyone cool off.

The minute that door closed behind him the cops started ranting to each other about how stupid he was and that he didn't have a clue. They also threw in a dozen or so curse words along the way to emphasize their point. Eventually, the comparisons were drawn between him and his father and how different they thought they were. I remember one cop said that his dad must be rolling over in his grave. At one point, the older of the two cops reached over JFK Jr's desk and grabbed a blank legal pad and a pencil. He started writing something down while the other cop continued to rant.

I am not a fan of the "flash back". However, for the benefit of younger readers, I must have one before going any further with this story. Back in the late 80's and early 90's, if you were growing up and watching television on a regular basis you have to remember a television commercial that aired as a public service announcement to keep kids off drugs. They showed this commercial every hour, on the hour, until you were sick of seeing it. The commercial showed an egg and a hot frying pan. You then hear the announcer say, "This is your brain" (he holds the egg) "And this is drugs" (a hot frying pan). Then the hand holding the egg, cracks the egg and drops it into the hot frying pan. You are then able to hear the sizzling egg while you watch it fry in the pan. The announcer takes a slight silent pause for effect and then says, "This is your brain on drugs, any questions?". Okay, flashback over.

Back in JFK Jr.'s office, the free flowing words of frustration and anger were evidently not enough for this gristly veteran with the legal pad. He was going to take it further and express his dislike for young JFK in art form. After several minutes of what looked like hard work on the legal pad, the veteran cop turns the pad around and shows a picture of an egg and under it reads, "This is your brain.". It also shows a frying pan which reads, "This is drugs." underneath that. At the bottom of the page the last picture is a crudely drawn picture of a man who had obviously been shot in the head. It read, "This is your fathers brain all over the fucking place. Any questions, asshole?".

After I picked my jaw off the floor and the other veteran cop stopped laughing, I realized it was their full intention to leave that pad on JFK Jr's desk in plain view for him to find after we left the room. Now, I'm all for a good laugh and a practical joke but this was too much. After much pleading and explaining what a bad idea this was, I managed to get then to destroy the picture and take it with us when we left to be thrown away outside the building. I wasn't leaving anything to chance with this one. I mean that was just wrong on so many levels.

It was a cold, sick joke and yet even things like these can teach you something. Number 1, it does emphasize how strangely the mind can work when frustrated and pushed. Number 2, it showed how a sense of humor can vary greatly from one person to the next. Lastly, it showed that it's never a good idea to piss off one of New York's finest veteran cops and not expect repercussions. Weird, what can I say.

28. A Penny For Your Thoughts

Have you ever gone to a checkout line in a small business and see that little cup on the counter filled with pennies? It usually is accompanied by writing that reads, "Leave a penny, take a penny.". This cup is there to spare a customer from having to break a dollar for need of a few cents or getting back a fist full of change in return for sale of something that is a penny or two over the dollar amount in price.

Cops always go to the same places to eat. Contrary to popular belief, it's not for a break in the price but because we like good food. Usually you are on the run and eat in the car between jobs. So when you do get to eat you want it to be good. It can be the only nice thing you encounter during a days work. It's a sort of escape from the job for a brief time. We had a bagel store on Broadway that we believed had the best bagels and the best spreads anywhere remotely close to our Precinct. The bagels and spreads were so good that we even overlooked the sub par coffee just to get the bagels. I used to joke saying that we drank their coffee just out of necessity to wash everything else down. Still, we didn't care. The bagels were that good!

Along with crappy coffee was the owner who was equally crappy. The store was owned by Koreans and I don't think they were accustomed to the whole, "Leave a penny, take a penny" thing, or maybe it was just their culture and the way they ran their business. In any case, they had a knack for charging you to the penny without ever so much as knocking anything off the price. There we were, regular everyday customers in full uniform, sometimes five or six deep and if the bill was five dollars and one cent and you handed them a ten dollar bill, they gave you back four dollars and ninety nine cents in change. Believe it our not, when you are a uniformed police officer you actually have less rights then the everyday citizen. You can't do or say the same things a regular person can. If you speak your mind like most New Yorkers do, people will say you are abusing your authority. Along with that goes the fact that people are quick to file complaints on cops, both legitimate and bullshit ones. The Department entertains them all and it just causes you more grief when you get one. In the end you end up biting your tongue a lot of times or swallowing your pride in instances when other people would voice their opinion or dislike. That's why the standard a cop is held to can make even the easiest task like buying a bagel incredibly difficult, frustrating or awkward.

While I will admit it did bother me a little bit, my feeling was nothing compared to what it did to my partner. While I thought of actually bringing in one of those penny exchange dishes for the counter, he took his frustration to a different level. The whole time in line to the cashier you could actually see his face get tenser by the minute. He fully expected the ill fated transaction to take place and was obviously agitated. I could see his face redden as he handed over his ten dollar bill. I swear I could see smoke seep out of his ears when he received four dollars and ninety nine cents back in change. He would grumble something inaudible (thank God) and go back out to our police van where he would combine a great breakfast with his agitated anger.

Of course, being cops who enjoy a good joke, we would have to stir the pot and get him going about it even more. I mean, he would rant about the Korean's for a good half hour without our instigating. Once we stoked the fire a little bit he would really get worked up, cursing like a sailor the whole time. We even went so far once as to tell him to go in and out of the bagel shop several times, with the same order and try to use up all their change, forcing them to cut people a penny break out of necessity for the change. This only got him more aggravated.

No matter where we were or what we were doing, we could set him off by raising the subject of the bagel store and how they would never knock a penny off the bill. Then we would sit back and laugh.

To the Korean's credit, I have witnessed them do this to more than just cops. In fact, as far as I could tell they did it to everyone I saw with the same type of bill. At least they were consistent about their business policies. Shortly after, my partner went to the Narcotics Division and left the borough but I bet that if I ever bump into him, I could fire him up just like before with a stroll down memory lane and the Korean bagel store.

29. Disappearing Ink

In the early 90's, hookers were everywhere in Manhattan. They walked around on the street corners in plain sight at late hours. They would stick to the less populated areas where there were a lot of warehouses or businesses that would typically close after dark and the foot traffic would cease. When they came out they were in full force and wore the wackiest outfits to get noticed as motorists drove by. I guess they had to advertise their "goods". Unfortunately, these woman helped coin the phrase, "They look good from far away but far away from good looking.". My partner and I would mess with them when we passed by. We would use the PA system and say things like, "Hey dreamboat...not you shipwreck"or "Hey cookie...not you crumb.". Some of them would laugh or smile and some would give you the finger. We laughed no matter what.

We often drove through those routes on midnights to get downtown to drop off a prisoner. When they saw the police car coming they really didn't move all that much. It was like they knew what cars would come to arrest them and which cars were just passing through.

When they did get picked up for prostitution by the local Precinct they usually got picked up in large groups. The local Precinct that had to deal with this issue would make prostitution arrests on a certain night. On that night they would go all out and grab as many as possible. Then they would kind of forget about it until the next mass prostitution arrest operation came around again.

These ladies of the evening would get booked at the local Precinct and then shuttled over to Central Booking for night Court. There they would be processed and pushed through the system in their own little processing center. Most of them would be put back on the street in less than 24 hours. Some would get held and sent to Riker's Island if they had something on their record like a warrant or a parole violation. In any case, everybody who was arrested had to go through central booking at some point.

My partner and I went down to central booking all the time to transport prisoners. We were the rookies on the midnight tour and because transports weren't exactly a desirable task, it was given to us a lot. Basically, when you had to transport you were stuck with someone else's prisoner and had to endure the perp they for the entire ride and for the lodging procedure. You had to accompany them through the system to the final destination of lodging your perp(s) with Corrections Department, where they waited to go to Court.

It was a nightmare of a process that took you through numerous security checks, locked doors, protocols and procedures. These stations were run at a snail's pace by some of the laziest people that the Corrections and Police Department had to offer. Many of these morons were jammed up and placed there for various disciplinary reasons. They were miserable people who made it tough on working cops who were just trying to do the job that these idiots weren't smart enough to do without getting in trouble in the first place. Many times you had to kiss their ass or hold your breath and hope for the best just to get out of there. You were at their mercy. They knew it and so did we. Only the New York City Police Department could take an important task like this and fill it with a bunch of assholes. To be fair there were some good people working there. Believe me, they were the minority and few and far between.

Transporting a perp was a long, boring, frustrating process. You do anything to make it bearable and get through it. You would very often find yourself talking about the weirdest and sometimes stupidest things with your partner just to pass the time. Sometimes you even converse with some of the prisoners who are waiting to get lodged.

In the main waiting area was a hallway that seemed to go on forever. At the end of this hallway is where you would check your prisoner in. The line of perps stretched all the way down this hall and stopped at the check-in spot. You would place your perp in line, walk down to check in and then go back to the spot where your prisoner was standing. You then would wait together until you get let in to proceed to the next section. Until you get let in you waited in line with as many prisoners you were lodging that night. There were two lines, cops on one side and perps on the other. The line moved slow and the whole area was hot, extremely dirty and smelled from stale air and God knows what.

Plenty of times while I was waiting to lodge my own perps, the local Precinct that dealt with the prostitution problem would bring in their catch of the evening. A chain gang of ten or more hookers would get escorted into central booking looking for lodging for the night.

Even way back then I always admired tattoos. This sort of crowd seemed to go hand in hand with ink, displaying a nice assortment of tattoos. Although I didn't have any ink at that point, I always enjoyed checking out other people's ink and thinking about the story that might accompany that tattoo. On occasion, if the person seemed friendly enough, I would admire their ink and even ask them why they chose a particular tattoo. Some of the stories were interesting and others were just spur of the moment, with no real meaning to the tattoos.

On this particular night I was waiting with two of my own perps when in comes one of the usual chain gang of prostitutes. They pulled up in line right along side me directly in back of my perps. There was at least ten of them and they ranged from not too bad looking to a complete nightmare in high heels. The nighttime definitely favored some of these women. They had what you would call "A face for radio.". The outfits on some of them were ridiculous. They ranged from fishnet stockings with micro mini skirts to what could only be described as fancy, frilly underwear. Looking at them, you couldn't help but think what these women were like before they got caught up in the life of being a hooker and all that went with it.

I was checking out some of the ink on these women and amidst the track marks on one particularly run down young lady of the evening was a pretty nice piece of ink. It was a collage of snakes and skulls with some nice line work and color in it. As I was checking it out and asking the girl a few questions, one of the older prostitutes, who was chained next to her said to me, "If you like tattoos, you would love mine, it's way better than that one.". I paused and was trying to imagine what it could possibly be when she continued to say, " You want to see it? It's a mouse.". Right off, I didn't think any tattoo of a mouse could beat snakes and skulls but said, "Yeah, sure let me check it out.". With that, a few other cops and I moved in closer to see this great mouse tattoo. The prostitute pulls down the top of her skirt near her hip and then moves to the other side and does the same. Neither move revealed a tattoo of a mouse or any ink for that matter. She continued to search for her tattoo in several places around her waist with no luck. At this point, I'm thinking, "Damn, this girl must be fucked up! How the fuck can you forget where your tattoo is?". Just then she looked at me and the other cops who were waiting to see the tattoo and said, "It's gone.". Before I could say what I was thinking, which was, "How could it be gone?" The hooker said, "I guess my pussy must have ate it.".

Immediately, she and the rest of the hookers and the cops around me started laughing. The laughter echoed down the long hallway and got louder and louder. What else could I do or say? I laughed as well and laughed pretty good at that. It was pretty funny and totally unexpected. It was also funny to see that even chained to a bunch of hookers under arrest, awaiting to be booked and put in holding cells, this lady still had a sense of humor. I have said it before and it's worth saying again, never lose your sense of humor in life.

Whether it was her way of dealing with the situation that she was in or whether she just had a legitimate good sense of humor, it was funny as hell. Once we all stopped laughing we all went back to our own individual tasks or the next step in the process. It was a bit of levity in a grim nasty place filled with dread. I think that moment helped everyone to continue on their own personal path that night.

30. Smells Like Home Cooking

When I was a rookie one of my foot posts was on West 125th Street in the middle of numerous businesses. Back then there were a lot of stores that are not in business anymore. One of the more notable ones was Woolworth's.

It was referred to as a "five and dime store" which was known for a good selection of bargain items. It was comparable to the hundreds of dollar stores you see all over the place today. The only difference was that this had a well known franchise name and a full service luncheonette inside as well. It was sort of the blueprint for today's value type stores. A few years later these stores just sold merchandise before they finally went out of business. The one in my Precinct still had a luncheonette inside the store up until the day it finally closed down.

Set up right in the center of this thrift type store was a quaint little luncheonette that featured a curvy, s-type counter that ran from one end of the dining area to the other. Beyond the counter was the grill and the area where waitresses could run back and forth dishing out a standard menu which featured an assortment of cheap meals, desserts and coffee. Nothing on this menu was expensive and it looked like a thriving business with a high demand for a hot cheap meal that was served up quick.

I remember seeing people shop in the store, then take a break at the counter for coffee, dessert or a complete meal and then continue their shopping before leaving. I also remember seeing the same people going into the store just for the cheap meal on a regular occasion. It tended to cater to people who were on a tight budget and the senior citizens who lived in the area.

A very common job that I would pick up on a busy street like 125th is called an "aided" job. An aided job is a call that goes into 911 as a service call which is not usually criminal in nature. However, sometimes the call gets entered into the system wrong and what gets dispatched as an aided could be the result of a crime. More times than not it was just a person who had fallen, got sick or had some sort of medical condition which required an ambulance and a trip to the hospital. In any case, when you are on a foot post you were expected to take these jobs so that the sector cars were free to handle the heavy runs that came over the radio. The majority of these jobs tended to be somewhat boring but they killed time and on rare occasions did produce arrests or something memorable.

One day when I was on that post right down the block from Woolworth's, a call came over for an aided. The 911 dispatcher stated it was an elderly woman who was sick inside the store. As soon as I heard that call I knew it was probably one of the regular senior citizens at the lunch counter who was having some kind of medical issue. I also knew no sector wanted that job and so I gladly picked it up and headed down to the location to see what was going on.

I stepped inside the store and a worker motioned me over to the luncheonette at the middle of the curvy s-type counter. There at the counter was a little old lady who looked to be about 90 years old with a distressed look on her face. I got some basic information from her and that she didn't feel well. I tried to keep her calm as we waited for the ambulance to show up. Due to her age, she would be in for a ride to the ER to get checked out just to make sure it wasn't anything too serious.

That day the place was packed. It was around 12 PM and the luncheonette was really busy. People all around me were enjoying bargain priced lunches. Through the crowd of hungry patrons came two EMS workers carrying a folding wheel chair to assist in the woman's transport to the ambulance. They came prepared and obviously got the call the same way I did. I briefed them on what we had and the EMS worker with the chair began to prep it for the lady to get in. The other EMS worker moved in closer to interview the lady himself and gather some more information as to who she was and where she lived. The people all around us at the counter looked like they were thrilled at the events unfolding in front of them as they ate their lunch. As boring as this job was to us, it was like dinner and a show to the diners and they kept right on eating and watching every move that was made, as if they were watching a TV show in their own house.

The second EMS worker leaned in and said to the old lady, "What's wrong ma'am, you don't feel good?". The elderly woman shook her head no and then promptly threw up all over the lunch counter from the end where she was sitting clear off the other end and onto the floor in the section where the workers would stand. The EMS worker stepped back a little and the person immediately to her right grabbed their food and walked to the other end of the counter and sat down at a new seat. The person to her left just kind of shifted over on the stool a little bit more to the left and just kept on eating. The whole thing was pretty gross. EMS helped the lady into the chair and carted her away, puke and all. I didn't stick around to see what type of cleaning measures were used to remedy the situation at the counter. However, as I walked away I did glance back to see that no one else bothered to get up to leave from their spot at the counter. The whole crowd of diners just kept right on eating in the midst of the puke, which I must say had quite a pungent odor.

I had never eaten in that place before and after that incident it would have been impossible to do so. Every time I saw that s-type counter all I thought about was puke. Even if I am at a totally different location, if it resembles the curvy s-type Woolworth's counter luncheonette, it reminds me of puke and makes me lose my appetite.

Shortly after that, whether it was a coincidence or not, they closed down the food counter and removed it from the store all together. Not long after that the whole store closed down and went out of business. The rest of my twenty years that location changed businesses several times but no matter what store reopened in that spot, whenever I went to that location, I was reminded of puke.

31. Honda's Salesman Of The Year

The Police Department sets up vehicle checkpoints for all sorts of reasons. License checks, DUI checks, seatbelt, cellphone or any other type of violation. They may say this is done for safety or to make the City a better place to live but in the end, it's either for the purpose of getting numbers, generating income for the City through the fines they impose or for making arrests.

One night me and my partner were out on patrol and the Sgt. called us to a location and told us that we were going to do a checkpoint for any noticeable violation. Me and my partner looked at each other and both knew it was going to be a long night with a lot of arguments between angry cops and even angrier motorists.

We got set up and started to stop cars, one at a time, and gave out a summons or two for whatever violation we could see. We felt we were doing okay and making some progress as we started to get a good little rhythm going and some decent numbers to show as well. Evidently, one of the Sgt.'s was getting pressure from the bosses above him and were pushing him to push the cops into getting more numbers at the checkpoint. In any case, he came out to our location to check out our activity. He felt we could work a little faster and get a few more summonses before the checkpoint ended. I tried to explain that some of these motorists really give you a "song and a dance" and that it takes a lot of time while they complain and make up these crazy stories as to why they were in violation. Of course the Sgt. said that he was a cop once too and it could be done faster and better and he even volunteered to show us how. He kept talking about how we were exaggerating and that the majority of motorists don't give a shit and never say a word. To him, the idea of people saying anything to get out of a summons was bullshit and he was going to prove it and show us how it was done.

With a bold look and a tough guy stance, the Sgt. turns to us and said, "Watch this" as he motioned for a white Honda to pull to the side of the road at our check point. The motorist did pull over and the three of us approached the vehicle. As we walked over the Sgt. said to me, "This is a ground ball. Look at his windshield, he has no inspection sticker. What's he gonna say? We got him dead to rights, quick and easy summons. No story, give a ticket and we move on to the next one, got it.". I didn't say a word in return, I wasn't sure if he was trying to convince me or himself.

We walked up to the window and the motorist said, "Can I help you officers?". The Sgt. said, "Yes sir, license and registration please. I see you don't have an inspection sticker on your windshield. We are going to give you a summons for having an un-inspected motor vehicle.".

With a puzzled look, the motorist said, "Inspection sticker? This is a Honda!" With an even more puzzled look the Sgt. said, "And that means what? Your car needs a valid inspection sticker.".

The motorist said in return, "This is a Honda Sarge! It's a good car, it doesn't need an inspection, it's a Honda.".

The Sgt. with clear frustration growing in his voice says, "Sir, this is New York. In New York every car needs an inspection, Honda or not!".

Me and my partner were both grinning as the motorist replied, "Not a Honda, it's a good car, it doesn't need an inspection. It's a Honda!".

The Sgt. looked at me and I just shrugged my shoulders and said, "It is a good car.". With that, the Sgt. just shook his head and walked away. I told the driver to get the car inspected as soon as possible, even though it was a "Honda". The motorist grinned and we all laughed as he drove away. We had to let that guy go. How could we argue with such logic? Besides, he got the Sgt. off our back for the rest of the night and that was worth its weight in gold.

32. A Cop Is A Cop, 24 Hours A Day, Seven Days A Week, Till Death Do We Part!

When you become a cop, you are a cop every day of your life until you retire or die. Even then, I guess your either a retired cop or a dead cop. So I guess once you become a cop, that's it. You definitely go through a change. Your lifestyle and the way you go about your daily activities also changes. From the moment you raise your hand to take the oath, the rest of your life is dedicated to the profession that you have chosen. Very often you find yourself saying, "I can't do this or that", because of your job. Certain things just don't fit into a cop's life and you have to avoid them. You are absolutely held to a higher standard and as such you have to pick and choose what you do and who you are involved with much more carefully than the average person. You now represent the New York City Police Department and that means you can't just do whatever you want or say whatever you want. If you do, you will find yourself in trouble with the job in a heartbeat. In a lot of ways when you become a cop you actually lose a lot of the freedom you had before you became one.

For example, when you are a cop, whether you are at work, home or even on vacation, if something happens in front of you that requires a police officers response you are expected to step up and take action. Most cops would do this sort of thing instinctively. The general population for the most part would and do run away at the first sight of trouble. For them that's okay and if someone differs with their choice to look the other way they can plainly say, "Who cares what anyone thinks, it's not my job" and carry on with their life. However, for a cop this would be considered unacceptable and either wouldn't happen or if it did happen, that cop is going to have to answer for his/her inability to help someone in need of assistance.

A few months before the 2001 terrorist attacks, I was on vacation and was using my time off from work to buy our new house. We were moving out of the City to the suburbs to accommodate our growing family's needs. A little more space, a yard for the kids and some distance between myself and the City I worked in. We managed to find a nice town that was not too far from work but far enough to have a noticeable difference from city life.

Knowing how much was involved in buying a house, I had saved my vacation time for that purpose. I knew there would be a lot of paperwork, home inspections and visits to lawyers and the bank to get the deal done. I knew I could never juggle all that and work so being on vacation allowed me to concentrate on the purchase and hopefully get it done as quickly as possible.

It was a nice house and the price wasn't too bad either. However, like all houses, there is bound to be a few things wrong with it. That's what home inspectors are for. I had scheduled an inspector to meet me and the wife of the owner to do just that. When I arrived at the location, the wife and her daughter were there and the inspector wasn't. The three of us went into the kitchen to wait for the inspector and spent some time talking about the area while we waited. After a short while, the doorbell rang and we assumed it was the inspector. It turns out it was the woman's husband. I knew from a previous visit with her that the two were in the middle of a nasty divorce. The husband had already moved out and the mom and her kid would move next after the sale of the house.

The mom looked out the window and said, "It's my husband. You wait with my daughter here while I go talk to him downstairs.". With that, the mom left to answer the door while I talked with the daughter who looked a little uneasy and nervous. After a few minutes, we could hear them talking and walking up the stairs to the floor that we were on but in the room next to us. They stopped at the top of the stairs in that adjoining room and continued to talk. I couldn't understand the conversation as it was in Russian. However, the talking turned into arguing and kept going until it was just short of yelling. The daughter looked at me and said, "Now they are going to fight. They always do this, that's why they're getting divorced. Let me go see what they are doing.".

The daughter had just cleared the room we were in and headed for the top of the stairs where her parents were arguing when all of a sudden, amidst the arguing, I heard a series of thumps followed by the woman's daughter running back into the room where I was sitting and frantically said, "My dad just threw my mom down the stairs.".

So much for vacation. I jumped up and ran down the stairs with the daughter right behind me. At the bottom of the stairs I see the mom lying on the floor in serious pain. She was holding her leg and crying uncontrollably. Standing over her with both fists clenched and the angriest scowl on his face was the dad. He was frozen, just standing there, watching over her. I immediately got between them and eased him back a little from the woman on the floor. With an outstretched arm, I slowly moved him back another five feet and kept him in place. He never took his eyes off the woman. I leaned over to the daughter and whispered in her ear, "Call 911.". Frankly, with the trance that he was in I could have yelled it and got no reaction from this guy. He was definitely in the red zone and just fixated on his wife who was still in pain on the floor. His arms were still straight down and hands still clenched in fists.

The question in my head was, "Did he know I was a cop?". I had never asked if the wife told him what I did for a living and I had never met him before. I knew that both the wife and daughter were aware of me being a cop and knew that I hadn't heard them shout out my profession to the husband as a hope of self defense. I had my service gun on me and this guy appeared to have no weapon as far as I could see. I quickly sized him up and could see that he was a short guy but stocky. He was a Russian immigrant with the accent and everything. He looked tough but he was about twenty years older than me. Although he definitely had the rage on his side I felt that if we got to brawling I could take him. What I didn't want to happen was to put myself in a position where I got caught off guard and this guy had an advantage over me. If that happened, being all alone, I knew I would probably have to shoot this dude as a last resort. I would be totally justified in that scenario but I was on vacation in the house I intended to buy. Not exactly the way I wanted to go.

At this point the daughter was upstairs hopefully calling the cops. I looked at the woman on the floor and I didn't think she broke anything, probably just badly bruised. There was no sign of blood and although she appeared to be in a lot of pain and was crying, she was moving and conscious. The dude spoke English so I was able to convince him to come with me out the front door and into the driveway. I had to make it seem like all he needed to do was to calm down and then he would be able to leave and everything would be alright. That's what I wanted him to think. The truth was that his ass was getting locked up for assault and going to jail. Furthermore, if he tried to leave before the cops showed up, I was fully prepared to sucker punch him as hard as I could and take him out till the cops showed up.

We went into the driveway and couldn't have been there for more than a few minutes when a State Trooper pulled in. It was a Canine Unit and in the back seat was a huge German Shepherd with teeth like a wolf. I remember seeing his big hairy head pressed against the closed window with all his teeth showing.

I had closed the door to the basement behind me as I walked the husband out but was sure to leave it unlocked. The Trooper got out of the car and I put my hand on the father's shoulder patting him to reassure him it was okay and to stay still. I met the Trooper half way and quickly identified myself as an off duty police officer. In a quiet voice I said to the Trooper, "Hey, I'm on the job in the City. I came to buy this house and this guy just threw his wife down the stairs. She is on the floor in the basement in a lot of pain, this guy needs to get locked up.". The Trooper asked me to stay with the husband while he went into the house to check on the wife.

I stayed in the driveway with my owner/perp and kept an eye on him without looking like I was watching him. I was just trying to keep him calm and in one place as we waited for the Trooper to return. All of a sudden, the Trooper came busting out of the basement door in a hastened manner with his cuffs out and made a bee line for the Russian going right for his wrist. The Russian, of course, moved his wrist and that's when the Trooper grabbed a hold of him. I quickly moved over to them and they were both already intertwined and doing the old two step dance across the driveway. The Trooper and I tried our best to pry his arm back away from his chest and that's when I heard the dog in the back of the Trooper's car going nuts. He was growling and barking and jumping on the glass. Subconsciously I must have been worried about that dog. I know it distracted me several times during the altercation and made me look over at it. I know why I was distracted. I remember a canine cop telling me that in some police departments the rear window of the police car where the dog sits works on remote control. The canine officer has a button on his belt he can activate and allow the window to drop and let the dog jump out and aid the officer if he is in a fight or needs help. When you think about it, it's a great idea. What good is a dog in a car that can't get to you to help when you need it most? It would be like having a gun with no bullets. The only problem is that these dogs are trained to know and help their master. In that respect, anyone the officer is fighting with could be seen by the dog as a perp. If I was that dog and saw my master and two other guys wrestling around I'm gonna bite one or both if I can. To the dog, me and the Russian were both perps. I have seen canine dogs in action and up close. They are big dogs and their bite is very hard and they don't let go until they are told to do so. I have also seen perps and everyday people who were bit by a dog and believe me, it's not a pretty sight.

Thankfully, he either wasn't equipped with that device or thought of my safety because the dog never came out of the car. In the next instant, the three of us tumbled to the ground and I heard that familiar sound of a handcuff clicking. We tried pulling his other arm around to the back area but this guy was a little overweight and was lying on top of his arm. I started to yell at him, "Don't resist, put your arms back, don't resist!". He would not budge one bit.

All of a sudden I could feel the Trooper let up on the dude's arms and then I heard the unforgettable sound of a taser being used. The taser makes a loud clicking sound which is usually followed by the perp groaning in pain. The perp would then tense up his or her body. If the perp was standing when hit with the electric volt, they would fall to the floor. This guy was already on the floor so he didn't fall down. However, he did go through all the rest of the taser effects. The Trooper hit him with the taser for a good 3 to 5 seconds and then we tried the cuffs again. The idiot fought some more and so he got the taser again. More clicking and groaning. Right in the middle of the clicking noise, the guy's daughter starts yelling, "He has a bad heart, he has a bad heart!". Not exactly what I wanted to hear from the background. I'm definitely thinking this guy is going to die from getting zapped right here in the driveway. Finally, with a few more zaps and me repeatedly telling him to stop resisting, he gives in and lets us cuff him.

He laid there on his stomach, cuffed in the driveway, as we got ourselves together. The dog was going ape shit in the car the whole time but stopped once the Trooper got up and looked over to him. Within a few seconds another patrol car showed up and an ambulance right after that. The second car took the Russian, who was now a perp and the ambulance took the mom out of the house on a stretcher with her leg and arm all wrapped up. The daughter went along in the ambulance with her mom. The Trooper and I were both fine, not a scratch on us. I went over to the ambulance to see the mom before she left. She was unbelievably grateful for me helping her and thanked me a dozen times. She gave me her house keys and said to just lock up after I leave with the house inspector.

I finished up my statement with the Trooper, finished my inspection of the home and phoned in my off duty incident to the job as all cops are required to do. Of course, the phone call wasn't good enough for the NYPD. I had to make the trip to a Bronx precinct where a Captain who had the duty of investigating the incident would interview me about the whole twisted tale. It took me several hours to do all that and finally get it put to rest with the Departments seal of approval as a "good incident", with no fault of my own and performing in the manner expected by the NYPD.

The good news was that the Commanding Officer of the Trooper that I assisted had made a call to the Captain who was investigating the incident and gave me rave reviews for my service to his officer. Additionally, I also made some decent overtime for the incident and the interview in the Bronx as well.

The following week I made another visit to the mom and her daughter at their house. This time I had the inspector's report in hand and was set to do some haggling over the asking price. The lady's daughter let me in and we went up to the kitchen. When I walked in I saw the lady sitting with her leg propped up and all wrapped from one end to the other. The woman also had her arm in a sling. As soon as she saw me she started thanking me again over and over. I told her that she was welcome and I was just glad that she wasn't more seriously hurt.

While I had her in a good mood I figured I should get back to the business at hand and use my home inspection report to haggle on her asking price. Before I could start to talk the woman stopped me and said, "I truly believe that if you were not there to help me and my daughter, that my husband would have killed us both that day. Thank you so much. I want to take ten thousand dollars off the price of the house if you still want to buy it". My mouth had to be open because I was floored by that statement. In police work you hardly ever get a thank you for doing your job. This was appreciation like I had never seen before. It was special to say the least.

The sale of the house went off without a hitch and with no more incidents. The family moved to another area of the State and in a few weeks I was called to Court to testify as a witness for the incident.

I was off duty when I went to Court for this case so I wore a suit and had my Detective shield looped on my pants belt but it was visible to the room as was my service weapon, when I took off my jacket. In the room was the Judge, the Defense Attorney with his client, the Prosecutor with the wife and the Court Reporter.

The judge said, "Be seated." and "Let's get started.". Quickly, the Defense Attorney said, "Your Honor, shouldn't we wait for the witness to get here?". The Prosecutor snapped back, "He is here your Honor!" The Defense Attorney said, with a questioning tone in his voice, "I see the Officer here but what about the witness?". The Prosecutor said, "He is the witness, he is a City Detective." The Defense Attorney said with disbelief,

"He is the witness!". He sunk back into his chair shaking his head. How that fact slipped by him I don't know. What I do know is that right after that they called for a meeting with the Judge and adjourned Court for the day. I never went back to Court for that case again.

I was told some time later that the Russian took a plea and did some time and had to go to anger management class after he got out of jail. I'm sure the whole incident helped out in the divorce case as well. Plus, he absolutely couldn't go near his wife or daughter ever again or would be looking at some serious time in jail for violating a court order.

When I told my family and friends that story they couldn't believe it. However, they also took the incident in stride as well. Truth is, they were all becoming accustomed to the life of a cop like I already was. Your family and close friends know the life that cops live. They see you carry a gun and badge back and forth to work or at parties or non-work related events. They know you carry that gun and badge at home in your neighborhood and to the store or the movies. They realize just like I do that even though you are off duty, you are still are a cop. If something happens, you will do the right thing and help out someone in need. No matter when, where, or what you are doing.

33. All The Work And Nothing To Show For It

In the mid-90's the Department switched from live in-person booking of new arrests to video booking. This was a typical NYPD move, to try and cut down on overtime and had nothing at all to do with moving ahead through technology. Proof of this could be easily seen in the quality of the equipment we used to facilitate the video booking. The cameras were of the worst quality imaginable. The picture was always blurred, frozen or working on an exaggerated delay. It was like watching one of those really bad voice-over Chinese martial arts films. If none of those malfunctions were taking place then the picture was out all together. The headset and mic was just as cheap and very flimsy. Very often it was broken or falling apart. The sound quality was filled with static and it would constantly go on and off or cut out all together. When you step back and consider the severity of the charges people were being booked on and that a person's freedom was at stake, you really begin to get disgusted with the whole set up. It was like the Department was making a mockery of your profession.

The old way of processing an arrest was always in person. No matter where you worked in Manhattan (in my case, Harlem) you would travel down to the DA's office which was in ChinaTown. You would draw up your case and then sign off on the affidavit, right then and there. For cops like myself, who worked further away, it did elongate the process a bit but it definitely went smoother. It was live and all parties were present. There was no chance of misunderstandings, electronic malfunctions or breakdowns.

One day I made a nice felony assault collar. It was close to the end of my tour and that usually meant some good overtime to process the arrest. The Precinct that did the video booking in the Manhattan North area was the 32nd precinct. It was a crappy little setup they just threw together above the Precinct garage. The equipment was shaky to say the least. The electronics were always "on the blink" and most of the time the setup slowed the process down rather than speeding it up. The 32nd precinct was about ten blocks away so the drive there was easy. Basically one avenue north and a few blocks over and I was there.

I finished my paperwork, punched out of my Precinct and told the Desk Sergeant I was going to draw up my collar. He gave me the okay and off I went. Even though I was on overtime I was in my street clothes and used my own car to get to the booking location. I wasn't more than five or six blocks away from my Precinct when something caught my attention. There, while I was stopped for a red light, I saw a crowd of about fifteen people with double parked cars. They were standing in the street and on the sidewalk arguing, yelling and lightly pushing and bumping each other as they argued. I could tell the argument was heating up and judging by the size of the crowd, it was the kind of situation that could get ugly real fast.

Most people would just pass right by something like this. Some people might call 911 but civilians have the luxury of deciding to make a choice to get involved or not. I was a cop and although I was off the clock for regular police work and in civilian clothes I still felt compelled to do something. The fact that it looked like it was getting worse by the minute made me want to do something all the more. I knew a sector car would eventually roll up and this looked like something they might not be able to handle alone.

To emphasize the difference between being off duty and the disadvantages that come with that, it's important to understand that along with being in civilian attire, which keeps you from being recognized as one of the good guys, I also had no radio, no vest, no back up weapon, no partner and only my off duty five shot revolver which had no extra ammo. All this, against what appeared to be a crowd of fifteen to twenty angry people, a couple of cars and an unknown of any possible weapons. In the Academy they teach you a car can hold a lot of things that can kill you. Cars are dangerous in more ways than people believe or even think about.

I took a quick look to see where I was and noticed that although I was close to the border between my Precinct and the 32nd Precinct, we were definitely in the 32nd precinct. I knew that the way the crowd was growing and carrying on that someone was eventually going to call the police. This meant with all likelihood, unless a patrol car just happened upon this dispute, the unit to be dispatched would be a 32nd Precinct car. We were in the southern most part of the 32nd Precinct and chances are the responding unit would come from the north end, driving south toward my location to get to the job. It sounds like a lot of guess work but when you think about it, it's all about cutting down the odds and giving yourself and the other cops the best chance possible for success and possible survival. I thought that if I could swing my car around I could keep an eye on the crowd till the cops arrived and maybe provide some good information as well as backup for them. I was in a unique position to see the start of this argument and what person, if any, committed a crime or should be arrested.

I made a quick u-turn and double parked about two or three car lengths away from the very last car that was parked and involved in the fight. I checked my rearview mirror and saw that way off in the distance one cop car was slowly coming down the avenue toward us. I looked back at the crowd and saw that the argument appeared as if it was heating up even more. It seemed like all of a sudden the yelling was a little louder and some screams were mixed into the overall noise as well. Standing in the middle of the crowd was a tall man, dressed in black and holding a small gun in the air and moving about the crowd, scaring people back by pointing it at them. With every couple of steps he would lower the gun to his leg and then quickly pick it up, pointing it at several people and then put it back up in the air again. This guy was wildly whipping the gun around the crowd and looked to be extremely unstable. It was at that point that I became extremely fearful for the responding officers. What I feared most was that because this guy appeared sometime after the argument started, the call might have been dispatched as just a verbal dispute with no information of a weapon. In that case, the responding unit, would not be aware of any weapon in the crowd or how bad the argument had escalated. Additionally, this fight was taking place very close to the corner. What if a unit came around the corner blindly? They could roll right into gunfire or even force a deadly confrontation without any kind of notice or preparation.

I quickly started to exit the car and as I did so I noticed the patrol car that was in the distance was coming from the direction that I had hoped they would come as they approached the scene of the fight. As I exited my car I leaned on my horn and got enough of the crowd's attention so that they noticed the police car getting closer. I stayed partially hidden by my car door and watched the crowd and especially the dude with the gun. Some of the people got up on the sidewalk out of the street. Some walked off in different directions. The cars stayed put and double parked. Most importantly, I watched the guy with the gun as he casually placed his weapon into a small leather pouch he had around his neck and zipped it up. This move was a stoke of luck for us. By placing the gun there, not only would he be unable to draw it if he wanted to but he absolutely didn't notice me watching him do it. He must have felt secure placing that gun into that pouch with the cops about three blocks away. In all likelihood he was probably thinking there is no way in hell they saw him do that. Proof of this was the fact that he didn't leave but instead hung around right there in the street behind the double parked cars.

I took a good long look at him and made damn sure I could identify him and then walked to the rear of my car and waved to stop the cops as they approached the scene. I quickly showed them my shield and told the cops what I saw. I told them to follow me into the crowd and we can walk right up on the perp with the gun and jump him quick while the gun is still in the pouch around his neck.

The cops and I did just that. As we walked up towards the perp he was acting real cool like nothing was wrong and all he was doing was standing there hanging out. He definitely felt secure with that gun tucked away. He had an almost arrogant demeanor as he stood there in the street behind the car.

Without hesitation or warning I walked right up on him, said, "Police." and pushed him right onto the trunk of the double parked car, face first, right there in the street. He looked like he was stunned from that action and while the cops grabbed his arms, I grabbed that pouch, unzipped it and pushed the butt of the gun (a small revolver) out just enough so it was visible to the other cops. I snapped the leather band as I yanked the pouch off his neck and then handed it to one of the uniformed cops. Quickly I turned back to the perp and helped the other cop cuff the dude up. The whole incident took less than a minute.

With that the crowd went pretty silent. They also knew he had that gun and were probably confused about how we knew he had it around his neck. Once the perp was secured in the back of the patrol car, I told the cops I would see them back at their Precinct so that I could give them my entire statement. I quickly jumped back into my car and took off as quietly as I could with out any other civilians seeing me leave. I definitely did not want anyone to see what I was driving or what my license plate was.

Back at the Precinct, I saw the cops bringing the perp into the station house and in front of the Desk Sergeant. There I got a better look at the gun when it was presented to the Desk Sergeant. The gun was a fully loaded, black, .32 revolver with a snub nose. It was a nice little revolver that could do some damage. Now it was one more gun off the street and a nice arrest with the best type of witness you could have, a cop.

I gave the two cops taking the arrest my whole statement and they were pretty amazed, as well as pretty happy. It's not everyday you get handed a gun arrest without doing any work and having a cop as your witness for Court. It didn't matter to me, I had a collar of my own and this little incident prolonged my stay and increased my overtime.

The next day I told some of the cops in my Precinct the story and they were amazed to hear what had happened. One of the cops said, "You better keep in touch with those cops or they won't even put you in the write up for a medal and that's the least you should get for doing all the work." I told them that I didn't really think about that but also told them that if they did put it in for a medal, how could they not put me in the write up? If it wasn't for me, that guy would have walked away at the scene with that gun still in his bag for sure.

Later that month, I met those two cops at Court for the case. Once the DA got the story she worked out a quick plea deal with the perp's attorney. They had this guy over a barrel. His attorney knew he was caught red handed and could only get a worse outcome by going to trial. From what I was told, he got a pretty good deal with very little time and probation. That's not a bad deal for getting caught with a loaded firearm in NYC.

Later that year, the 32nd Precinct had their list of service medals announced in the Department Orders which lists all the cops from that Precinct and the medals they have earned. I was nowhere to be found on that list but both of those cops were on it. When I finally caught up with those two guys and asked them about it, they said, "Oh, we put in for it but we never got anything for that arrest.". I just looked at them and said, "Really." They were the worst liars I had ever seen. Besides the fact that I saw their names on the list, there is no way in hell that we wouldn't get recognized for a gun collar. Especially one where I was involved while off duty, on the way to handling another arrest. I guess it just goes to show you how people everywhere are out for themselves, cops included. The whole public perception of police always sticking together is true to a certain extent. However, in the end you have to remember that cops are people too. Like in all lines of work and walks of life, there are good and bad. You can never let yourself fully trust anyone just because of who they are or what they do.

34. Cops Say The Darnedest Things

On one of the occasions when my partner was out, I was assigned a substitute who not only didn't have a partner for good reason but was transferred to our Precinct on what the Department called a "scholarship". In other words, he was dumped on us for some disciplinary problem or negative reason. Sometimes you're told straight out why the cop was dumped in your command. Sometimes you have to figure it out on your own. In both cases, it's just a matter of time before it becomes common knowledge to the entire Precinct. The word on this cop was that he was a bit of a nut case. Supposedly always doing crazy shit and saying things that kept getting him in trouble, both on and off the job.

And now I'm saddled with this guy for the tour. In my mind I know this is not good. I know that when one cop in a car fucks up, it always drags the other cop into it in some way. I was going to have to watch this guy closely and hopefully avoid any really serious problems where he could get us both in trouble. In other words, I was going to have to babysit this nut job for the whole day for my own good.

So, there we are cruising the streets and as you might have guessed I was doing the driving. You just can't let anyone get behind the wheel with this job. Especially some cop who has a reputation for being a nut. If you get a reckless cop driving in the City, you could get killed or kill someone real quick. The intersections in Manhattan are unforgiving and I wasn't taking any chances. You combine the fact of this cop's history with the amount of cabs, traffic and pedestrians and it is common sense to keep him on the passenger side of the vehicle.

Our sector covered the area around W125th Street and it was the busiest street in the Precinct. It had a lot of foot and vehicle traffic along with a lot of petty crimes and quality of life issues. These problems were mixed into the area and included both the commercial businesses as well as the various vendors that were lined up and down the street.

Anyway, we were doing some routine cruising along the main street and got flagged down by one of the local vendors. As soon as we pulled over to him he started blurting out the details of a minor argument he was evidently having with a customer over his last transaction. From what he told us it seemed the customer was giving the vendor a hard time and although I don't recall the exact transaction or subsequent problem, I do remember it was obvious the customer was being incredibly unreasonable in his demands of the vendor.

As I said, I was driving and the vendor was standing on the passenger side. I knew I was babysitting this cop so I decided to sit back a little and let my temporary partner for the day handle the argument. By doing this I could see what type of cop he was and how he handled some of the everyday, bullshit jobs we encounter on a regular basis. From that interaction I could get a better read on whether or not I could trust this cop to be able to handle a heavy call if one came later in the day.

So there I am, sitting there while my partner was getting the story from the vendor. It was obvious my partner also had the same idea about the customer being an asshole. In fact, as more of the story unfolded, it was becoming clear that the customer was not only being an asshole but appeared to be trying to take advantage of the vendor and his apparent good nature. As the vendor's story came to a close, my partner told him to wait on the sidewalk and then called the customer over to his side of the car.

The customer started ranting and raving as he walked up to the passenger side of our car, yapping about the bad deal he got and how he had been cheated and how it happens to him all the time. Blah, blah, blah and on and on he went like a broken fucking record with no end in sight.

To my partner's credit, he was pretty patient as he explained to the customer the deal he was getting and how it was more than fair. My partner repeated this at least three times. Like clockwork, all three times it was clearly explained how he was getting a very fair deal, he started his nonsense complaints all over again from the beginning. It was becoming painfully obvious that this guy was unwilling to bend or realize that he was actually going to come out ahead of the game. His attitude and stubborn personality just wouldn't let him see the big picture. On top of that, he looked like a greedy person. He was the type of guy who wanted everything in return and more. To sum up what type of person my partner was dealing with, I will repeat an often used phrase a Sgt. on the midnight tour used to say all the time when talking about someone you just can't please. The Sarge would say, "You could give this guy breakfast, lunch and dinner in bed and he would say, what, no mints?".

To my partner's credit, his own baggage not withstanding, I think I could have done only slightly better talking with this asshole and trying to work out a solution to mediate this argument. In fact, ironically enough, my usual everyday partner at that time was not a people person at all and would probably have done even worse than the substitute partner I was with on that day.

Eventually everyone has their limit and we have a job to be complete. We obviously can't stay there all day handling one job. Not everyone is going to be happy and that's the way it is. The longer this dragged out the more hot under the collar my partner began to get. I could see him getting frustrated with the customer and before long my partner and this guy were in a full blown shouting match. I listened as my partner tried his best to show him he was being stubborn, unreasonable and demanding when there was no need to be. Unfortunately, by this point, this guy was like a brick wall. He was ranting and carrying on, not receiving any information, just repeating his same silly point of view.

The shouting match came to an abrupt end with the customer and my partner cursing each other out and my partner threatening him and giving him an ultimatum by telling the dude to, "Shut the fuck up and get the fuck out of here or I'm going to lock your stupid ass up. Now go ahead and try me, motherfucker!". With that the customer stormed off and the vendor nodded a "thank you" as we pulled away.

There was a good five minutes of decompression/cool down quiet in the car. When the steam stopped coming out of his ears I looked at my partner and said, "Man, that guy was an asshole.". To that statement my partner responded, "Yo dude, I'm black and let me tell you, there are black people and there are niggers and that guy is a fucking nigger.".

I was shocked at the statement and never expected that, even from this guy, who is supposed to be a head case. I mean I knew he had a reputation as a bit of a psycho and was always supposed to be getting in trouble for things he said and did, but I didn't see that one coming. When I picked my jaw up off the car floor, I thought to myself how grateful I was that he didn't say that to the guy's face. I had been down to CCRB enough times by this point in my career and I didn't want to have to touch that, as a possible allegation with a ten foot pole.

All in all, he actually did use a great amount of restrain and handled a difficult person pretty well, given his past history and propensity for getting in trouble. Bottom line, it was over and I was very grateful. We got through the rest of the tour without incident and even though the rest of the day was uneventful, I told the Sergeant that I can't work with that cop anymore. When the Sgt. asked, "Why?", I said, "Personal reasons and can we leave it at that?". What was I going to say? The Sergeant was black as well! Later that year, that cop got arrested and was fired for an off duty incident. I didn't have to worry about working with him again anyway.

35. CCRB and The Michelin Man

When you become a cop they tell you that getting civilian complaints is part of the job. The Department doesn't like when you get them but it is definitely understood that it is going to happen sooner or later. Eventually every Cop gets one. In fact, if you are an active cop you may very well get quite a few of them throughout the course of your career. I think in my career I probably got twelve to fifteen. Considering I was a cop with just over twenty years, all on the street, and over eleven hundred arrests, that's not too bad.

In any case, the first time you get one it is a little nerve racking to say the least. In your mind you know you are new and on probation. Someone has just said you did something wrong. Meanwhile, there you are trying to do your job and serve the community and you get a complaint. Sometimes you'll even get a complaint when you get hurt making an arrest. In those instances you truly feel like police work is a thankless job.

For me, and probably most of the cops who receive complaints, they come from the perp you arrested as a means of trying to get even with you for locking them up or to get you off their back. It doesn't matter what the complaint is for or who made it. The City entertains all this bullshit and you have to go down to CCRB to see some asshole investigator who has no idea about police work and what you go through on a daily basis. When you are down there they are quick to look at your history but I never heard them talk about the complainant's history. This is the one venue where recidivism doesn't mean a thing.

I must have been on the job about 6 months when I got my first civilian complaint. It was in fact from a perp I had arrested. I don't really recall the complaint itself other than the usual reasons a perp would make a complaint. The majority of those instances are usually for allegations of abuse of authority, unreasonable force or false arrest.

When you get a notification for CCRB word gets around. When you get one as a rookie it gets around even faster and when it's your first time going to CCRB, it's really big news to the rest of the Precinct.

I was walking into the back entrance of the Precinct when a few of the veteran cops from the late tour stopped me and said they had heard I was going down to CCRB for the first time. To them this was big news and it was almost a good thing. In their eyes this was like a rite of passage or a way of showing you were turning into a real cop. It also told them you looked like you were going to be the kind of cop they liked, active and not afraid to handle your business on the street. To them "zips" and "house mouses" didn't get complaints. They assured me it was nothing to worry about and went on to say how stupid the CCRB investigators were. They told me these investigators were fresh out of college, civilian investigators for the City who have no idea about performing investigations or asking the proper questions to get the true story. I have to say, the whole conversation did make me more at ease. Before I left these cops, one of the old timers who I had heard was down to CCRB dozens of times said, "Hey kid, just before you walk into the room at CCRB think of the "Michelin Man.".

For the benefit of any younger readers, the Michelin Man is the cartoon character who represents the Michelin Tire company. He is a cartoon man who is all white and is made solely out of tires from head to toe, including his arms and legs. If you really don't know what I'm talking about, stop for a moment and look up the picture of the Michelin Man on the Internet before you read the rest of this story.

So there I am walking away, confused as hell, thinking to myself about why should I think about the Michelin Man before I go into CCRB. In the back of my mind I know how wacky these guys on the late tour are so I kind of dismissed it and kept walking. I was still a little nervous about the complaint as I headed down to CCRB. I really didn't want a complaint on my record this early in my career and was hoping to beat it and get it taken off my record.

Unfortunately, I found out later that these complaints never come off your record. It doesn't matter whether you win or lose or are found guilty or innocent. Once they are in your file they are there for your entire career. From there they just pile up and unlike the person who makes the complaint, the Department looks at your past history to see how many total complaints you have in your career. These complaints then work against you as you try to advance or move out of the Precinct to a nice detail.

In the 90's, the location of CCRB's building, was on Houston Street. It was an old building and was a bit of a ride to get to by public transportation. The only good thing about its location was that it was in walking distance to Katz's Deli. Katz's was an old fashioned Jewish Deli with the best corned beef and pastrami I have ever had. Naturally, I found out about this place from an old time Sergeant I had to drive to CCRB several times for his own numerous civilian complaints. Bottom line, it was a great place to either celebrate a victory or drown your sorrows in good food after a crushing defeat. Either way it was a place that made you forget about CCRB and all the bullshit that went with it.

I left the Precinct early because I didn't want to be late. I guess I was a little paranoid and felt these investigators would be grading me on everything I did to determine an outcome. I went though the front door and followed the signs up to the appropriate floor and walked to the outer door that read "CCRB" on the frosted glass window. I took a deep breath and started to open the door when all of a sudden I remembered the midnight guys and the old timer who said to think about the "Michelin Man" before I go into the office. Even though I really didn't know why I should do it, I pictured the cartoon image in my head and turned the knob to enter the office. I stepped through the door into the reception area and there sitting at the reception desk where every cop had to sign in, was a female midget.

It was immediately clear to me why the midnight cop told me to picture the Michelin Man. The receptionist was an average size midget and she had wrinkly rolls of skin like you would see on a chubby baby. It was similar to the Michelin Man who has the same appearance but in the form of tires which are stacked up to represent his arms and legs. I couldn't help but think of the similarity and also wondered how many cops have spontaneously laughed at the sight of her just because they were told to have that image in their heads before they walked into the room. I have to give myself credit because I did not laugh but probably was a little shocked for a moment. In any case, the sight of her definitely slowed me down a little, as I processed everything in my head. The receptionist, in response to my not moving fast enough, yelled out that I should move quickly, get out of the doorway, sign the attendance book and get my slip to show what I was there for.

She said all of this in a quick and nasty tone, kind of like barking it out to me. I remember thinking that really she was more like a Shar-Pei than the Michelin Man. In either case, she did not seem like a very pleasant person to deal with. It seemed odd to me that the Police Department would put someone like that in a place like CCRB. It almost made me feel like they had her there as some sort of test and that maybe we were all being videotaped to see how we handled her and what we said back to her when she got nasty. After a few moments, more cops came through the door and she was equally nasty with each one, again barking out the same list of statements. None of those cops laughed either but some also looked a little confused. I remember checking her out without making it look like I was checking her out. All of a sudden she reached out her hand to give me my "list of allegations" and as I was reaching to get it she barked out in a loud nasty tone, "Let's go, you gotta reach over, you know the midget can't reach all the way over the desk.". I probably should have laughed at that, whether it was a joke or not, but I didn't. Instead, I just remained a little dazed by the weird reaction, took my paper and sat down. I continued to check her out as I was sitting in the waiting room and I noticed that I could see her little feet dangling off her chair. I also remember seeing her use a ruler to retrieve the papers coming in on the fax. With each one that came in she would stick the ruler under the sheet of paper and kind of sling it to her hand and then snatch it down to her desk. She had amazing dexterity in her stubby little fingers. When she had to get off her chair to leave the room it looked like quite a chore as she struggled to go either up or down and had to include a little hop to complete both tasks.

As more time passed and more cops came into the room, the place was really filling up. It almost seemed like she was getting nastier with each new cop who came in. With one cop in particular, although I couldn't make out the entire conversation, the receptionist seemed to be especially nasty in her exchange of dialogue with the Officer. The looks on their faces and the muffled tones just seemed express that they were at odds with each other. This cop looked like he had age and experience on his side. He also looked like the kind of cop who had been to this place a bunch of times and was not intimidated or nervous. It would make sense that this cop would be the one who would not take kindly to the receptionist's nasty demeanor. The cop got his paper from her and sat down all the while continuing to mumble under his breath. He was quickly joined by another cop from his Precinct and the two began to have a conversation that I could tell was about the receptionist and her attitude.

The receptionist's phone ran again. She quickly answered it and at the end of the conversation, the phone, which was prominently place near her at the edge of the desk, was slammed down on the receiver. With a sour puss on her face she hopped off the chair and made a bee line for the adjoining office. While she was out of the room, the cop who seemed to have the most problems with her got up from his chair, went over to her desk and moved her phone all the way back to the rear end of the desk. He quickly sat back down with his partner and I could see both cop's trying their best to hold back their laughter while they waited for her to come back into the room and to her desk. By now, almost all the cops sitting in that room knew what the cops did and were all watching the door waiting for the receptionist to return. You could practically feel the anticipation in the air. Within a few seconds the receptionist came back in and climbed back on top of her chair. It wasn't long before the phone rang and she stretched out her tiny arm in an attempt to answer the phone only to realize there was no way in hell she was going to reach it in its new position. She went into a tirade, cursing and yelling, saying something like, "Who the hell is the smart ass who moved my phone back?". She kept saying the word "asshole" as she got her handy fax ruler and used it to maneuver the phone close enough to her hand and fling the receiver part towards her so she could pick it up and answer it.

I tried my best not to laugh but several cops who knew what was coming next burst out laughing as she continued to call all cops, a bunch of assholes. It was a mean joke but that's what happens with police officers sometimes. They are an odd group and want respect like anyone else. When they don't get that respect there can be some awful repercussions. I've noticed that cops can be a vindictive bunch and also tend to have a good memory of who has crossed them. On top of that they are a patient bunch and will wait for an opportunity to get even, acting with great improvisation whenever the moment presents itself.

Years later, I was still making my periodic trips to CCRB for more bullshit complaints. Eventually they moved the office to lower Manhattan all the way past City Hall, far from Katz's Deli. One day I noticed the nasty receptionist wasn't there anymore. When I asked what happened to her, the new receptionist told me she had cancer. Later that year I heard she died from that cancer. It makes you realize that the lady must have had a rough life. She definitely had her reasons to be unhappy in life. Whether or not she was right or wrong for displacing her feelings on the cops she dealt with really didn't matter now. Maybe her life and all her hardships made her act the way it did. Maybe her problems caused her anger to spill over into her work life. Whatever it is it's another example of how lucky some people are and don't realize it.

36. In With The New And Out With The Old

When you are a rookie, inevitably some old timer is going to say how the job has changed, how it sucks these days and how much better it was years ago when he first came on the job. If you stay on the job long enough you find out that you will end up saying the exact same thing to a rookie just like they did. The Police Department is a never ending cycle. Cops come and cops go. The job changes but this necessary change is closely linked to the evolution of the society you serve. At the same time this society is changing, your perspective of the job changes as well. What sounds like something that isn't so good seems to be a lot better when you have done it for ten or fifteen years. Then, all of a sudden there is a new way that doesn't seem as good as the old way. This is the point where you will tell a rookie how much the job has changed and that it now sucks repeating those famous words you once were told years ago. In either case, you will find yourself adapting to and dealing with them with ease. You will continue to adapt until you either just can't adapt anymore or your time comes to retire and leave the job.

One of the biggest changes I saw towards the end of my career involved CCRB and the way cops were handled during the investigation process. This was one of those changes I would tell a new cop absolutely sucked and was definitely better when I was a rookie. When I first joined the Department, the Union and the Police Department seemed a lot stronger. The Union seemed to call the shots when it came to dealing with the cops and their rights and the Department seemed like they always backed the cops up.

Before I retired it seemed like the Union was getting pushed around and had lost its ability to negotiate with leverage. They always seemed to be a step behind and the Department was being second guessed and scrutinized for everything. Cops were being accused and disciplined for more complaints and the Department was cracking down on everybody for everything.

Don't misunderstand me. I am not talking about cops who are corrupt. Fuck those guys and put them in jail. They aren't cops, they are perps with badges. I could care less if a dirty cop got locked up or even died. The reality of it is that cops like that make it harder on the good, hard working cops. What I'm talking about is the kind of stuff that I was a victim of. Plain and simple, a bullshit complaint from a piece of shit perp who has twenty or more prior arrests and gives you a problem everyday on your beat or sector. When you finally catch him dirty and lock his ass up, he has nothing else better to do then make up some phony story for a civilian complaint solely for the purpose of getting even or to get you to leave him alone so he can go back to conducting his criminal business. The Department entertains it and even judges you on how many complaints you have, regardless of the type or origin of the complaint. They never look at the character of the perp making the complaint but, instead, put your integrity on trial as you defend yourself and possibly your career.

When I was a rookie, the investigators didn't seem to have free reign to ask and have you answer a bunch of arbitrary questions. There were guidelines and representation for cops who spoke up on your behalf, halting any excessive investigation, especially for the bullshit complaints. The Union Representatives had intimidation built into their whole demeanor, attitude and the way they went about their business. These Union Reps made it known to the CCRB investigators that this was a cop they were investigating. It was made clear that cops serve the city for people like them, the public and that we demand respect. They let it be known through their actions and their words that they are not going to let anyone defame a cop, especially allegations of some perp low life who got locked up, decided that it wasn't fair or that they didn't do it. Just like every other perp in the city of New York.

Years later, before I left the job, the CCRB investigators had become very "ballsy". Their whole attitude and sense of authority had changed. The Union Reps had changed too. More often than not, they didn't seem to know what to allow or object to and stayed way too quiet during the investigation. They also didn't appear as tough as the old time Union Reps. Plain and simple, the game changed and the parties involved seem to switch roles quite a bit, like a shift of power. It is a real shame and it is a detriment to the police officers who get these types of complaints. If there is one thing those old time Union Reps knew, it was how to play the game.

I really don't remember the substance of my first complaint other than it was the result of an arrest. I think being a rookie and getting a complaint was traumatic enough and I must have blocked the details out of my memory. However, clear as a bell and as if it happened yesterday, I can remember the Union Rep who handled my complaint. First of all, I can tell you that it appeared that he handled the whole investigation with ease and a sense of authority. He had a definite air about him. It wasn't arrogance but more like entitlement. The way he talked and moved told everyone this is who we are and this is the way things go. If you don't like it then go fuck yourself because we are not hear to please you. It was amazing to watch and I took it all in as if it was a lesson in the Police Academy.

While you wait for your representation you get moment to look over the charges or allegations made against you. They were written on paper in short statements without details. Usually it's three to four allegations and if the complaint was a result of an arrest, it's usually for abuse of authority, excessive force or false arrest. These are the types of complaints you receive from yet another perp who "didn't do it". Anyway, you read your list of allegations and let your stress levels get good and high while you wait for the investigation to begin.

It's easy to pick out the Union Reps from the rest of the cops because Union Reps wear nice suits and are much older than the average cop. Back then, all these guys had at least twenty years on the job. I didn't know my Rep personally. I had never seen or met him before but when he checked in with the reception area to get a list of the cops he was there to represent, I knew he was the Rep for the police officers.

As I said, he was dressed in a real nice suit, clean shaven and looked to be about fifty years old. He had a briefcase and a newspaper under one arm and his list of cops in the other hand. He took a quick look around the room, looked at the list one more time and then quickly exited the room.

When he reappeared he just had a sheet of paper and a cigar hanging out of his mouth. He made his way across the room and the way he moved made him look like he was either in charge or at the very least important and vital to the success of what was happening in this office. Anyone he interacted with gave him total respect and he seemed to be in control every step of the way.

He stopped in front of me, looked at my name tag and said, "You and me kid, let's go.". I followed him into a small room with two benches and a table in the middle of the room. On the table was blank paper and a few pens. We sat down and he introduced himself and then lit his cigar. It was one of those long thick cigars that really stink. This was during the years when you could still smoke indoors but I would be willing to bet he would have lit up regardless of any law. He really didn't puff on it all that much and it seemed like it was going out but he kept it in his mouth anyway as he read my list of allegations. It definitely added to the effect and look of a gristly old veteran cop with years of wisdom and experience handling the situation at hand. As I sat there, I could only imagine all the stories he had heard and all the cops he had defended down at CCRB over the years.

He finished reading the sheet and said, "This sounds like bullshit, so what happened?". I told him the story to the best of my memory and also told him I brought all my arrest paperwork in case he needed it. He smiled and said, "Okay, put that paperwork away. Don't say anything about that and don't say anything at all unless I tell you it's okay, got it?".

With that he left the room and returned a few minutes later with the Investigator in tow. At that moment I really didn't feel nervous because the whole event seemed to be on cruise control with me just going along for the ride. I stayed in my seat checking out the Investigator as he came in. He was a young, nerdy looking guy with a legal pad, a folder with my name on it and a tape recorder. He set all that down on the table in front of me and sat down across from the two of us.

He said hello, introduced himself and pressed record on the tape recorder. In a very official tone he read his name and had me and my Rep state our names. He continued with the date, the allegations and some other information regarding the incident. He then said, "Before I start the questioning, I would like to ask the Officer if he remembers the incident and if he is willing to make a voluntary statement regarding the incident before we start.". I turned slightly to look at my Rep for coaching and he simply put his hand up as if to say, "Don't say a word.". Then, in one breath, he said to the Investigator, "He don't know nothing about nothing from nothing and he's got nothing to say regarding the incident.".

From that point on, the whole thing was pretty much over. In the minutes that followed, I hardly said a word and when I did it was a simple, "I don't recall.", "I don't know.", "yes.", or "no.", all of which was coached by my Union Representative. Furthermore, we provided no documents or evidence of any kind and it was clear the Rep was in fact saying through his actions, "If you or any investigator wants anything, then go find it out for yourself. We are not helping you to hang a cop." I could tell by looking at the Investigator's face that he was used to this style of mediation and treatment. He appeared trancelike and was just going through the motions of the investigation. He appeared as if he wanted to get this done as much as we did.

That was what the police Union was like at one time. It was powerful, as were most of the City Unions years ago. At the end of my career and in a trend that seems to be continuing, the Unions were losing their power and effectiveness and the Reps you get today seem to be lost or scared. Maybe a little of both. Just before I retired I remember reading about dozens of cops who were being put on special monitoring for excessive complaints. A lot of those cops were not only getting numerous complaints but were being found at fault as well. That never would have happened in the past. At least not to the extent it was now occurring. Like the old timer said to me years ago, "The job is changing. It used to be a better job years ago.". I spoke those same words to countless rookies just before I retired and they will too some day. The cycle goes on.

37. Waffles Anyone?

Some calls for service are listed as "aided" cases. Usually these calls are medical in nature and non-criminal. However, like most of police work, you never know what you are going to find when you get to a location. It really is one of the best things about the job. It never gets boring because you never know what you are going to encounter and no two jobs are ever the same. Sure you might get a couple of thousand calls for domestic fights over the course of your career but they will all have something unique about them. This holds true for all the jobs you handle.

One day a call came over as an aided case and the information only stated that it was a burn victim, nothing more, nothing less. From the information it didn't sound like much. In your mind, however, you always tell yourself not to get complacent. You never know what can happen or what the job could really be. Besides that, I am a true believer that you can learn something from every job and the more jobs you handle, the better you will be at doing police work.

It's for that reason that even on a bullshit call like this, if you are not doing anything, you would back up the unit that has the job. If it turns out to be nothing, no big deal. You can always leave the responding unit to handle it. If it turns out to be something else, then you will already either be there or on your way to lend a hand.

For this call we were the back up unit and it was a slow day. Being that we were close by we took the ride over and met the responding unit outside the location. It was in one of the more skelly buildings in the Precinct and it was on the top floor. We took the elevator up to the top floor. On the way up, the unit that was assigned the job did the usual tasks of letting dispatch know we were there, checking the call back number and trying to ascertain further information and get an ETA on EMS.

We exited the elevator and were met by a man who says he is the husband of the person who needs EMS. The guy looked like a straight up junkie and looked as if he just finished whatever drug he was doing. His eyes were red and he had trouble focusing on us. His speech was slow and a little fucked up and when we asked him to lead us to his apartment, he paused for a brief moment as processing the request took effort. Once he got moving, he had a slight sway in his step as he slowly led us down the hall to his apartment. On the way to the door we asked him what happened and he said, "My wife got burned on the stove.". A lot of fucking help that was. We asked if he could elaborate a little more but he didn't answer in more than an inaudible mumble.

It's important in any job to get as much information as possible. In this case it was extra important. What we didn't want was to find out that she burned herself on the stove after he stabbed her in the back or some other wild event had taken place. Reluctantly, we accepted the limited information and because there were four of us and this guy was half baked, we felt secure enough to go in to the apartment and check this lady out.

We walked into the apartment and it stank of dirt, smoke and some other God awful smell that I really couldn't place at that moment. That was until I saw the lady on the floor. She was half dazed and semi-conscious. She had nasty burns on the side of her face, head and ear. The smell that I couldn't quite place was burned hair. The part of her head where her hair line began was burned pretty bad and quite a bit of hair was melted off. She also looked like a junkie and the only reason she wasn't moaning in pain was because she looked like the junk she was on was still racing though her body. She appeared to be very far away at that moment. I couldn't help but wonder what color the sky was in her world at that very moment. Still, I didn't envy the pain and agony she will be in when she comes around in the hospital later that night when that shit she's on wears off. On top of all that, she won't even be able to get high while she is recovering in the hospital either.

Between the limited information we got from her junkie husband and from what we could tell from the kitchen, this loser took a hit of heroin and who knows what else and got herself really stoned. For some reason, after that she decided to try and cook on the stove top. The burners were still on when we walked into the kitchen area and there was food that was laid out to be cooked. Evidently, she must have nodded out and fell over onto the open flame on the stove. You could actually see the grill marks on the side of her face and head where she hit the stove as she went down for the count. She looked like someone drew a waffle shape on the side of her face. The only thing missing was the butter and maple syrup. What a sight. It looked real painful too. With all that she was still lucky her little accident didn't make her go up in flames and set herself and the rest of the apartment and building on fire.

The primary unit called in the details to the dispatcher so that the arriving EMS unit would be aware of what they would be dealing with. Other than that, all we had to do was hang around until EMS showed up, do some simple paperwork and get a little more information from the husband, if possible. Once EMS got there they would wrap her up and take her to Harlem Hospital and the job is pretty much done.

We got all the information that we needed from the husband and believe me, it was like pulling teeth. Every time there was a pause of conversation for more than a minute or so the husband would nod out. Each time he came out of it or we gave him a shake, to wake his ass up, he was a little more fucked up than the time before. In between this guy's nodding periods, the four of us were basically just standing there with the wife on the floor on one side and the husband against the wall on the other side.

Before long, partially out of boredom and partially out of the frustration of dealing with idiots like this or just the morbid sense of humor that all cops possess, we found ourselves cracking jokes about these two losers.

They were the types of jokes that people hate. Those lame types of improvisational jokes that are so bad you laugh just because they are in fact that bad. Once you get going you try to top the last bad joke with an even worse one. Among the jokes were: "That's using your head!", "That guy must have been really hungry.", "Now ear this, now ear this, the stove is very hot.", "Boy, what a hot head!", "I guess that's his old flame.", "No, I said an ear of corn!", "Should we send her to the hospital or to IHOP?", "I don't know about you but I'm craving waffles." and on and on they went. Even when EMS arrived, if someone thought of another stupid joke they just blurted it out. EMS was looking at us, shaking their heads in disapproval as they wrapped up the lady for the transport. I bet they found themselves doing the same thing in the ambulance on the trip to the hospital.

When you stop and think about it, you know it's not funny. It's insensitive and mean but these type of jobs happened on a daily basis and we dealt with them the best we could. It's not an excuse but it is a reality of doing this type of work. It becomes another mechanism for helping you to get through the continuous flow of jobs you get through your long career. In the end, the job was handled and you move on to the next one.

38. The Children Are The Hardest To Forget

When you have the job of a police officer or firefighter, or if you are active duty armed services, you are going to see dead people. If you are opposed to this then these lines of work are not for you. Not only are you going to deal with the dead but you will deal with their family, their friends and all the other facets of that person's life. They will become a part of your memory. You will do and see things involving the deceased that the normal everyday citizen would never even think of doing, imagine doing or want to do no matter what the compensation.

I was called countless times to a location where I found myself moving, searching or standing watch over a person who was dead, dying, or unconscious due to a medical or criminal incident. I have seen people who were cut, stabbed and slashed. Some had visibly broken bones or missing body parts. Others had bullet wounds and some just died from simple old age.

In every case involving death, no matter how involved you actually have to get, you tend to get used to being around it pretty quickly. After a while it really doesn't faze you and it just becomes another part of the job. When you first see a shooting or stabbing victim, the wounds appear almost stage like with a fake quality to the persons body and their injuries.

Like all things, however, there is the exception. Without a doubt when talking about death and actual dead bodies that exception comes when you must handle a job where the dead body is that of a child. Whether it's an emotional attachment because you may have children of your own or simply because it is a child that we as society view as helpless and dependent on adults for safety. In the end it is not a pretty sight and the image can stay with a person for a long time. When you have that personal involvement, it makes it all the more difficult to handle and forget about.

In over twenty years of police work, all on the street and all in Harlem, I have dealt with death on a consistent basis from month to month throughout the years. Some months are worse then others and you may get longer periods where you handle a lot of jobs involving death. Some months are quiet and you can go through several months with very few of these incidents. In the end, I guess it all averages out to a consistent steady flow of various types of death. Even now, as I'm writing this story, I can vaguely remember several really bad homicides that I had to handle in some capacity. You would think that those jobs, the especially gory ones, would stand out in my mind one hundred percent. They don't, and that could be a part of being a cop and forgetting enough of your work to continue on for more than two decades of police work. For some of the older ones the details are even fuzzier. Thanks to the exception when dealing with kids, two jobs that deal with the dead stand out like they happened yesterday and yet they were both fifteen years ago or more.

I was still in a sector car doing patrol work with less than five years on the job. It was early in the morning and I remember just finishing my bagel and coffee. My partner and I were parked somewhere close by to the call making entries in our memo books when the job came over the radio. The job was assigned to us and the dispatcher stated the job as, "a baby not breathing". The building was on West 112th Street and I knew exactly where the building was because it was right on a corner spot where there was heavy narcotics sales day and night. We would often chase drug dealers into that very building and I had arrested dozens more both in front of and inside for drug use as well.

It's important when you are driving to a location to know exactly where you are going and to know where to pull up. You also need to know the flow of the traffic throughout the City as well as the quickest way to beat that traffic in order to respond as fast as possible. I wasn't driving this day, I was the recorder. The recorder handles the radio and the paperwork for the day. My partner at that time did most of the driving and in this case it was a good thing. He drove like a stuntman for most of the time, even on routine patrol. With this type of job I knew we would get there as fast as possible even if he had to drive on the sidewalk to get there, which he did quite frequently anyway.

When you hear the word "CHILD" or "BABY" associated with a bad incident it makes you react much differently than the everyday normal jobs involving adults. You give everyone the best you can on a daily basis but there is something about a young child needing help that makes you go all out and then some. There is a real sense of urgency in your response. Almost a desperation to help.

We pulled up right in front of the location and we already know the job was on the fourth floor. In a call like this you obviously are not taking the elevator. Elevators are too slow and unpredictable. Besides, four floors is not much to run up. No sooner than we stopped, we were out of the car through the half broken front door and raced up the run down stairs. Once we hit the fourth floor we headed right for the apartment and went right inside through the wide open door. Not only did we know the apartment number but it was the only door on the floor that was wide open, as most calls for service are.

I entered the apartment first with my partner right behind me. The mom was screaming and shaking in the outer room saying, "My baby is not breathing, my baby is not breathing.". I didn't see any other adults in the apartment as I went into the rear bedroom and right up to the crib. The baby was face up and had a little dried fluid coming from one corner of her mouth. It was a little girl. She was a newborn, maybe a few weeks old. Her eyes were closed and her nose had crusty fluid as well in each nostril. As soon as I saw her body, I knew she was dead. She was pale and rubbery looking and she was cold to the touch. I looked at my partner and said, "Get an ETA on EMS real quick.". He immediately did so and did it loud enough for the mother to hear. We did not let on to the child's true condition to the frantic mom at this point. We wanted her to think her child had a fighting chance. You can't just blurt out that sort of thing without any support for her from family or friends to comfort her.

Within a seconds time, dispatch was radioing us that EMS was pulling up in front of the building right now. My partner told dispatch to let EMS know that we had a baby in distress and that we were coming down with the baby. I picked up the lifeless little body of that little girl and straddled her on my forearm. I held her close to my body between my stomach and chest area and ran out of the apartment, right past the mom and down the stairs. My partner stayed behind to help the mom as best he could and try to find another adult to stay with her until we could locate some family to help her deal with this awful situation.

In a matter of seconds I was down the stairs and barreling through the font door. EMS had the back of the ambulance wide open and were on the the top step waiting for me to hand the baby off to them. They looked like they had everything set up for treating a child in distress, and I quickly passed the infant to EMS and they quickly closed the doors with the baby inside and me outside the ambulance. After that, the feeling of helplessness settles in a little more. I already knew the situation. I couldn't do anything in that apartment to help, nor could I do anything else now. While EMS was with the little girl, I just sat on the back step of the ambulance and wondered what the mom was going through back in the apartment. I also thought about how bad it was going to be to have to tell her that her baby was dead.

A few seconds later the baby's mom appeared outside of the building with my partner. She was still screaming and crying for her little girl. We tried to tell her the best we could that EMS was doing everything that they could to save her little girl. It was all a show but it had a purpose. All these steps we took were for the sake of the mother. She was going through a tragedy and needed a process to do it with. We couldn't just hit her with the news about her little girl that fast. Like a funeral wake, it's a piece of the mourning process that people use to accept the bigger picture that someone they love is gone. In this case, she saw her child rushed out the door of her apartment to EMS. She knows that it's not good. The ambulance is not moving either. This is another step that is preparing her for the worst. By the time she gets the bad news you hope she is in a little better shape and better prepared to accept the fact that her baby is gone. Perhaps by the time she got that news some family or some sort of support system will have shown up to help her cope with this tragedy.

I can still see that girl's face and picture her there on my forearm. She was so tiny that she fit right there on my arm from elbow to wrist. Her legs and arms would have hung down and swung freely if I didn't hold them up and in towards my body as I ran with her. Things like that are moments you don't forget. They are hard to deal with but you just do it. EMS told me later that she died in her sleep not too long before we got there. They called her condition SIDS, something that happens to newborns. As a consolation, EMS later told me they really appreciated me running the baby down the stairs to them. They said if nothing else, it made a difference in the perception of us trying to help the baby. They said although we all knew the baby was gone, it helped the mom to see people attempting to save her chid and that the baby fought till the end. It felt good to contribute in some way. The way we figured it we may not have been able to help the baby but maybe we helped the mother a little bit.

I remember the woman's apartment was a mess and very dirty. I'm sure the mom had a lot going on in her life and a lot of issues to go along with it. Now she had one more to deal with. I felt really bad for her. It was obvious she was already struggling before this happened. Could this be what sends her over the edge completely? At the time of this incident I was a young rookie cop, not married and with no kids of my own. Even at that point in my life it still hits you hard to see that happen.

Just seeing a dead baby is one thing. I guess you could tell yourself how it doesn't look real or that it wasn't that bad a sight. Even though you know that's just not true. Its that personal connection from having to physically touch that child that takes on a whole different level. It certainly packs an emotional aspect and a realness you can't ignore or play down. If you are a parent that feeling is multiplied for sure.

You finish the job and continue your career. You see more death, some worse, some not so bad. Your personal life changes and that changes how you feel and react to what you become involved in.

Years later, I was married and had a child of my own. With that change in my life I began doing the same job except from the perspective of a married man with a child. It was shortly after my first son was born that I was involved in a second job which involved a child's death. Now, as a parent, the situation took on a whole different meaning.

It was on West 118th Street and the child was about five years old. The call was a child who fell from an open window. The call was listed as an accident but in Harlem in those days, there were no safety gates on the windows and no window guards to prevent a child from going out on the fire escape. The fact was that I frequently saw people, both kids and adults alike, sit out on their fire escape and use it as a sort of patio. A lot of residents used the fire escape to get the air they couldn't get from living in a hot, cramped apartment that had no air conditioning. Life is different in the City and especially in areas where the population is struggling to get by. Some people never realize what life is like outside of their own neighborhoods.

When a call like this comes over it can either be a surprise or it can reveal the hard truth. This one revealed the hard truth and unfortunately we all knew what we would find when we got there. The call stated a child fell out of the fourth story window. On the way over you are thinking to yourself: at four stories with ten to twelve feet a floor, your talking a forty five to fifty foot drop. Best you can hope for is grass or hedges or a lucky fall. However in your mind, you're not feeling so good. The call said "child" and that is not what you ever want to hear. Reality begins to set in.

The location was a row of buildings that were all attached and built in the same design style. The front of the buildings that face the street had windows and fire escapes but that's not where the accident occurred. The building also had a courtyard to the side with a sitting area with tables and benches. Unfortunately, there was no grass in the courtyard and it was made mostly of blacktop. The child was lying in that courtyard. We were led around to where the child was lying by building security. This building was an assisted housing building and they were known for having problems between tenants so unarmed security was hired to help out. When we arrived, one security guard and a neighbor were holding the frantic crying mom and a second guard led us to the child.

The child did not look bad in a gory sense of the word. Unfortunately, I had seen bodies in much worse shape. However, this was a little boy was only about four years old. That in itself makes for an unforgettable sight. He was unconscious and looked like he had scrape marks on the visible parts of his body. He looked as if he was unconscious and not dead but when one of the other cops felt for a pulse, they couldn't find one and he was not breathing either. With that, EMS came running down the sidewalk and immediately went to work on the little boy right there. I could hear crying and screaming coming from the front of the building. Several bystanders looked visibly shocked and frozen as EMS did their best.

Within a few minutes, we were all helping to lift the lifeless child carefully to a rolling stretcher. EMS quickly removed the child to their ambulance and did whatever they could to save that child. We all knew there wasn't anything for them to do. The little boy was gone. The look on some of the emergency personnel who couldn't hide it told all you needed to know about that little boy.

After the child is in the ambulance the officers handling the job have to get back to actually doing what goes along with the job. Obviously, there would be an investigation and the officers will need to try and calm down the mother and attempt to find out what happened. Basically, it's a lousy job to handle and it could have been an avoidable death. It's the kind of job that is both depressing and infuriating at the same time.

At some point the mom was told the grim news and the child was removed to the hospital. The mom was taken by police escort to the hospital as well. From there the detectives would take over the investigation, just to be sure that it truly was the accident it seemed to be. If possible, they would also arrange for the mom to see her baby one last time.

In the gap of time between the child being removed and the ambulance going to the hospital, you could see several cops who were there at the scene and actually did take part in physically dealing with the child now making phone calls in the Precinct. I imagine they were all doing the same thing that I did, call home and check on your own family. It's not the type of call where you tell the whole job to your spouse. It's the type of call where you act like you had a moment and called just to see what's new. You hear the voice or voices you need to hear and you hang up and go back to work. I don't think it's possible to handle a job like this and not think about your family. That one phone call can help you be a little more at ease and allow you to concentrate on your work again. Don't misunderstand me, that phone call or even going home that night and being with your family is not going to make you forget what you just saw. However, without that little check on your own family and that little break in the action, you could be working in a fog till you end your tour and that can be dangerous. In a way it helps you cope with what you just dealt with and then hopefully be able to leave it at work. In a career full of memories, some things are better off forgotten. Trust me, it's easier said than done.

39. Something Smells Fishy

Every EDP job presents a unique incident. The great thing about police work is the variety that each job gives you. Some EDP jobs can be violent and some can be funny and harmless. Some are simply just weird and leave you scratching your head. They are all pretty interesting.

We had several halfway houses in the Precinct. Halfway houses are places where people who need supervision but not confinement get counseling while they live in groups. They are put into work programs, learn trades and are integrated back into society. They want them to become productive members of society while they get the treatment they need to succeed in the world. They are not supposed to be violent or commit criminal acts. They have house rules, curfews and staff who try to make sure they are living in accordance with the program guidelines, taking their medication and visiting the appropriate medical facility if the need arises.

That being said, whoever thought that putting a bunch of people on various psych medications under one roof was good idea needs to have some medications of their own.

We were constantly getting called to that location. It seemed like every other day we had to go there to either subdue a person who stopped taking their medication, break up a fight or mediate an argument between staff and a patient or just between patients.

One day, like clockwork, we again get called to this halfway house for an EDP call.
I will never forget the name of that place, it was called the Weston House. It always reminded me of a place for fancy type living. It wasn't even close to fancy. It was four floors and the levels had been cut up into several small rooms where the residents live. They had communal bathrooms, eating and social areas. They also had rooms for treatment, counseling and medication. The residents seemed to come and go pretty freely but had curfews and supervision. Some of the residents seemed fine, others looked like they were a little off and there were a few that looked like ticking time bombs just waiting to go off.

The call we got that day was for a resident who had stopped taking his medications and was acting strange. That's all the information we got from the dispatcher. Vague to say the least. The NYPD has rules about EDPs and just what makes them an EDP. The rules also state whether or not these people can be removed from their location whether they want to go to the hospital for help or not.

Simply stated, EDPs must be a danger to themselves or another before we can force them to go to the psych ward, especially if they don't want to go and it comes down to us using physical force to remove them. Merely acting strange is not going to cut it where forcible removal is concerned. This is New York City, who isn't strange. We might as well remove half the City's occupants if that's the only criteria we are going to go by. We would have to talk to this individual as well as the caller and get a better read on this particular EDP.

When we pulled in front of the location, it was just my partner and I. By the time we got out and made it to the front stairs, a backup unit with two more cops, the Sergeant and his driver showed up. Most of the EDP jobs would bring the supervisor around to check out the situation. The Sergeants are the ones who would make the final decision, if the EDP is borderline, as to whether or not he/she gets a free trip in the ambulance to a rubber hotel room. The supervisor is also the only one who carries and uses the taser gun if the situation calls for it.

We were met in the downstairs hallway entrance by the resident supervisor who tells us that the man in question has not been taking his meds and as a result is acting very strange. The obvious question I had to ask was, "What do you mean by strange?". To this, the resident supervisor went on to tell us that the man has been acting funny, saying weird things and doing things that are not consistent with his personality and his normal behavior when he is taking his medication. I looked at the Sarge and said, "Can you lead us up to his room so we can talk to him?".

Being this information was as vague as the original radio call, I asked all the necessary questions to help us handle the job. Questions like, "Does he use any non-prescription drugs?", "Is he violent?", "Are there any weapons in the apartment that you are aware of?", "Has he done this before?".

Just basic questions we would ask at most jobs in an attempt to cover all the bases and keep us safe, just in case. The resident supervisor gave us the answers we were looking for but we still weren't sure if this warranted a forcible removal if the man objected to going to the hospital.

We get to the EDP's door and we didn't hear any sound from inside. I looked at everyone one last time and got the "we are as ready as can be" look. I knocked on the door and announced us as "the police" and that we needed to speak to the man. In response a voice said, "Just a minute, I'm coming.". So far everything sounded okay. The door opened a crack and the man on the other side said, "Yes, can I help you?". I replied, "We need to talk to you, sir. We are here with your resident supervisor and we need to ask you a few questions. Can you open the door and let us in?". With slight hesitation he said, "Okay, come in.". He stepped back from the door allowing us to push it open and enter the apartment. We entered the room and found the man standing there totally naked, looking at us as we were looking at him.

He was about six feet tall and very thin. He had crazy hair like Einstein only longer and more of an afro look to it. It was sticking out in every which way and matched his eyebrows. He had no facial hair and black frame glasses. If you took away the fact that he was naked and his hair was wacky, he had the look of a very intellectual type of person, sort of like a teacher or college professor.

"What's wrong?", he asked. We all kind of hesitated with that question considering we should be asking him that very same question. He was standing there in a manner as if he was totally clothed. He wasn't attempting to cover himself up nor seemed to be embarrassed one bit. He wasn't holding a robe, a towel or near anything that could remotely be used to clothe or hide himself. His stance had a confidence and comfort to it which was definitely "strange".

"Well", I said, "The supervisor here said you haven't been taking your meds and that you have been acting a little different lately.". He calmly responded, "Well, I don't know what he's talking about. I have taken my meds and I feel fine and everything is normal as always.".

Holding back laughter, I said to him, "And you don't feel a little different than usual?". The man shook his head and replied, "No, except that you guys are questioning me and now I'm a little nervous but other than that I'm fine".

This guy was either completely unaware or truly felt that what was happening and the manner in which it was happening was just fine and dandy. At that point I had to ask about him being naked and see what he would say. Asking that question could be the one thing that brings out everything that is causing this guy trouble. It also is a question that you don't find yourself asking too many times in life. For both these reasons I asked, "Sir, do you realize that you aren't wearing any clothes and that you don't seem to be bothered by that at all?". He quickly responded in a very confident manner, "No clothes? I'm in my house! What's wrong with that? I can do that in my own house, can't I?".

In a strange way he was right but I pressed on and said, "Yes Sir, but there are several strangers here and you don't seem bothered by that at all.". He shook his head and said, "No, I don't see that as a problem and there is nothing wrong with that.".

While we talked to him some more, the Sergeant spoke to the supervisor who was adamant that this man was off his prescribed medications and needed to go to the psych ward to get reevaluated and treated before he got worse. The Sergeant interrupted the man as we spoke and relayed the information he just received, as well his intention to send him to the psych ward for evaluation.

The man did not get violent, or really angry. Instead, he protested not about going to the hospital but that he was going to the hospital without the benefit of a shower first. He kept repeating how he needed to shower first before he could leave his house. No matter how we tried to impress upon him the fact that he would be fine without the shower, he just kept shaking his head saying, "I must be stinking like an old fish. This is embarrassing!". Being naked wasn't embarrassing him but being smelly was. Yeah, he was nuts!

We rounded up some clothes for him and let him continue to complain the whole time while he slowly got dressed. After each article of clothing he put on, he would again say, "I'm stinking like an old fish." and "I'm so embarrassed.". He must have said those words and asked to take a shower a dozen times before we got him dressed, cuffed and on his way to the hospital.

I would see that same man walking the street from time to time after that incident and he looked a little odder each time I saw him. After a while, he disappeared from my Precinct and I never saw him again. I often wondered about certain people like that who just disappear. What became of that guy? Did his treatment work and is he better or is this guy walking around the streets of NYC, stinking like old fish!

40. Technology vs. Crime

It's funny how advancement in technology can cause certain crimes to go away while others are reinvented so that they can continue to be committed under the new system. It seems that the harder you try to improve or upgrade a particular area or public service, there is always some dirtbag who is going to figure out a new way to take advantage of it and rip it off again.

When I was a rookie cop in the early nineties, the subway system in NYC was still operating on subway tokens. The turnstiles were pretty much the same as you see them today, except at the top where today's Metrocard gets swiped there was a little coin slot. In that slot went your token, which you bought from the clerk at the booth on the station platform before you entered the subway system. The token resembled a small gold foreign coin and it changed in shape and style over the many years that it was in use.

In those days if a crackhead needed money they would target the stations where the police didn't patrol as much or crowds were a little less frequent. They would also target these stations between the shifts of the officers to cut down the chance of getting caught. If they felt safe or if they were so strung out that they desperately needed money for more crack, they would rip off the turnstiles in one of two ways.

The first way was by using a "slim jim", not the food but the tool used to unlock a car door when a motorist accidentally locks their keys inside. You might have seen people, tow truck drivers or locksmiths use this tool to unlock a car door. For those of you who have never seen one, its nothing more than a thin piece of pliable metal that you would maneuver up in the outer door frame till you hit the door lock and pop it open. Crackheads would take this same tool and cover it in glue. They would then snake it into the coin slot and down into the receptacle inside the turnstile. There they would fish around until they felt the tool get heavy. They would then slowly pull the tool out and pick off the tokens that stuck on. Sometimes they could get a few tokens at a time. They didn't care how long it took. They would stay as long as needed or until they felt like they might get caught. Once they were done, they would clean the tokens off and sell them at a bargain to commuters to get money which they promptly spent on more crack. Some of these crackheads would sell those tokens right there at the very turnstile they got them from to riders as they were entering the platform.

The second way was done by "token sucking". A token sucker was a crackhead who would target a relatively busy platform with a lot of riders entering the subway. They would go to one of the turnstiles and stick some sort of an item or foreign object into the coin slot. They would then push the object down into the coin slot as far as they could go without the item going into the receptacle box inside the turnstile. The token sucker would then step back and wait as numerous riders put their token into that turnstile to enter the subway. The token would not drop through to the inside box and would not operate to permit the rider entrance to the subway. The rider would go complain to the clerk on duty who would let the rider enter through the security gate. A few seconds later the same thing would happen again with the next rider. This would keep going on until the tokens would back up in the coin slot all the way to the top where the tokens would be initially placed. By the time the tokens backed up all the way to the very top, the number of tokens that could be stuck inside the slot might be six or seven deep. When no more tokens could be placed in the turnstile the token sucker would then go to the turnstile, put their lips over the slot and suck as hard as they could. They would suck the few tokens at the very top out of the hole into their mouth or until they clear the opening at the top and are able to snatch the token out of the turnstile with their fingers. When they can't get any more tokens out by using this method, the token sucker would hang back again and wait for more subway riders to build up the number of stuck tokens and then try it again. They would do this several times just like the other method, until a clerk would see what they were doing, someone calls 911 or if a cop came along scaring them away.

Just like the other method of stealing tokens, the crackheads would then sell the tokens at a discount in order to buy more drugs to get their daily fix. The next day it would start all over again.

Today, the subway system uses Metrocards. Just as technology enabled the City to abandon tokens, technology has forced criminals to find new ways to beat the system.

I remember talking with transit cops right after the subway started using Metrocards. They told me that the criminals that work the subway had figured out a way to bend and manipulate the cards so that when they were swiped it would fool the machine and be used multiple times. These criminals were now selling "swipes" instead of tokens.

I can only imagine what the criminals of today are doing down in the subway. One thing is for sure, whenever you have a change in a particular system a change in the criminal activity is not far behind. It's sort of a play on the old saying, "Anything man can make, man can break.". Along with that, goes the other saying, "Necessity is the mother of invention.". It's weird to think about crime as something that people would intentionally work at to become better or in order to overcome an obstacle but they do and it will definitely continue in the future.

41. Can You Spare Some Change?

When you work in a small unit concerned with certain areas of crime which routine patrol doesn't really handle, you get to do things that are unique and interesting. You get to work outside the box and create ways to handle a problem. That's when police work really becomes fun.

For a number of years I worked in a unit called community policing. Along with addressing the various complaints of the community, we also had to address numerous quality of life crimes as well. When you talk about handling quality of life crimes and complaints, you start to pick out all the little things that happen on a daily basis in the City. They are not hard and dangerous crimes but the little things that are everywhere, annoy everyone and can really drag a location down. In some cases, if you get enough of this type of behavior, it can drag a neighborhood so far down that criminals begin to feel as comfortable as an everyday hard-working citizen.

There is a theory in police work called "The Broken Window" theory. The idea that if you let a house go with small imperfections, such as a broken window, it will slowly look more and more rundown and begin to have an overall appearance of disregard and abandonment. In relation to a community or neighborhood, if the criminals see an area going down in quality of life standards, they will equate this to lack of police patrol or enforcement. The criminals begin to see this as an opportunity. They become comfortable committing crimes and begin to engage in that behavior regularly and with a feeling of entitlement. Once the area goes too far for too long in this manner, it will change the dynamic of the neighborhood in the same way that a home would eventually be condemned when it falls apart. Once this happens, the community will abandon the area and the area is lost. From there on out it would be a constant battle and struggle to get the area back to where it once was.

One of the first areas to fall during a period of high crime is the subway. Less cops patrol them and by design it is so much harder to patrol as well. It's underground, poorly lit and just not a pleasant place to be especially in some of the lesser traveled stops along the subway route.

In those stations where police don't frequent or in the really busy areas where there is a lot of action, one of the more frequent quality of life crimes that we addressed were "turnstile jumpers". Also known as "fare evaders" or "fare beaters". These are the people who will just hop over the turnstile and enter the subway without paying for their fare. It's no coincidence that these same people are the ones who commit most of the crimes. They usually have long rap sheets and are often found to be in possession of weapons, drugs or have outstanding warrants at the time of their arrest.

In any case, these people, just by their blatant criminal actions, make other people feel uneasy. They walk around with an attitude like they own the City and very often are quick to cause problems in the subway system and on the platforms. Along with jumping the turnstile and avoiding to pay the fare, these people will also freely commit other various violations without even thinking about it. These are the people we target down there in the subway.

Of course, you can't just stand there in uniform at the turnstile and expect these losers to jump over right in front of you. They are criminals but they aren't all together stupid. They aren't looking to go to jail just to beat the fare. They will, of course, use some discretion to avoid arrest when possible. Some subways have a lookout room that is within eye view of the turnstile and you can see everything. The problem with that room is that most of the regular criminals all know about that room and avoid those stops as a place to jump over the turnstile. Additionally, these perps will wait untill the train comes in and then jump so they can go right on the train instead of hanging out on the platform for too long. If you are in the room watching, by the time you get out the door and reach the other side of the turnstile, they have either gone into the train as the door closes or they run back out of the subway at the sight of you. Then they're gone, to the streets above or as transit cops say, "to parts unknown.".

To get the job done sometimes you have to think outside the box and be a little creative. If uniform patrol or looking out of a room isn't going to cut it then you have to be out in the open where you can see and react to whatever is going on around you. You have to get close to the action. You have to hide in plain sight.

In our Precinct we had an old manual wheelchair that was left behind by a perp with a leg injury. The cops who handled that collar borrowed the old wheelchair from a local area hospital and never returned it. That thing must have sat in the police break room for months. It seemed like a great opportunity to put that wheelchair to some good use so I asked my Sergeant about using it down on the subway platform and he was all for it and loved the idea.

I went through my old work clothes and picked out some old paint splattered, dirty, ripped jeans, an old faded military jacket, a dark hoodie to pull over my head and some real old work boots. To finish the disguise I had that old wheelchair and a crushed, wrinkled take-out coffee cup which would appear as a beggars cup once I was set up at the turnstiles on the train platform.

I was dropped off at the station that was south of the one we were targeting. You should have seen the look on the faces of the passengers on the platform when I carried the wheelchair down a flight of stairs, through the service gate and onto the platform to wait for the next train. When the train pulled in, I was already in the chair and rolled into the subway car to go one stop uptown. It definitely was a weird feeling being in that chair pretending that you really need it. Some people may say it's bad luck to sit in a wheelchair you don't need. I didn't think of it that way. To me, it was just another tool to use to grab some bad guys. It wasn't the first time I had done something like this. Over the years I had used all kinds of different methods and props to get the job done. That was always the bottom line. Get the job done.

I got to our target station and rolled out of the subway car and over to the part of the platform that was directly in front of the turnstiles right after you pay to enter the system. From this spot, I literally had the best seat in the house. Not only could I see someone evade the fare but I could also get up and easily grab them afterwards. My backup team was in that little lookout room I mentioned earlier. They weren't right on top of our set up but close enough to help if I needed it. I was glad to have backup. When you do some of these plain clothes operations you find that you can't carry the same equipment as you can in uniform. While I was carrying two guns, I had no extra ammo, only one set of cuffs and no other weapon such as a nightstick or pepper spray. As for a radio, I had one but it was off and tucked away under my jacket and they really don't work that good in the subway anyway. I was also dressed like an ordinary person, not a cop. In this case, I looked like a bum. That was worse. What New Yorker is going to help a bum? Most New Yorkers wouldn't help a priest in trouble, let alone what I looked like.

The subway is a dangerous place to begin with. If you start a fight with a perp you're really pressing your luck to come out in one piece. The immediate threat is the platform itself and the possibility of falling off onto the tracks. The drop off the platform is pretty high, probably six feet. The tracks are dark, as is the tunnel and besides the threat of electrocution, you also have trains pulling in all the time. When the trains come into the station the operators really can't see down below to the tracks until they are right on top of something. By then it's too late. If you fall onto the tracks while the train is pulling in, there is no way they will be able to break and stop in time. When I was in the Academy they showed my class a man who lived in the subway tunnels and walked across the tracks all the time. One day he looked left and not right and got run over by a train. It was not a pretty sight. I remember the morgue tech pulling down the sheet just about a foot or so and revealing the man's foot. When he pulled the sheet down a little more, we found out that his foot was not attached and they had it laying there next to his head which was dented in at the top. The rest of him was cut, torn and crushed. It's a lot of metal coming down the tracks. Here, more than anywhere, you have to pick your battles and be sure you can handle what's in front of you. Like most times, you do what you have to. Dirty fighting is definitely allowed and in this environment the only thing that matters is survival.

There I am, set up in my wheelchair, looking as disheveled as can be. I'm not vocally begging but between the crushed up coffee cup in my hand and my clothes, I definitely look the part. In fact, I must have looked too much like the part because quite a few people walked up to me and put change into my crushed coffee cup. The way I figured it, I didn't ask anybody for money. If people want to assume I'm a beggar, then so be it. I wasn't going to say a word to blow my cover. Besides, what could I do anyway? I was in full view of the public, it's not like I could protest to getting change from a stranger. I was playing the part and the general public was corroborating my part. This one guy gave me a dollar in change and walked away, only to return in a few minutes. He came back and told me he needed the change for the bus and traded me the quarters for a dollar bill. What could I say? I just sat there and continued to watch the turnstiles.

After a half hour or so and a few dollars in change, one of the cops from my Precinct entered the platform in civilian clothes. He was done with his shift and was heading home on the train. You should have seen his face when he saw me in that chair on the platform and in that get up. To his credit, he didn't blow my cover or say anything to me but he looked like he was ready to burst as he smiled and walked past me to get on the train. The next day he came and shook my hand at work and said that I really looked good out there. I told him how great it was to be working like that. It really was great. It was like the sort of stuff people watch on television. I was doing things in those years that millions of viewers tune in to see on various cop shows these days.

Like all enforcement, there are things that baffle you. The confusing thing about people who jump the turnstile is that nine out of every ten who do it seem to always have the money on them for the fare. In fact, one guy we arrested had a hundred dollar bill on him. I don't know why they do it. Maybe it's the thrill of it or the feeling of beating the system, I guess. All I do know is that a lot of these fare beaters have outstanding warrants for arrest and have drugs and weapons found on them when the are arrested. Why a person in that position would risk getting grabbed by the cops is beyond me. Then again, who said criminals were smart?

A few times during the arrest I did get to see the look on the faces of the other riders who saw me get out of the chair, walk over and arrest a person who just jumped over the turnstile without paying. I don't know what was more classic, the look on the perp's face or the passengers who saw the whole thing transpire. I wish we had it on video to watch later on at night.

The best of the bunch that night was the guy who came into the subway and walked up to the turnstile, looking all around the platform. He was obviously trying to check the whole platform for cops before he decided to jump over. It was hard for me not to laugh watching this fool as he leaned way over and looked to the right, then leaned over and looked all the way to the left. The jackass even stood on his toes to see past me across to the other side of the platform looking for a uniformed cop. Once he was done looking all around he must have felt secure because he hopped over without paying and casually walked over to the benches and sat down. That's when I casually got out of my wheelchair, walked over to him and placed him under arrest. He was stunned and said, "Where did you come from?" He didn't even remember me sitting in the chair right in front of him. He actually started to argue with me and the backup team saying that he didn't hop the turnstile. He carried on for a while until he saw me get back in the wheelchair as they took him away in cuffs. After that, he stopped talking and just shook his head. I couldn't help but think to myself, "Where else can you get paid to do this kind of work?".

When all was said and done, we must of had about a dozen fare beaters under arrest. That meant a successful operation, with good numbers the boss will love and shitload of overtime for me and the team. Also, I had a couple of dollars in spare change, from the good hearted, compassionate citizens of New York which I spent on a well deserved cup of coffee and a few donuts.

42. It's A Miracle...I Can Walk!

Sometimes you have a good idea so you use that same idea on a different problem to see if it will work there as well. Once it's successful, the idea goes from good to great. When you are lucky enough to try something unusual and have that success, you have to milk it for all it's worth. Take the idea and run with it, as far as you can. Some of these ideas can't be used too frequent or repeated at all once the word gets out. It's for that reason that if you have the chance to use it before the word gets out, you have to really take advantage of that opportunity.

You would be surprised how fast something can spread on the street. Especially in an instance where you catch a guy while using a tricky method. It will definitely get around out there. There were plenty of times when we grabbed someone on the street by using a slick method and had perps in the street walk up to us and ask us about it the next day. Some of these mutts were ballsy too. They would come up to you and tell you how they heard this or that and that we pulled some sneaky shit out there. Their tone was like they were pissed off but still giving you respect at the same time. The attitude from these guys wasn't the problem. The problem is that each time you go into your bag of tricks and grab someone by using a real clever method, it gets harder the next time because of how the word of our trick spreads. It gives all the other perps a warning and let's them know what to watch out for.

We had been experimenting in the subway, using a wheelchair as a prop in order to catch turnstile jumpers. At that same time, the Precinct had a real problem with a bunch of guys selling those knock off bootleg compact discs all up and down the street. These guys weren't hardened criminals, they were more like illegal vendors. However, the law regarding this type of merchandise fell under counterfeiting and because of that they could be charge with committing a crime and not a violation. Additionally, most of the legitimate store owners complained about these guys because they set up on the sidewalks in front of their stores. The manner in which they set up caused hazards on the sidewalk, scared away potential customers and sometimes even stole business from the stores. The legitimate business owners, the people who pay taxes, have a direct line to the politicians. When they make the call the wheels get moving and then we have to take care of business out there.

Some of these CD guys were out there so much that they were almost famous for what they sold and how they never got caught. Some of these guys had quite a name and reputation. They were also hard to catch. They would be gone in a flash at the sight of a uniformed cop and seemed to have a sixth sense about plain clothes cops coming for them. When they ran they were like lightning as they flew down the street. On top of that, not only were they fast but they thought nothing about running through crowds of people, pushing down old ladies or kids and even running straight into moving traffic on the busy streets. You could hear and see cars screeching on their brakes to avoid hitting these guys. I have seen some of these guys jump and run across hoods of cars and break through vendor's tables to get away. Still, they were on our list of things we had to crack down on and make arrests in order to show we were doing something about it.

Like always, if you need to, you reinvent the wheel to get the job done. One night it was particularly cold and we were wrapping up another successful operation down in the subway using our wheelchair prop to round up some fare beaters. We were pretty much done. Our police van was filled to the gills with perps and we were going to call it a night. Being that there was no room left in the van for me, the Sarge and the wheelchair, we decided we would walk back to the Precinct which was only a few blocks away.

Before we started to head back, the Sgt. had a great idea. He wanted to push me in the wheelchair across the busiest street where these guys selling the bootleg CD's were set up. We bundled up to hide our faces and hoped that with the disguise of the wheelchair we could get close enough to one of these guys to grab them before they went running down the street.

I hopped into the wheelchair and pulled my hoodie down to block my face. The Sgt. had a scarf and a hood as well to cover his face. Off we went across the avenue in search of a bootleg collar. No sooner were we a block away from the subway, when who do we see but one of our regulars who is known for being super fast and hard to catch. This guy had run from dozens of cops and just couldn't seem to be caught. Part of the reason he was never caught was his method for looking for cops. If you watched this guy, you saw he never stopped looking up for the cops. No matter what he was doing or saying he seemed to constantly scan the area up and down and behind him. He looked more nervous than some crackheads I've seen out there on the street. Believe it or not, that same nervousness is what finally got him caught. He survived for so long because he was a nervous guy, because he knows, or thinks he knows what the threat is. He was afraid of police running up on him, not a couple of bums with a wheelchair. In this case he took for granted that what was in front of him was real and harmless and let down his guard or never had his guard up.

The Sergeant faked a limp and pushed my wheelchair right up to the edge of the floor mat where this guy had all his CD's laid out. I told the Sarge beforehand to let me move first, then he could come in for the kill behind me. I began to innocently make believe I was checking out the various CD's that were closest to me. At this point, the perp was on the other side of the mat, across from me, maybe three feet away. I would look at one CD then put it down and slowly pick up another to look at. When I could I sneaked a peak at the guy to see where he was looking. This guy had no clue who we were and never looked at us the whole time we were in front of him. I waited for him to look back and forth, obviously checking the street for a cop and then as I leaned over to put the CD in my hand back on the mat, I made believe I was reaching for one a little farther away. I then sprang out of the chair, directly towards him, slamming him into the parked car behind him. When we hit the car I heard the dude scream in fright. If I wasn't locking him up, I would have laughed my ass off right then and there at that very moment. Even funnier, along with that high pitched girlie scream, he made some sort of spastic motion like when someone jumps out at you and catches you totally off guard. Like clockwork, the Sgt. moved right in after me and before the guy knew what hit him, he was on the ground with both of us crushing him between the parked car and the cold concrete curb of the sidewalk. I wanted to make sure this guy wasn't getting away so I quickly put a cuff on and we dragged him level with the sidewalk and easily finished the job of cuffing him up. After that, all that was left to do was to pick up all his CD's and call for a transport to the station house.

Within seconds a car showed up and took the perp and the CD's back to the station house for us. Across the street from where we made that arrest was a Dunkin Donuts. The Sarge said, "Get in, it's on me.", as he pointed to the donut shop. He wheeled me over to the donut place and we had a cup of coffee and a donut while we laughed our asses off with him sitting in the booth and me in the wheelchair. After we finished our coffee and donuts, he rolled me back to the Precinct to take care of our days catch.

When we got back to the Precinct we went to the holding cells and the CD perp was sitting on the bench in the cell. He had his shirt off and he was sweating like a pig. He still looked visibly shook up and in shock. The cop watching told us that he looked like he was going to pass out when he came into the Precinct. As he sat on the bench he kept telling us how we scared the shit out of him, and that we were fucked up! The whole time he was saying this he just kept shaking his head and drinking his cup of water one of the cops gave him to calm him down. We both laughed as we walked away. There was no way in hell we were feeling sorry for that guy.

The next day we were back in uniform doing some routine patrol on the same strip where we busted the CD guy the night before. A couple of shady characters came up to us and told us how they heard what we did and how we dressed out on the street last night. They continued to say how they heard we bagged their boy who never gets caught. One of the guys said, "I heard you guys looked like a methadone addict pushing a crackhead in a wheelchair. That's some fucked up foul shit y'all pulled.".

That's when you're know your doing your job right. Our huge smiles were too much for those dudes as they cursed some more and walked away. We were more than pleased with the outcome of our little experiment. Even though "the street" seemed pissed off at us, it really is like getting some respect. That kind of work keeps the perps on edge and lets them know that if we want you, eventually we will find a way to get you. The perps seemed mad because now they were uneasy and have lost some of their comfort zone. That's exactly what we wanted. If a criminal becomes too comfortable at doing his thing, you have lost control of the street and the respect that goes with it. It's the respect that may just one day save your life.

43. Not What I Expected But I'll Take It Anyway

   You would be surprised how sometimes you set your sights on one thing and end up with something completely different. It just happens that way. Sometimes you literally walk into an arrest or incident you weren't expecting. That constant unknown that comes with police work is the reason I always told younger cops that if you work hard, the collars will come. If you are constantly looking to get involved you will find more collars than the cops who sit back and let the job come to them. Police work is not solely a job where you can expect to sit back and just handle the radio. Yes, there are plenty of times where the radio will direct you where to go and what to do. However, I always felt that in between those times a good cop needs to be proactive and physically look at the street and, at times, dig out what may be hidden out there in front of you. The cops who don't take that initiative miss out on a lot of really interesting and unique moments. These are the cops who just go through the motions. They have no idea what they are missing out on.
   One day I was determined to get this guy who I had noticed hanging around on the corner a little too much. I could tell he was dirty just by the way he went about his business. He was the type of guy who anyone could look at and tell that he was up to no good. He was always looking around and appeared nervous like he was waiting for something bad to happen. I would see him hanging out and talking with people who I had arrested in the past for drug possession and clients from the methadone clinic which was right down the street from where he stood. However, having him pegged for a dealer or someone who uses or possesses drugs isn't good enough for an arrest. Situations like this remind me of Denzel Washington, in Training Day, where he says, "It's not what you know, it's what you can prove.". For me to get this guy, I needed to see the deal go down and get him dirty.
   I always loved to go up on the rooftops to get a good sneaky vantage point. With a good pair of binoculars you would be amazed at what you can see. It was easy. You see a busy corner with someone who strikes you as a possible perp, like this guy, and you find a nice spot to peek on him and the entire corner as well. When I watched a corner, I would watch and divide that crowd on the corner into two separate sets. The first set contained the people who stuck around and just lingered there and for no apparent reason. They were stationary, not leaving the corner but interacting with

everyone who came to that corner. The second set were those who would come to the corner, talk to someone and leave quickly. They usually wouldn't return. Once they left it was for good. From this, you can begin to think in terms of dealer and seller and train your view accordingly. Once you have established your possible players you wait and hope you see the deal go down. At this point, most people would think you just watch the possible dealer. Not so. In fact, sometimes you learn more from than buyer then anyone else.

Junkies have a unique way about them. They have an uncontrollable impulse where they just can't help themselves. They have to look at the drugs they just bought in their hand. In this respect, they remind me of kid who goes to a toy store. They know what they just bought and they know its theirs. They know that its in the shopping bag and they are taking it with them. Still, what do kids do? They can't wait till they get home to play with the toy. No sooner do they get out the toy store door or in the car to go home and they are annoying their parents to take the toy out so they can play with it.

Junkies are the same way. They have to see the crack, dust or dope as soon as they can. So, as they walk away from what looks like a possible drug deal, if you train your binoculars on their hand you have a great chance at actually seeing what they just bought. A good tip off is to look at the junkies hands and zero in on the one that is balled into a fist. No one walks down the street with balled fists, especially with only one balled fist. Watch that fist and train your sights as they will without a doubt lift up that fist to their face area and take a look to check out the goods. Now you have something. You can do this a few times and confirm not only who your dealer is but what he's pitching out there as well. If you have a backup team helping you out, you can tie up those loose ends and grab all the players/junkies to better your case. If you are alone, like I was on that day, you go down and grab the dealer by himself and make it a possession collar with intent to sell drugs and call it a day.

After a half hour I had seen several transactions and was able to see the color of the top of the crack vial in one of the junkies hand. I was even able to see which pocket the dealer was taking the drugs out of and where the dealer kept his stash supply hidden behind the pay phone he was standing next to. All that was left was for me to go down to the street and scoop him up.

I remember trying to get some backup prior to going down but it was a really busy day with a lot of jobs coming over the radio. Just as I had thought to myself that I would try again to get a backup unit in a few minutes, I saw the dealer go to his stash, pick it up and begin to walk off the corner. That was all I needed to tell me he was leaving the area and might not come back. I knew I couldn't wait for backup and had to act fast so I ran down to grab this guy by myself. I flew down the four flights of stairs and out the front door towards the corner I was watching. As I came out of the building, one of the local street thugs began doing a warning call yelling, "FIVE-O", to warn the area of police presence. That warning, combined with me moving quickly and with an obvious purpose, would cause anyone who was dirty and heard the warning to run off, including my would be dealer.

One quick glance over his shoulder and he was off like a shot. However, he didn't run down the street but instead he ran across the street into a the storage center. This storage center had more than five flights of stairs. The building was very wide and inside were hundreds of little units with each having a metal roll down gates as a door. This guy had a head start on me and once he got through the front door he would be very difficult to find. He obviously had a reason for going in there, which meant he had an escape route planned. I quickly decided that I would go in after him anyway and take a shot at catching him. I figured if I didn't see him within the first few flights, I would consider him lost and try again another day. I already had set myself up for disappointment. I knew catching him was remote at best and even if I got lucky and did find him, he would have thrown away any drugs on him. Without any evidence, no DA will draw up your case no matter how many observations you saw beforehand.

I entered the building and listened for movement, hoping for help in the direction I should go. There were four sets of stairs and numerous hallways with turns. It was dead quiet inside that place and that's not good news. I went up the nearest flight of stairs to the second floor and listened again. This time I thought I heard some faint sound coming from the end of the hall directly ahead of me. I ran down the hall as fast as I could and saw a roll down gate for one of the storage units in the up position. I carefully peeked inside and saw one guy inside but it wasn't the guy I was looking for.

The unit was large, probably the biggest size they had. It was approximately thirty feet long by thirty feet wide with tall ceilings. The guy I saw inside was by himself sitting on a crate, reading a newspaper, in the rear of the unit. The room was set up like a store with an aisle going all around the sides with displays set up all along the walls and in the middle. The displays were set up on boxes and they consisted of every type of sneaker, shoe and boot imaginable, in every color and style you could think of.

The guy in the unit was using the storage facility as a makeshift store to sell bootleg footwear of all types. To the eye, this stuff looked just like the real thing. However, when you really look at the items closely you could see imperfections and cheaper material that you would never see on the costly real versions found in the stores. These imitation items can't be sold in a regular store for all the public to see. Plus the people who run these underground shops can't afford the rent even if they could sell them to the general public. The storage unit is an instant, cheap version of a footwear store. This guy sells out of this unit just like a regular store but does so by word of mouth. This location was one block off of West 125th Street and 7th Avenue and word of mouth in that area was all you need to have a thriving business. People came in, did their shopping and left. It was a cash business with good prices and no hassle. Until now that is.

The guy looked at me with an "oh shit" expression and I told him to stay put and don't move. I quickly cuffed him up before he could think about running off. I wasn't going to lose two collars in one day, that's for sure. I got on the radio and called my Sgt. to the scene. He got there pretty fast and came with a police van, trying to think ahead in regards to transporting the merchandise. When we looked more closely at the contents of the room, we realized that one van wasn't going to be enough unless we made several trips back and forth. We had way more than a van load here. In fact, we filled up the van to the roof and two prisoner transport vehicles twice to get the job done. We had thousands of shoes with street value in the tens of thousands of dollars.

Most people don't realize that this is in fact a crime and in this case it gets written up as a felony charge because of the amount and value of the merchandise. Luckily, I was in a Quality of Life Enforcement Unit at this time and we had some good contacts for representatives of various brand names for both clothing and shoes. These people were more than happy to either come down to the Precinct or send us a fax to prosecute this guy for using their trademark illegally. This guy would get charged with possessing fake merchandise and selling the items without permission of the company who manufactured the shoes or sneakers being duplicated.

The representative from the boot company was the best of all the ones who helped us out. He came down to the Precinct and verified the merchandise as a copy of their style and using their trademark without permission. He gave us a signed affidavit to state everything in print to pass on to the ADA for court as well . While he was there in the Precinct, the perp says to him, "That stuff ain't fake, it's the real thing.". The representative said, "If it is real, how do you sell it so cheap? You're selling it for a fraction of the retail price it goes for in any store.". The perp said, "I get a good deal and I pass it on.". The whole time he said this he had a big smile on his face. The representative didn't so much as flinch at the statement but instead took a hacksaw out of his bag and promptly cut the boot in half right in front of the perp. He turned the halves toward the perp revealing what looked like a very cheap inner makeup that even the untrained eye or anyone with common sense could see. The representative further corroborated his action when he took an already cut version of the "Real McCoy" boot out of his bag and put then side by side for a comparison with the perp's merchandise. It was like night and day, with no comparison between the two models. The perp's smile vanished and ours all grew.

I remember that it took what seemed like forever to load, unload, voucher and put all that evidence into storage. I think I was seeing shoes, boots and sneakers in my sleep that night. The perp was long gone to Central Booking before we ever got done with all the processing. I was on overtime for most of the day and into the night for that arrest. After a while I couldn't wait to be finished and go home. It was a lot more work than I had wanted or anticipated and definitely more work than the original drug collar would have been. I learned a lot that day about the bootleg market by talking to the various representatives and doing the paperwork for all that merchandise. It was a collar that perhaps wasn't the greatest but it was unique and something that doesn't come around too often. When it's done, it's in your arsenal of experiences and you can draw from it for future incidents. It definitely wasn't something I had started the day looking for but like everything else I have gotten involved with over the years, I made the most of it and tried to learn from it as best as I could.

44. Make A Problem, Fix A Problem

The Police Department has a way of tracking just about everything. Everything except themselves, that is. There are a lot of big bosses on the job. The ones I'm referring to as "big" are those way at the top of the rank and file. The Inspectors and Chiefs of the NYPD. The majority of these bosses have forgotten where they came from and how the job really works. They also seem to forget that they were once doing the very things they now condemn cops for on a daily basis. In some instances, these top level bosses are so far removed from everyday police work that they have actually become the root cause for a lot of the problems they now try to eliminate. The problem is that they just don't see it that way. Either that, or they are in denial and misplacing the blame to justify their actions and their jobs.

If some of the communities where these problems are occurring took a closer look at the Department's policies and practices, the communities would be outraged. Furthermore, they would be justified in ordering an investigation, filing complaints against the actions or at the very least ask why these practices continue to go on.

Sometime after I became a cop, probably around my five year mark, I remember hearing from my supervisors how the Department was going to step up their monitoring and really keep tabs on cops who seem to rack up a lot of civilian complaints. They made statements, both public and private, that they were going to reduce the number of complaints cops received. A real statement of disapproval for a cop who receives civilian complaints. This trend continued throughout my years on the job and although I had learned a great deal about reducing my own complaints from some really great cops I worked with, there were still plenty of cops who just seemed to attract bad incidents. Very often these incidents would result in a civilian complaint.

Some of these complaints may be justified but I believe that number to be very small. The majority of these complaints, just like the ones I had received in my career, come as retaliation from the very criminals you arrest on the street. Unfortunately, no matter what the reason for the complaint, it was still just another complaint to the department and they didn't want them regardless of the reason.

Police officers are familiar with the term "CYA". For the benefit of the civilians who may be reading this book, it stands for "Cover Your Ass" and this is exactly what the Department was doing by starting this paper trail and keeping a record of how many complaints each officer had. All this counting and monitoring was done in anticipation of that one bad incident that might get national coverage and negative press. If a cop went "off the reservation" so to speak and did something to really embarrass the Department, the Department could pull out their lists and graphs and explain how they know all about the officer in question. They could show how they have been monitoring him or her and would probably use the incident for the final nail in this cop's coffin. In the public eye, the Department could spin it so they come out of that bad incident a little better than just being blindsided by the number of complaints the officer received.

The Department even went so far as to put a Chief in charge of calling the cops into his office, with his CO and his ICO, to scare him or her into doing better and getting less complaints. The Chief threatens them with transfers, special monitoring and even termination down the road if the problem persists and gets worse. The cop has to stand there and get berated without any representation or ability to justify his or her record. It is a classic case of only saying what the boss wants to hear or speak your mind and pay the consequences. As I said, your supervisors were there with you but you couldn't look to them for help. They were equally afraid to speak up and are only looking out for their own jobs.

It's ridiculous to hear some over the hill, company "yes" man who hasn't done police work in decades tell you how it is. This talk, as if it was going to change that officer's way of policing, would be better suited to come from his/her peers or other officers who have been there and have experienced the same problems. A working cop who can take these cops aside, talk to them about a few changes they can make to better their situation and make their job easier and more enjoyable. Instead, they get this old, antiquated, miserable, power trip of a person whose sole purpose is to hear him/herself talk as he/she scares a cop into going from active to inactive to just avoid another complaint and a repeat trip to his/her office. This boss didn't cure the problem, he created another one instead. If these chiefs weren't hiding in their offices, playing dictator of a third world nation instead of being out there in the streets, they might see how their own actions keep causing the same problem to repeat itself time and time again.

The way I see it, the job and bosses like the ones I mentioned are responsible for a great number of the complaints and for so called "bad cops" becoming the way they are. They might not see it this way or want to believe it's true and I'm sure they would have an answer as to why I'm wrong but I will give my opinion anyway.

When I graduated from the Police Academy, I went straight to my assigned Precinct. No side trips, no NSU, no special privileges or cushy Precinct. I was sent to the place I spent my entire career in the NYPD. I had no hook, no influential friend or family on the job with any connections. So, I went to what the Department considers an undesirable Precinct assignment. A place where only two types of cops go, cops with no connections or cops who get into trouble.

You can plainly see the problem this creates. Right from the start, without even being on the street, the Department is already telling you that if you have no connections you are going to a place nobody wants to go. You will quickly hear cops say, "That place is a shit house." or "What a dump!". All the negative comments will come out as people hear where you have been assigned. The Department even has labels for the Precincts regarding their level of crime. A high crime Precinct is referred to as an "A" house and then as crime levels decrease the other Precincts would be called "B" or "C" houses. A "C" house would be those cushy Precincts where the cops with connections end up. Cop's assigned to a Precinct considered an "A" house, would often joke and say, "A, B and Z house". The joke being that the cops in those easy houses were sleeping from boredom and catching some ZZZ's. In any case, these labels and standards set the tone early in a cop's career. It has to affect some cops in how he/she perceives and works for the community he/she is going to be asked to serve.

When you get to your new Precinct you naturally want to find out about your command and the community. You ask old timers and veteran cops what the deal is and what the area is like. In my command, I found out pretty quickly and was told straight out, in no uncertain terms, that you are in what the whole Department calls, "a dumping ground". Evidence of this is seen by the number of cops who have been literally dumped there from various other commands and details after they fucked up one way or another. Punishment for these cops along with whatever discipline the Department gave them as far as suspension or loss of vacation time, was an all expense paid trip to their new Precinct assignment for the indefinite future. How can the Department not realize that they just told over two hundred cops that their Precinct is considered punishment?

I never had the chance to actually survey all the other Precincts, especially the "Z" houses but I'm willing to bet there weren't any cops who were dumped there and probably very few cops like me with no hooks or connections. In twenty years I saw dozens of cops get transferred into the Precinct with some story or black cloud over their head. Whether it was minor or something serious, it was always some kind of trouble that got them sent to our Precinct. The story on that cop always came out and was eventually told to the troops. The story always followed them, no matter where they went. In the NYPD phone calls are made quickly, and in a matter of hours your news is all over the Precinct.

The point is that it's obvious that Precincts get labels. Be it good or bad this is a problem that gets compounded by transfers of problem officers who are being punished. This is all done while the Department overlooks the cops who are in those Precincts for no other reason than graduating from the Academy.

Robert K Merton, a 20th century sociologist, is credited with coining the phrase, "Self Fulfilling Prophecy". In his book, Social Theory And Social Structure, he defines this term as, "A false definition of the situation, evoking a new behavior, which makes the original false conception come "true.". In other words, a positive or negative prophecy, strongly held belief or delusion declared as truth when it is actually false may sufficiently influence people so their reactions ultimately fulfill the once false prophecy. An example Merton uses is, "Roxanne falsely believes her marriage will fail, her fears of such failure actually cause the marriage to fail.".

By comparison, in the case of the NYPD and their labeling of Precincts as "dumping grounds" or places where "nobody's" go, along with the constant transfers into the Precinct of cops who are jammed up as a form of discipline. The Precinct is now transformed into a place of punishment and all of this negativity is absent in those other cushy, hook houses where cops with connections go to work.

It seems obvious that Merton and anyone with any kind of intelligence and a conscience would plainly see that if you continue to label and operate a Precinct as a "shit hole" or "dumping ground", it has to have some type of negative effect on the personnel assigned there. After a while, I truly believe that the cops who are subjected to this long enough will begin to look at themselves, the job and the community around them from that same point of view. Once a feeling like this develops, it could be difficult, if not impossible to correct.

Yet, with all that working in the background, here is that idiot Chief who is going to stand there and preach to a cop standing before him/her about how he or she needs to stop getting complaints. I wonder how many transfers that Chief signed off on "dumping" a problem cop into that Precinct. As far as I'm concerned, bosses like that are just as guilty for the CCRB as the cop who got the complaint.

The whole time all this is going on the community is the real victim. The only difference is that they are kept totally in the dark and never told things like the ratio of "dumped" cops to officers assigned right out of the Academy. How do you think they would feel if they knew the department thought of their community and treated it like a "dumping ground?" What would the community say if they knew that "problem" cops were routinely "dumped" into the precinct that serves them

Even if the department didn't verbally call the precinct those negative names and it isn't literally written down somewhere, actions speak louder than words. All the community needs to do is to look at the numbers and they would be outraged and rightfully so. It goes to show that you don't necessarily have to be smart to be a chief or any other high ranking boss in the NYPD. You only need to have a few lucky Saturdays, where you pass the test to reach the rank of captain. After that those bosses can get promoted all the way to the top of the ranks on merit, or demerit, as it might be in some cases. Definitely demerit in this case.

45. Runners High

Being on bike patrol in Manhattan was great. It was like being part of a special team or unit who got to do things the majority of the police force couldn't do. It was also a great way to see and hear the street in real time as it unfolded in front of you. It was like being a civilian riding through high crime areas and seeing street life without the perps holding back for fear of the police. Sometimes, you felt like you were invisible or the perps looked right through you without recognizing who you were.

I was the first bike cop in my Precinct and it took the general public a long time to get used to the idea of cops on bikes. Even the uniform was different and this definitely helped to aid in your "disguise". I can't even remember how many times people would say, "Oh, you're the police." before they would talk to me at the scene of a crime or if I was responding to a 911.

Because of this ability to hide in plain view, a great deal of the collars I made on the bike were because the perps just couldn't recognize me as a cop until it was too late. There were numerous times when I would roll right up on a perp and even as I was right in front of him he was trying to look around me to check for any cops in the area. It was actually pretty funny when it happened. At the same time it provided us with a great edge that regular cops just didn't have. You get real close to the action. You get to see and hear how the street works. You catch bits of conversation and interactions that most cops never see or hear. All this became stored data in your head that you could use at a later time to help you identify more players on the street. You began to pick up things that other cops missed and make even more collars than before.

On top of everything else was the stealth and speed a bike gave you. You could zip around street corners faster than the perps would anticipate or without being noticed until the very last second. You had tremendous closing speed and were already in motion in the event that your perp tried to run from you. If they ran, you absolutely had the advantage hands down, especially if they didn't have the chance to get off the street and had to run down the sidewalk or in the street.

I remember this one time I saw a guy dealing weed from down the block. I was hiding behind a truck and had my travel pair of binoculars out. As clear as day I saw him deal a few bags of weed to some dude then just ease back against the wall. He was just leaning there, setting up to use this spot for more sales and looked totally at ease.

It was one of those days where I was alone and didn't have a backup unit. I was looking for an easy collar and this was it. I really didn't care about the buyer and just wanted to grab the dealer and whatever he had and that would be good enough for me to call it a day.

Somehow, this guy got tipped off that I was down the block. Either he saw me or someone gave him a heads up that I was down the block watching him. In any case, he all of a sudden got really nervous looking and started to walk off before I got up to him.

As I got closer to where he was standing he started to walk faster. From there, for every foot I drew closer to him he walked that much faster. I knew he was going to bolt so I flipped my pedals around so I could use the foot straps that were on the other side of the pedal. These foot straps, also called cages, loosely secure your foot onto the pedal so they don't slip off. As any biker knows, these cages allow you great power to not only push but pull up on the pedals equally strong. With this kind of pedaling you build incredible power and speed with each stride.

No sooner had I placed my feet in the pedal cages, the dude all out started to run down the street away from me. The problem he had facing him right from the start was that he didn't live in the area. He had no building to run into to get off the street. Additionally, he had made the mistake of dealing on an avenue that was almost entirely made up of commercial establishments. There was no way he could run into one of those places to hide so his only option was to just keep running down the street in an attempt to get away, hoping he could out run me.

He started out running on the sidewalk and then in the street. A few strides later, he was back on the sidewalk again looking over his shoulder each time to see if I was still behind him. I was right there and closing in with each stride. It's amazing to see how fast he was running and the energy he was exerting to stay at that pace. The whole time he was busting his ass to stay in front of me, I was a few car lengths behind him and felt like I was just coasting, nowhere near tired. Honestly, I was behind him by design. You want the perps to run a little because it tires them out. For every step he took he was using a lot of energy. This energy he is burning will play out as an advantage for me when I finally decide to take him down and cuff him up. If this should turn into him resisting arrest or an all out fistfight, I will have the edge because I'll be less tired. The loss of energy in attempting to flee always becomes the great equalizer.

All of a sudden, I could clearly see that his stride was beginning to slow down. I could actually see him beginning to tire. His posture started to look slouchy and beaten down. On top of that, he had nowhere else to go because he made a turn onto an avenue that had more of the same makeup and nowhere to hide. His stride slowed even more and now he was down to a light jog, at best. His arms were down by his side and I could hear him breathing hard and really laboring to keep his body in motion. It was getting close to the time to end this.

I pulled even with him and looked him dead in his face and said, "Whenever you're ready to stop, let me know, okay?". Of course I said this with no strain in my voice and no gasping for air like he was. I was simply riding alongside him as easy as can be. With a half defeated and half look of disbelief on his face, he went from a light jog to a fast walk and then finally to a complete stop right near the hood of a parked car.

In one motion, I hopped off the bike and shoved him face first onto the hood of the car. He actually seemed grateful for the landing/resting place because he was wheezing like an emphysema patient. I quickly and easily cuffed him up and then let him lay on the ground to catch his breath.

While he was on the ground I quickly searched his outer pockets and found what I was looking for. In that pocket he had a big ziploc bag filled with 25 to 30 smaller ziploc bags inside it. Each small ziploc bag was stuffed with marijuana. The size of the bags were nickel bags. For the non-pot smoking population reading this, they were called that on the street and typically cost $5.00. Although I have arrested some weed dealers who claim their shit was the best and charged more for the same size. They smelled real strong too. The odor was easy to smell through both bags. This guy lost some good, skunky shit that day.

Later, in the Precinct during the booking process, I found a couple of hundred dollars on the dealer as well. Everything becomes evidence. The drugs, the money and anything we think can help us with the case. Obviously, he wouldn't get the weed back but the money he could actually get back if he fought the case and for some reason won or the Court ruled that the money was not proceeds of the crime. However, this was misdemeanor weight and not something he would get serious time for. Most times, if these guys plea bargain the case they pay a fine or do community service. It's true that most times they do get off easy but we get the last laugh. By copping a plea to the crime, they are admitting the crime occurred. As a result, not only did they lose their weed but also the money marked as evidence. In some cases this can be a sizable amount and a good way of teaching these guys a lesson.

It was an easy collar, made easier by using the bike instead of running after this guy to catch him. I made some overtime and got a number as well. The perp lost his weed, his money and his freedom for a day or so. Things don't always go that smooth but they do tend to go your way a lot more when you are given a way to do the job in a better, smarter fashion. There is a saying that cops used, "Work smarter, not harder.". I definitely used that advice whenever and wherever possible. It makes sense and has paid off time and time again.

One night on the midnights we were all doing our routine rounds when a call came over for a burglary in progress at a commercial establishment on the 125th Street strip. When we pulled up, two other units were already on the scene. Those units had their patrol cars pointed at the side wall of a clothing store. Their headlights were on high beam and they were standing in front of their cars with their flashlights out.

My partner and I got out, curious to see what was going on. When we reached the other four cops, we could see that someone had broken a small hole in the side of the building to enter the store. The perps went right though the outer wall and now there was a clear entry point leading into the store. Evidently, the perp must have triggered an alarm from somewhere inside the store after they broke the hole and entered the location. The question now was, did the perp or perps who did this get stuck inside the store or did they have time to get out before we showed up?

The unit assigned the job tried the call back number but the only further information was from the alarm company who stated they were just notifying 911 of the break, not responding to the scene. As far as the owner or the employees, there was no way of contacting them or getting them to the location until they opened for business, which wasn't for several more hours.

The hole in the side of the wall was very small. I'm not sure of exact dimensions but from the look of it you had to be a small and slender person to squeeze in through the hole. Looking around at the cops at the location you could just see that the years of experience came with years of extra pounds. The old cliche of the cop and the donut was screaming at the top of its lungs. In one motion the collective group looked at the tiny hole and then looked at me. One of the two cops originally assigned the job said, "Hey, you could fit through there. Why don't you slide in and check it out?".

On the outside I said, "Yeah, sure.". On the inside I'm thinking, "Yeah, great idea.I'll crawl through a tiny hole into a dark store where a perp could be waiting to ambush me. That sounds great.". In reality it was something that sounded very stupid and very dangerous. Of course I did it.

It's amazing the process your mind goes through when you do these types of things. Immediately you begin to rationalize the whole thing. You begin to think about the situation in a way that takes the danger out of the scenario or at least cuts it down to the point where the odds are stacked in your favor. Instead of how they really are. Before long, the whole thing sounds like a walk in the park to you and you are actually looking forward to doing it.

It turned out that the hole in the wall was not only small but much smaller than we had first assessed. In reality, not only was it too small for the big burly veteran cops but it was tight for me as well. I had to take off my duty jacket, bullet proof vest and gun belt so I could wiggle and slide myself in through the hole. Entering the store, head first with no protection and completely vulnerable brought the reality of the situation immediately back to me. Except at this point it was too late to turn back or rethink the plan. I continued to slither through the broken concrete hole and dumped out onto the floor inside the clothing store.

Once I had cleared the hole and got to my feet, the cops on the outside handed me my trusty six shooter and my flashlight. That was it. I was alone in the store and nothing else was coming in behind me. I took a good couple of minutes to stand still and just listen to hear for movement but there was none. Everything was quiet as could be. Meanwhile, the cops outside the hole stayed close to the entry point so they could hear everything and kept calling to me every few minutes to see if I was okay. I remember thinking about that later and thinking, "What good would that have done, if I got jumped inside?". They say hindsight is twenty twenty but at the present moment, inside that dark store, I carried on with my job anyway.

I couldn't figure out where the main light switch in the store was so I used my flashlight to see and it was extremely dark. The metal roll down gates in the front were solid and let no street or moonlight in at all. In a methodic and slow manner, I looked in every aisle, corner and separate room I could find inside that store. After about twenty minutes of looking around in the dark, I felt like I had covered it all pretty well. We collectively came to the conclusion that this guy was either not in there or hiding too good to find right now. I passed my gun and flashlight back out to the other cops and retreated back out of the hole and put the rest of my uniform back on. Within a few minutes of getting dressed, the Sgt. showed up. With nothing else that we could do, he had the sector car that was assigned the job stay and guard the store until the owner showed up in the morning.

Evidently, the owner did get notified of the break in and showed up at the location within the hour. He unlocked the gates and put on the lights and this time we all searched the store together. It turned out that not one thing was stolen from the store and no one was in the store either. We figured the perp who broke through the wall must have gotten spooked and cut out before he was able to finish the job or take a single item. The only loss was for the damage of repairing and now fortifying the wall to prevent against future breaks.

I never did anything else like that again. Don't get me wrong, I have done other stupid things that I also later regretted or thought better of after sitting down to think about it. Just not like this one though.

Situations like that hit you later on when you are sitting at your locker at the end of your tour or driving home by yourself. You begin to think about the job and replay the event in your head. You begin to think of what you did good or bad and what you would have done differently if you could do it over again. It's times like that when you realize how lucky you are that things turned out the way they did. You also contemplate how horribly wrong things could have turned out as well. Like everything else in this job, you learn from what you do. Good or bad, you have to take something positive away from every situation and store it away for use at a later time. Luckily for me, I was able to learn this time without dire consequences and be around to reflect on it.

47. Frequent Flyer!

I loved working in Community Policing. We were always allowed to work on long term problems and come up with unique operations that we put together from start to finish. From these operations we got great numbers, great overtime, some real great experiences and we made our bosses look good as well. We never minded making our bosses look good because they were great bosses. The way we figured it, they were good to us so we were good to them. I think it's pretty much the same in every line of work. People never mind working for a boss who looks out for you, shows they care or are sincerely grateful for the work you produce. My bosses were exactly that. Our team worked our asses off and they rewarded us with overtime, time off and the freedom to conduct these special operations in the future.

These special operations kept the job fresh and interesting. While the majority of the lazy ass, patrol cops were content sitting in a radio car and chasing the radio all day, I was working in plain clothes, disguises and sneaking around alleys and rooftops to catch the bad guys who were not readily visible on the street. I must say, there is something really gratifying about catching a perp who is sneaky and works behind the scenes to conduct his/her criminal actions. These perps feel that they are smarter than the average cop and have figured out a way to be a successful criminal. In some cases, maybe they are somewhat smarter. They probably do get collared less than the average on-the-street criminal. However, in the end they all eventually get caught.

It was also great to have to work at making a collar, not just responding to the scene you were dispatched to by your dispatcher. Showing up at a address you were directed to and cuffing a person who is waiting to be arrested for what they just did kind of takes the thrill out of the job. It's like the difference between hunting for your food or going to the supermarket. The end result may be the same but it's the road you take to get there that makes all the difference in your work. I took this job because of the variety and excitement. That's what separates it from almost every other job in the world and what made me love going to work so much. They say a person who loves his job never works a day in his life. In my mind, with regards to police work, truer words were never spoken.

Sometimes when you are trying to sneak around or catch these perps by being sneaky, you need to "hide in plain sight". Perps are both smart and stupid at the same time. They're stupid because they believe crime is an okay way of life but they are smart enough to know they need to watch out for the police. They aren't going to just commit a random crime without checking for the police or at least taking a look around the area they are planning to victimize. Just as we are looking for them, they are looking for us. It's a simple game of cat and mouse.

In areas such as the subway, you can't expect to be standing out in the open if you want to catch someone who is trying to sneak in without paying the fare. If all you care about is deterring that crime, then by all means stand there in full uniform like a wooden indian and you will scare all the would be fare evaders away. However, when your boss asks for some numbers, or results, to show that the Precinct is in the subway and enforcing the laws to combat rising crime, you will need to bring in some bodies as proof. These turnstile jumpers might be bullshit collars but they show enforcement. In the Police Department, the saying is," If it isn't on paper, it never happened.". In the Department's eyes you could spend your lifetime in the subway, scaring fare evaders away. Yet, the first time crime spikes in that subway, it's like you were never there at all because you have no proof that you were actually working down there. You can't show what you prevented. You need to show results on paper and bring in some bodies to prove yourself.

Subway platforms can be a tricky place to work. There isn't a lot of room like on the street. Not only are they dangerous but hiding down there presents a real challenge. If you don't do something to blend into the location it's going to be real hard to get the perps who are committing the crimes to do it while your there.

We had a subway stop in our Precinct that was getting whacked with robberies, assaults and all kinds of quality of life issues. Once this spike in crime was brought to the C.O.'s attention, he naturally went to our boss and told him to do something about it and to get the results fast. The Commander needed results that he could take with him to show the Chief before the topic came up at the next meeting he would have to attend in regards to the crime in our Precinct.

I had a couple of contacts with the local transit cops who covered that subway line and worked out a date and time where we could target the area together. We made it a joint operation between our two units and hoped for the best. If it was a success, we would have what appeared on paper to be a well executed plan of action between two units in the

Department to solve a common problem. The bosses would be happy and we would stand to get some collars and overtime for ourselves. More than that, we would be looked upon favorably and be able to do even more of the same later on down the road.

The only problem we had was that the station we were working had very little room around the turnstile area. There really was no where to hide and watch the turnstiles without being seen or looking obvious to all the would be perps. We knew this was going to be both a problem and a challenge but we prided ourselves on working outside the box and getting results when asked to. All that was left was to put a little plan together and make it happen.

We met with the unit from Transit before we started the operation. There were two of them and two of us who would be physically working the platforms. We figured the best way to work it was to each take a side of the train platform to work on. They picked the uptown side and we would be across from them on the downtown side. Upstairs close by on the street we both had a van standing by to take our collars out of the subway for us and hold them until we were done with the operation.

During the entire meeting the unit from Transit looked at me and my partner a little funny and at times seemed as if they were actually going to start laughing. When the meeting ended and we headed out, they grabbed us and asked if we were going to hide in the nearby janitors closet or go way down the platform all the way to the end to hide as much as possible. After talking with them a little more, we found out they felt we weren't going to be able to catch anyone. In fact, they were worried we would scare away the perps on both sides of the platform because we were going to stand out too much and give the operation away.

At this time, in Harlem, the community was still predominately black. The two cops from Transit were also black. My partner and I were white. While I am often mistaken for Spanish/Puerto Rican, there was no way my partner looked anything but white. The transit cops figured they could hang out right near the booth in plainclothes and make a killing because they fit into the surroundings and general demographic of the area better than we did. To them we were way too obvious, even in civilian attire and not only were we going to be unsuccessful but would probably hinder their results.

As they say, "This wasn't our first rodeo.". We were both experienced veterans who had taken part in tons of operations before this one. Additionally, a lot of those previous operations were much more difficult and had bigger obstacles than this one. Not only were we not worried about being "obvious" but had already planned to use it to our advantage. In my mind, if we are in an area where we were that obvious then we had to play along with it, exaggerate it and be even more obvious. We had to "hide in plain sight.". We needed to take the thought of the perp possibly seeing or making us out as police out of the scenario. We planned to once again try something new and think outside the box.

When a perp is going to commit a crime that is pre-meditated, they are going to check for two things in the area they plan to victimize. First, uniformed cops who happen to be doing random or directed patrol. Second, people in plainclothes they believe are cops attempting to blend in and not be seen.

So, even a cop like the transit cops we were working with who believe their ethnicity allows them to fit better into the surroundings can look like an obvious plainclothes cop. These cops can give themselves away by looking a little edgy or watching the set way too hard. They could be too clean cut or wearing the wrong clothes given their assignment. In the case of a subway station, a smart perp will wait for one train to pull out before he hops over. After the train pulls out, he would take note of who is left behind on the platform. He would then ask himself, "Who's still hanging around and why didn't they get on the train?". If everyone else on the platform leaves and two guys stay behind a bell goes off in the perps head. The obvious question is, why are they still there? The perp will most likely take a better look at these two guys and try to figure out if they are cops. Smart perps know cops usually work in pairs, especially in the subway. It's enough to make the perp nervous and cause them to leave. They will probably walk to the next station and try again.

We assured the two transit cops not to worry about us and that we would try our best not to fuck up their operation. We agreed on a preset time to stop the operation and agreed to meet back at the Precinct to count the catch of the day. They both had big smiles on their faces as we all set out for the subway. The two transit cops went right down to the subway and camped out together near the turnstiles in what looked like to me and my partner, an obvious place to be watching the turnstiles. In my estimation they did not look like subway riders at all but more like cops pretending to be subway riders.

Prior to the operation, my partner and I made a stop at the local supermarket. We didn't stop in to get groceries but instead cleaned out the assortment of free newspapers and advertisements that are always offered in front of the store. Before going down to the subway, we retrieved these flyers and papers from our van and then headed down. Taking positions to both the immediate left and the right of the turnstiles, we began handing out the flyers to everyone who entered the train. With this ruse we were able to stand right in front of the turnstiles, in clear view and watch the whole platform as we handed out the flyers. We didn't even know what we were handing out nor did we care. It didn't matter. It did however give us a great view and an optimal vantage point.

One by one perps would come down the stairs and look around the platform. At times even stretching their necks over the turnstile to look for police in either uniform or what they felt were obvious plain clothes cops. Once they did their check and felt comfortable the coast was clear they hopped over the turnstile to the other side without paying the fare. That's when we gave the token clerk on duty in the glass booth the signal to hit the release button on the service gate. Calmly, we put down our papers and easily strolled through the gate onto the platform and locked each one of these guys up.

Each time we made an arrest I looked over to the other side of the station to see what if anything was happening over there. Each time I looked, I didn't see anything of an enforcement nature going on. Meanwhile, we would quickly call for our backup team to come and remove the perp so we could set up again and wait for the next loser to come along. And the losers certainly did come along and at a pretty good clip at that.

By the time we ran out of handcuffs we had at least a half dozen perps stored in our transport van waiting to get booked. We decided we had enough perps for this operation. We were more than happy with how many we had and figured we would call it a day. All that was left was to meet up with our Transit counterparts, see how they did and get their numbers for our report.

What we found out was that the transit cops only managed to get one perp for fare evasion to our seven arrests. Needles to say, the cops from transit were both surprised and a little annoyed that we beat them at what they felt was their own game, on their own turf. The conversation between us didn't last long and they hurried to get out of there and away from us.

We could have rubbed it in and we had the right to do so. In all honesty, they learned their lesson and would have to face the truth when they had a chance to talk or think about the whole situation later on. The mere fact that they had to go back to their boss and their Precinct with stats that showed us being much more successful then them was punishment enough.

Meanwhile, our boss was overjoyed at the numbers we brought in. Naturally, he spun the operation to show how we were aggressively attacking subway crime. He presented it as his idea at the next meeting with the Chief and got some praise from his superiors. As for us, we got the usual numbers, overtime and the freedom to not only do that operation again but a bunch of new ones in the future. We had created some more trust with the bosses and it paid off for years to come.

48. That First Step Is A Doozy!

A good rule of thumb in police work is that if you see someone out on the street after two AM, chances are they are usually up to no good. Of course there is always the exception but I am talking about Harlem, in the early 90's. Crime was at an all time high and law abiding citizens just didn't go out at those hours. If you factor in the general condition of the housing developments and the area surrounding them, you would almost guarantee being a victim. The bottom line was that you weren't going to come across a great deal of hardworking, honest people out and about on the midnights back then.

That was one of the reasons why I always felt police work was easier on the midnight tour. I don't mean the work itself was easier, I mean having to discern between perp and civilian is easier. It almost took the guess work put of policing. On day tours, you really have a diverse crowd to deal with. Criminals can just blend in and walk amongst the decent people, using them as camouflage to commit their crimes. However, the later it gets, the advantage comes back to the police as the streets get thin with traffic.

In most areas of Manhattan there are at least some housing developments. Some Precincts had more than others but every Precinct had some type of housing development in their area to contend with. These developments were a clear mistake made years ago by the City and they are continuing to pay for those mistakes today.

By design, city housing developments are set up to fail. You can't cram that many people in one area and expect good results. On top of the number of people living there you have an inordinate amount of them who are low income or subsidized by the government. It doesn't take a brain surgeon to figure out that mixed in that group, more so than in affluent areas, will be people who commit crimes on a regular basis.

Additionally, the way these buildings were designed keep the police from patrolling effectively and proactively. In some cases, the courtyards are removed from the street and the entrances hidden so well that just getting to them in a tactical manner is a task in itself. The height of these buildings gives the perps a clear visual advantage. Not only can a cop or patrol car be seen coming a mile away, you also have the danger of having something thrown at you from the top apartments or rooftops.

One of the first things I learned when responding to a housing call was the need to always take a look at the rooftops when you were driving or walking towards them. If you didn't, you could be a victim of "air mail". "Air mail" is any item that the residents of the buildings you are going to decide to throw out the window or off the rooftop at the responding police officers. Air mail could be just about anything they decide to throw at you. Chairs, sofas, bottles, used diapers, you name it and I've seen it get tossed at responding police and emergency personnel.

One night, we got a call of a dispute and shots fired from the roof of a housing project at the north end of the Precinct. When we pulled into the courtyard, everything seemed quiet. In a way it was almost an eerie quiet. Like the quiet you get when something bad just happened before you got there and now the area was laying low and watching to see what would happen next.

There were six of us and we all went up to the roof of the supposed building in question. We went in through the back door because it was tactically better as an entry point. We often did this to get the jump on any bad guys who were lurking around or had the idea of running out the back in an effort to flee the scene. By going in this way we could catch someone by surprise and sometimes the element of surprise is all you need to stay safe, survive or get the upper hand.

Up we went to the top floor landing. This particular group of buildings weren't particularly tall. Probably only eleven floors in total including the last set of stairs leading to the roof. We carefully listened at each floor the whole way up and took special care before we entered the roof. With our guns and flashlights out, we were ready to walk out on the roof and check it out. We had done all the things a cop should do prior to going into that type of situation. Tactically we were as sound and as ready as could be. With everyone ready, we entered the roof.

Aside from the doorway and the elevator room we could see there wasn't anyone on the roof. We quickly checked the two blind spots and they were secure as well. We fanned out to get a look at the neighboring rooftops, as well as a look at the street and the courtyard below. Within a few seconds, I heard one of the cops say, "I got a gun here.". We all ran over to see what the cop found. There lying on the floor, near the ledge of the roof was a Glock semi auto pistol. It was unusual to find a gun like that, on a rooftop and especially a Glock. In the early nineties, these guns were still relatively new to the market and we didn't really see a lot of them on perps or found lying around on rooftops. Anyone who knows about guns knows the Glock is largely made out of a very durable plastic and was a new concept in the U.S. at that time. We were more accustomed to getting perps with revolvers and older style pistols made of metal back then.

While some of us studied the gun as it laid there on the ground, other cops were still looking around the rooftop, for other unusual stuff that might also be up there. Other cops were still checking out the buildings across from us as well as the courtyards to see if anyone was particularly interested in our finding. That's when one of the cops in our group said, "Hey, look down there!".

What the cop was looking at and referring to was a person or what was left of a person lying motionless on the top of the awing that led to the entrance way of the front of the building. Even from that height, in the dim light that shone down from the building, it wasn't a pretty sight. This was of course an eleven floor drop and I'm sure it looked at lot worse close up. Either way, this guy was obviously dead.

When we went down to the area where the body was we found another Glock on the pavement below and it was broken in a few pieces. It looked like it took the ride down   with the guy who was sprawled out on the top of the awning. It appeared as if it had suffered the same fate as that guy as well. I guess Glock's plastic guns, like the human body, can only take so much. There also were nine millimeter rounds from the gun scattered in the grass and on the walkway which evidently had come out of the broken magazine, which was also in pieces.

The roof was marked off as a crime scene and the gun that was up there was left in its place and guarded for the investigators. Down below, from the walkway, the only thing visible when you looked up was the person's left leg which was dangling over the side of the awning.

It was still the early morning hours so not many people had come out of the building yet. However, after it started to get noisy with cops and crime scene detectives, residents started to come around to see what happened. Being that you could see the body from the windows on the front of the building the Sarge had us put a sheet over the body until CSU got there and did their thing. Once they were done, which could take a while, the body could be removed. In the meantime,the front door way was blocked and the entire entrance was taped off from the general public. From that point on it was a waiting game until the investigation was complete and the meat wagon showed up to take the body to the morgue for an autopsy.

My partner and I were told to resume patrol considering they had enough cops to cover the crime scene. Afterwards, when ever we left a crime scene like this one, we always found ourselves spending a good deal of time talking about the job we just left, theorizing at what might have actually happened. We would take the facts that we saw at the crime scene and fill in the blanks with the unknowns. Later on we would talk to the detectives to see how close we were to what actually happened. It's a good game to play. It makes the time pass on an otherwise quiet night and it helps to sharpen your reasoning skills, logic and thinking like both the cop you are and the perp you would love to catch.

Needless to say, you could come up with a million ways that this crime could have happened and believe me, my partner and I went through about a hundred different scenarios. I think we stopped guessing when one of us brought an alien life form into the equation. Now, rather than list a bunch of those here, which were all wrong by the way, I would rather you, the reader, put down this book for a moment and come up with you own conclusion. When your done, read on and see how close you came to the actual truth of what happened that night.

Later in the week, we got the whole scoop from the detectives who worked the case and had put all the pieces together. It seems that the person on the roof was not solely a victim but rather a perp who became a victim. Evidently, the Glock on the roof was his but not rightfully his. The detectives told us the dead guy had stolen a case of Glocks from a gun shop in upstate New York. They also told us they had information that he was attempting to sell them in Harlem that night. Why he thought the rooftop of a housing project in Harlem was a good place to do that is a great question and one that no one had the answer to. Of course I'm sure he felt secure selling guns while carrying a gun of his own and probably never expected to get thrown off the roof. Yet that's exactly what happened after he got jumped, beaten and shot.

The detectives tracked his information back to his car and found it parked just a few blocks away from the crime scene with the rest of the guns from that case in the trunk. He must have parked it there and met his killer(s) on the roof. From there his sale went bad and ended abruptly. If the beating and the gun shot didn't kill him, the fall surely did. I guess this guy had it coming and he obviously didn't think he was in any jeopardy. I guess he forgot that when you deal with criminals you never know what to expect and can never trust one either.

I remember saying to one of the detectives, "Well, gunshot or not that eleven floor drop must have killed him instantly, right?". He responded, "Kid, it wasn't the fall that killed him but the sudden stop at the end.".

49. Bush League

When I was in community policing, we had an office we worked out of to do all our paper work and make all our phone calls. The office was located in the back of the Precinct, overlooking the rear parking area and back door entrance. That avenue was less traveled than the avenue in the front where the general public came in to file complaints and talk to the detectives. Still, cops were coming and going through this area on and off around the clock.

Parking for cops personal cars was angle parking, anywhere around the perimeter of the Precinct. The Precinct was built on it's own little block like an island right between two avenues and two streets.

The timeline here is Harlem in the early 90's and the crack was still running rampant along with the steady flow of heroin, dust and marijuana, which never seemed to go away. Needless to say, this mix of drugs created more than its fair share of undesirables in the area. If you remember one thing about a crackhead, you will remember how crackheads will steal just about anything that isn't bolted down and that they can make a buck off of. No sooner do they make that money, they run to their local dealer, buy more crack and get high again. If you are too young or have never seen a crackhead first hand there is an accurate but comedic depiction of what a crack head looks and acts like available. All you need to do is watch an episode of the Dave Chappelle show where he does his skit about "Tyrone Biggums". These skits are hilarious and not far from the truth about the real crackheads who roamed the City in hoards back then.

This particular story took place on a day tour, around midday. Not exactly the time of the day a person thinks of when you picture a crime being committed. A lot of the cops in the unit still took this time of the day as their lunch break. Like I said, it was generally quiet around that time and a lot of the cops used their lunch break to get caught up on paperwork so they had the afternoon hours to go out and hunt for collars. I guess there were about six cops in the office doing various things. Some of the guys were eating, some were reading reports and others were updating their notes. Everybody was pretty much busy in their own world at that moment. All of a sudden, we heard one of the cops say, "Hey, look. That dude is taking shit from a cop's car!". In today's world, I guess some people would call that profiling. I call it an obviously strung out, bummy looking, crackhead going through what in no way could be his car, getting caught red handed.

On the front dashboard of every cop's personal car is a bright colored placard that has the plate number and the Precinct to which the cop is assigned. Although we didn't know which cop in the Precinct owned the car there was no doubt in anyone's mind that this was a cop's car and did not belong to the dude rifling though it.

With a flash, the cop who saw it happening first was out the door of the office in an all out run. I mean he left vapor trails behind him as he left the room. Instinctively, I think the rest of us all went to the window first to see for ourselves before running out as well. That extra minutes time gave the lead cop who was already on the move a head start. The group motion of several cops going to the window all at once in unison was all the movement the crackhead's eyes needed to raise him up, alert he was about to be busted and got him running from the scene. Even in his cracked out state of mind I'm sure he knew he was stealing from a cops personal car and definitely didn't want to get caught by the owner or other pissed off cop.

Almost simultaneously, the perp started running just as the cop in the lead had exited the rear door of the precinct and headed straight for the him. At that point, the rest of us were now in motion, charging out the back door in one group, scaring the shit out of the desk Sergeant and any civilians who were in the station house at the time.

As we exited the rear door at what seemed like a great distance, we could see the crackhead tearing ass down the street with the lead cop hot on his heels. We took off as fast as we could and at this point we had a good distance to catch up to the two of them. The street they were on led to a nearby park. Once they reached the park, they would basically have three choices. They could go left or right on the avenue or jump the fence and enter the park. In any case, once they reached the avenue, they would be out of our sight if they turned in any direction. I think we all knew we had to do our best to make up the lost ground and keep them in our sight as much as possible till we caught up with them.

When the crackhead and the cop reached the avenue where the park was, they turned to the right and disappeared out of sight. It seemed like it took hours for us to reach that corner but in reality it was only seconds. Our pack of cops turned the corner and we saw nothing at all. No crackhead, no cop. There weren't even any civilians walking or driving to ask for help. We were all dumbfounded. We had gained a great deal of distance at the end and should have definitely been able to catch a glimpse of them on the avenue long before the next available street. We all stood there sort of helpless, looking around in all directions, hoping for some kind of hint or help as to where to go.

All of a sudden we heard faint noises that seemed pretty close by. We all stood quiet as could be and looked around. Again, we heard the noise. This time it sounded more like moans or groans. We turned towards the park where the sounds seemed to be coming from and there across the street we saw a wide, full bush that was moving slightly without the help of wind. We couldn't see anything around or behind that bush but saw a white colored arm bent at the elbow, going up and down and in and out of our view. On each down stroke, as the elbow disappeared from our sight, we heard that same moaning and groaning sound we heard before. It was accompanied by a slight thud each time it disappeared behind the bush.

We ran across the street and hopped the fence as fast as we could. As we came around the other side of the bushes, there was the cop sitting on top of the crackhead, punching him repeatedly at what ever part of his body presented itself as a good target. If it wasn't for being a little winded and pissed off at the guy we probably would have been laughing. We quickly helped to cuff the dude and stand him up straight. He looked bruised and battered but he was conscious and could walk on his own. The cop was fine except for being a little tired from the impromptu workout. We all headed back to the Precinct to find out which cop owned the car this guy was breaking into. Once we found the owner and made a list of what the crackhead took, or tried to take, we booked him for the petty theft at the Precinct.

After it was all over and we were back up in the office, we did start to laugh about the whole incident. The sight of that cop's arm and the sounds the perp made as he got tattooed by punches was an odd thing you just can't forget. It's often that way in police work on many jobs. The odd things stick with you forever and seem like they just happened yesterday. Yet, in between these stand out moments you handle thousands of jobs and incidents which come and go and you would never remember even if someone recounted the incident back to you at a later date.

Lunch time and being in that office was always different after that. We all found ourselves being a little more vigilant about peeking out the window every so often for weeks to come. I would like to believe that the crackhead learned his lesson the hard way and turned over a new leaf. However, the truth is that crack made these perps do things without thinking and created a way of life for them with very little self control. I'm sure that dude did something similar or worse than stealing from a cop's car in the back of a Precinct after he got out of lockup.

50. Batman Almost Strikes Again

For quite a while I was like the jack of all trades in my Precinct I thoroughly enjoyed these years. I was given assignments that no one else wanted or no one was any good at. In reality, it wasn't so much that the other cops weren't any good at it but rather that many cops didn't have the drive to try something new that was out of their comfort zone. I had no problem putting in that extra effort needed to perform some of these tasks. Through hard work and good results, I quickly became known for handling these jobs, getting results and even getting an occasional chance to work out of other Precincts.

Fencing operations were one of the jobs I enjoyed the most. One time I got to dress in character as a perp who was attempting to sell stolen headlights to businesses that would possibly use these items. The main targets would be auto repair shops and auto body repair shops. Like everything else in the world, there is also a market for stolen items. The items in this market are constantly changing to meet the current needs of society. What may be hot or in demand today is obsolete or deemed of little value tomorrow. The very advancements in technology that society enjoys also creates the need on the market. These items tend to run their course and then seem to burnout, or end just as a new item will pick up and begin right where the previous one left off. The perps on the street became facilitators of these needs and did their best to feed the supply. Their crimes created a cycle that can go around and around for a great deal of time before law enforcement can interrupt those criminal activities.

I am dating myself but I remember cable boxes as one of the first items I went around trying to sell to unscrupulous businesses. They were the old style ones with the fake wood look to them. They were among the first type of cable boxes back in the days when there were only a few channels available and people had ways of getting free illegal cable service. All they needed was a box to hookup the free service. Today that need doesn't exist and there are people who wouldn't know or understand that people would buy these items off the street whether they thought they were stolen or not. There was a need for that item and it thrived for a short time.

Another hot item during that time was car headlights. There were particular models that had the headlight unit designed in such a way that they were able to be taken out relatively easy, right on the street, with minimal tools. We had crackheads who would hit one street and remove the headlight units from several cars parked on the same block. In the morning we would get several calls in a row for the stolen headlights. I remember doing patrol, driving down the street and seeing all the cars parked in a row with missing headlights. We knew they had just been stolen that night and we were expecting phone calls in regards to the thefts in the morning when the owners woke up and saw what happened overnight.

As a result, these people will have to replace those units. Some of the owners will go to the dealer and pay top dollar but some people will look for a cheaper method of replacement, like a salvage yard or their local chop shop. Some of these owners were hit more than once and were probably worried about getting hit again in the future. You can't blame them for trying to cut costs on replacement.

Of course, some of the salvage yards were dirty operating as chop shops or taking in stolen parts to resell and make a profit. Evidently, this headlight theft was occurring a little too frequently and the Department wanted to do something about it. That's where I came into the picture.

Prior to this I had done a whole bunch of undercover plainclothes stuff where I had to either buy or sell stolen and illegal items. I had a lot of success and the majority of that success was in my own assigned Precinct. Inevitably, just as a narc detective eventually has to come out of UC work, my time was also coming to an end. I had made a lot of arrests and the streets were beginning to know me a little too well. Soon it would be to the point where either I wouldn't be effective or it could be to risky to try some of the things I had done and gotten away with in the past.

These operations were always more dangerous for several reasons. When you work these operations you really can't wear a bullet proof vest. It shows through too easily. Sometimes, if it's too hot, you can't even take a second gun for back up or a radio because it is too hard to conceal. In these instances you go without those items and work spot to spot with hand signals to the backup team waiting for you somewhere outside or down the block. The backup team would follow you at a distance between these locations. This type of setup obviously makes the work much more risky.

In an effort to give my enforcement duties in my own Precinct a rest but still do what I was good at, the Sarge asked if I would be interested in helping out the neighboring Precinct with a plainclothes operation. He explained it would be in response to the recent headlight dilemma the area was experiencing. Being we didn't have too many auto shops of our own, he felt it would be great to help out the neighboring Precinct which had plenty of them. I loved this work and it sounded like a good plan to me.

I knew going into this operation that we weren't going to get credit for any arrests or any positive enforcement that came as a result of our work. In fact, they told us up front that all data was going to be forwarded to the Auto Crime Division who would follow up on the investigation.

In reality, what we were doing was narrowing down the field of possible suspects for Auto Crime to focus on. From there, they would continue the investigations, using our intel on just the spots where we had positive hits and really clean house. In other words, we would point the finger at the dirty spots and they would lock them up.

What did I care? I loved this work. It was fun and I got to do things no other cops were doing. I was helping another unit to make some unusual collars, got some good OT and gain some great experience in the process.

This particular Precinct I would be working in had a lot of body shops, mechanic repair places and auto parts stores. Some of these places were in areas that were a little shady or in a spot that lent itself to criminal activity. However, you can't go on looks alone. God knows there were plenty of establishments I had been in over the years that looked fine until you got into the kitchen or behind the counter. It's what happens beyond the public areas that count. Once you get past the everyday workings of an establishment, everything can change real fast.

It's for that reason that you have to go through the motions and check each place to see for yourself what is actually going on inside. That's just what we intended to do, check each spot. We had a list of the first three places to check for possible illegal activity. Two were auto repair spots and the last one was a auto body place. I had met with the Sarge who was to be in charge and she seemed nice enough. Next, I met with the unit from the Precinct putting all this together. It's really important to let the uniform or plain clothes cops who will back you up see you in your civilian attire. The last thing you want is for them to mistake you for a perp on the street if the shit hits the fan and you have to draw your gun. I was not trying to get myself shot, especially by another cop.

I was dressed in my best bummy clothes outfit and hadn't shaved for a week or so. I looked as good for the part as possible. The Precinct outfitted me with a heavy duty contractor garbage bag that had three headlight units inside. The headlights were the ones that were being stolen on the current hot list and definitely in demand.

Between the disguise and the garbage bag over my shoulder, I was good to go. We headed out to start the operation. The three places we were going to hit were relatively close together. I was grateful for that, being that the headlight units were not that light and the bag they were in made it seem even heavier, as it was a little hard to carry.

The Sarge decided to give me two back up cops to ghost me from one spot to the other. I had talked with them ahead of time and told them I would be fine going into these spots by myself. I knew I could handle myself, had enough experience to do the job and just needed them to stay outside and just listen for any unusual sounds or 911 calls that may come from the location. Other than that, they were to hang back, wait for me to exit each location and make eye contact in between the spots.

The first spot went pretty quickly, in and out, without anything happening. It didn't seem like the kind of place that would take part in illegal stuff. For a business related to auto repair, it was very clean and very busy. With that many customers, I doubt they would risk getting arrested and jeopardizing what looked like a thriving business. I left that location with no sale. I exited the location, gave a nod to my ghost and walked off to the next spot.

The next spot actually showed promise. It was a little slower, as far as customers were concerned, and much grimier looking. The counter guy looked a little seedy as well. When I approached him about the parts, he seemed interested but told me he couldn't do anything without talking to the boss first. He told me the boss would be back tomorrow and that I should come back then. Since this place seemed promising, we would have to file it as a place to return in the future and try again.

Again, I exited the location and made eye contact with my ghost before heading off to my last spot for the day. This last spot was an auto body repair place. It kind of looked like an oversized garage from the front. It had a big roll down gate that was in the down position and the gate appeared to be locked at the bottom. Next to the gate was a single wood door to enter the location.

Once inside, I saw a few cars that looked like they were in various stages of repair. Way in the back of the location, was what looked like a service counter. I made my way inside and towards the back taking note of the layout as best as I could, looking for anything suspicious. When you do these operations, you try to take in as much as you can. Checking the layout on the way in and remembering as much detail about the establishment is key. If you get a positive hit, you will most likely need a warrant to hit the spot in the future. You definitely want to be able to give the entry team as much information as possible. The type of information you want to remember includes but is not limited to the amount and position of doors, windows or any additional rooms in the building. Aside from that, anything else you can remember will be helpful as well. Basically you try to take in and remember as much as you can.

At the counter, two Spanish guys were talking to each other and although they were speaking Spanish, it seemed that one was a worker and one was the boss. When I got close enough for them to see me, they stopped talking and looked at me.

I asked for the boss and the guy on the right said, "Yeah", in a real quick and nasty tone. I went into my routine, telling him that I had some headlight units for sale and wanted to know if we could make a deal. The price you get for the stolen merchandise doesn't matter. If the guy thinks he's getting a good deal or even if he believes he just ripped you off because he got such a good price, it's fine. The crime involved does not depend on the price of the item or how much the buyer or seller haggles over it. However, the one thing you must absolutely do during the deal is let the buyer know that the items they are about to purchase are stolen. Now, don't misunderstand me, you can't just come out in a super obvious manner and say the items are stolen. You have to remember, you are not a cop in their eyes and you want it to stay that way. If you start talking in civilian/cop mode and not perp mode, you're going to set off this guy's inner alarm and the possible sale is going to go right out the window. You have to say it in a way that it comes across tactfully but clearly as stolen. You have to do it in a way that when it goes to Court you can repeat the way you said it to the Judge or the jury and they will also feel that it was clear these items were stolen and the perp should have known better and not have purchased them.

So, I did my best and truly felt I definitely got my point across that these headlights were stolen. After that, I can tell you without doubt that the guy who ran this shop not only knew they were stolen but absolutely did not buy stolen stuff off the street. How do I know this, you ask? Because the guy became extremely agitated at the realization that the items were stolen and I was trying to sell them, to him, in his shop. I mean he wasn't just mad, he looked like a volcano ready to erupt. He started yelling, screaming and cursing at me in Spanish and English. He started slamming his hand on the top of the desk while he continued to yell and curse. At this point, I closed up the bag and slung it back over my shoulder. It was obvious this guy was running an honest shop and I wasn't getting a sale here. I tried to calm the guy down as I prepared to make my exit. I began to tell the guy it was okay if he didn't want them. I also let him know that all I wanted to do was to leave. At that point the guy reached under the counter and while I feared for the worst, I was very relieved when I saw that it was an aluminum bat in his hand and not a gun or knife. I know that sounds weird to be comforted by seeing something that could just as easily kill you but it did. In my mind, I still had a chance to get out without either identifying myself or pulling out my gun and protecting myself.

I knew this guy was steamed but I have to admit that I didn't think he would grab a weapon. On the inside, I was wondering if my ghosts could hear the ruckus and if they were going to come through the door at any moment. I was also thinking about my way out of this place if that didn't happen and I was on my own. The door to get out was a straight shot backwards but what bothered me was whether or not there were any rooms I passed that may have workers who were coming to see what all the yelling was about. The last thing I needed was some idiot worker who was trying to impress his boss by punching me in the face or jumping me from behind. I also was thinking whether or not this fool would really try to assault me or would he attempt to just hold me for the police as a citizen's arrest. Lastly, what if he does come at me? He could definitely kill me with that bat, no question about it. I would be totally justified in shooting this guy to protect myself but I didn't want that. Especially knowing this guy is nothing more than a stand up guy with a bad temper who was pissed off about stolen parts trying to get peddled in his store.

I didn't say anything but motioned with my hands for him to calm down. I carefully picked up the bag, keeping my eye on him and his worker as well as listening as best as I could for anyone who might be coming up behind me. The two men were still on the other side of the counter and that was comforting. Distance equals safety in this line of work. I slung the bag over my left shoulder with my left arm and I pulled the bag all the way down across my chest so I could conceal the fact that I now had my hand on my gun, which was tucked in my waistband. As I stepped back towards the exit, the two men came around the counter but just stood their ground at that spot. Although I was amped up, I still didn't feel in immediate danger as they stood there with the bat and continued to yell at me, pointing at what seemed like the exit sign and the door behind me.

I slowly back pedaled as I kept my eyes on the two of them. I also glanced around the room quickly, just to make sure I wasn't going to be ambushed. With still no sign of my backup, I continued to walk backwards to the exit and stepped through the door onto the sidewalk. The two men inside never came any further than the public side of the counter and no one else ever came out to the street as well.

Once outside, I looked across the street and saw my two ghosts standing there, looking around trying to be as inconspicuous as possible. They obviously had no clue as to what had just happened inside the location. I quickly walked around the corner, ducked out of sight and radioed the Sarge that the operation was done and that we needed to get picked up at our predetermined meeting place.

Once in our van I gave my notes to the Sarge. She said,"Okay, one for the future and two negatives, right?". She continued, "You feel sure that the first and last place are definitely clean?". "Yeah, pretty sure.", I said. I had decided to keep the incident at the last location to myself. After all, nothing really happened and in reality if everyone did what that guy did, these crackhead assholes wouldn't steal shit because they wouldn't be able to sell it. It would force them to think of something else to steal that might be a little more difficult and perhaps they would get caught instead of getting away with an easy score.

I credit my success and ability to not have that confrontation come to an ugly conclusion on a few things. First, that store owner, although really angry, was really just an upstanding citizen. He wasn't about to commit one crime while avoiding another. Second, my experience and ability not to overreact or panic and make the situation worse. The wrong response in that scenario could definitely have fueled that situation and snowballed it into a tragedy on several counts. A different cop could easily have panicked, drawn his weapon and from there the possibilities are endless and most likely disastrous.

Cops say police work is difficult. Well, undercover police work is not only more difficult but much more dangerous. It definitely calls for the officer to rely much more on his or her own skills, not just for success but for survival.

I didn't let that experience deter me from continuing to work plainclothes or other undercover operations in the future. Instead, I chose to look at this incident just as I have looked at everything I have ever done in my career, a learning experience. I put it down as another notch in my belt, another experience to draw from and one more thing that I can look back on and know that I did it to the best of my ability.

Jargon and Police Terminology

10-4	Radio code for acknowledgement. Tells central dispatch that you received the job or information/radio transmission.
10-13	Radio code for officer who needs assistance.
10-63 or 63	Radio code for meal or going on meal break.
Aided Case	A call for police that is believed to be non-criminal in nature. Usually refers to a call for medical assistance when someone requires medical attention or removal to a hospital.
All Nighter	When a cop goes out drinking from the early evening till after the bar closes.
Brass/ Top Brass	Refers to the high ranking bosses in the Police Department. Usually referring to rank of Inspector or above.
Building Vertical	A directed patrol of a building from the roof to the bottom floor including checking each hallway, staircase and elevator in the entire building.
"Bus"	Another name for an ambulance.
CCRB	Civilian Complaint Review Board.
Central Booking	The area where perps are brought to be processed for a new arrest and then held while awaiting to be

released, bailed out, see a Judge or remanded back to a Correction facility.

Central / Dispatch	The operator who gives out the radio jobs or assignments over the radio.
Chop Shop	A location that accepts stolen automobiles or stolen parts and also cuts stolen cars into parts which can be sold illegally as parts.
Cocobolo	A type of cops night stick used by old timer's. Cocobolo wood is known to be extremely heavy and hard wood.
Collar(s)	Another name for an arrest(s).
C.O.	Abbreviation for Commanding Officer. This is the person in command of the Precinct. Usually the rank of a Captain, Deputy Inspector or Inspector.
C.S.U.	Abbreviation for Crime Scene Unit. The unit that collects and inventories all criminal evidence at a crime scene.
DA or ADA	District Attorney / Assistant District Attorney. An attorney who works for the City/State and draws up the criminal charges against a perp who has been arrested. The DA or ADA later brings that case to Court if necessary.
DUI	Driving under the influence. Usually refers to a drunk driver, not a driver who is high on drugs.
EDP	Emotionally Disturbed Person.
EMS	Emergency Medical Services (ambulance).

ESU	Emergency Service Unit.
ETA	Abbreviation for estimated time of arrival. This term is most frequently used when asking for a "bus" or needing to know how long before the "bus" gets to your location.
ER	Emergency Room (hospital).
Foot Post	A form of patrol where the officer works on foot and is usually given a defined area to patrol or stand at.
Hair Bag	A cop who has an extremely sloppy look or way of doing things. This cop might be fat, out of shape, or dirty in regards to uniform appearance but does not necessarily have a lot of time on the job. Although some hair bags act and may look like they have a lot of time on the job to go with the disheveled appearance, it is not a requirement.
Halfway House	A facility where people with emotional problems or chemical dependencies live in a group setting while they continue to get treatment, attend meetings and get help finding work or learn a trade as they attempt to re-enter society as a normal person.
Harlem Flounder	Also known as a slapper. A flat piece of leather which is shaped like a spoon and has a piece of pliable metal inside from top to bottom. The top end is weighted and is used to strike a person and can cause serious pain and injury.
"House"	Shortened term for referring to the Station House/Precinct.

House Mouse	A cop who is full duty but never leaves the Precinct for patrol duties. A cop assigned to permanent clerical duties inside the Station House or some other police facility. Cops who do patrol and make collars generally dislike House Mouses.
ICO	Abbreviation for Integrity Control Officer. Every Precinct has one and it is usually the rank of a Lieutenant that holds the position. The ICO is the supervisor who handles a great deal of the disciplinary action the officers in his command are subject to.
Jammed Up	When a cop gets into trouble for something he/she did wrong either on the job while performing his/her duties or something from his/her personal life while at home. These incidents usually lead to disciplinary action.
Mace	A chemical agent in a spray form, used as a less lethal device to subdue a perp. Mace was later replaced by Pepper Spray which has the same effects with less risk of damaging the person's eyes.
Nocs	Abbreviation for binoculars.
NSU	Abbreviation for Neighborhood Stabilization Unit. This was a unit where rookies where assigned when they came out of the Police Academy. Although they reported to one Precinct in particular, they would rotate and service three to four Precincts in one given area on a daily basis. Later this was changed from NSU to FTU (Field Training Unit) where they would now be assigned and service one

Precinct on a permanent basis without rotation to any other Precincts.

Old Timer	A veteran of the Police Department with significant time on the job. Generally around or over twenty years on the job.
O.T.	Abbreviation for Overtime. Work that extends past your scheduled tour and gives you a higher pay rate for those hours.
PCP/ Angel dust	Phencyclidine, a highly addictive and dangerous drug.
Perp	Short for perpetrator, means any criminal.
Riker's Island	An island located between NY and Queens where Riker's Island Correctional Facility is located.
"Scholarship"	A cop who is sent to an undesirable Precinct or assignment because he/she is in trouble or is being disciplined for doing something wrong. A cop in this situation is said to have a "scholarship" to that Precinct. Cops will say, "that cop is here on a scholarship.".
Scripts	An abbreviation for prescriptions. Referring to the actual paper prescription pad a doctor would write and give to a patient for prescribed medications.
"Set"	The immediate area surrounding the location of a street dealers operation.
Skell or Skelly	A dirtbag, a loser, a perp, a dirty person, or criminal. A run down place or apartment can also be referred to as skelly.

Subway Vertical	A directed patrol of the subway, platform, token/metro card booth and the immediate area surrounding the subway station.
Taser	A less lethal device which shoots two hooks or barbs into a person that are connected to wires which run back to the taser. The operator of the taser can then engage the taser by pulling the trigger and shock the perp into submission. These tasers can also be used by just making contact with the individual instead of or in lieu of using the dart system.
Tour/ Tour of Duty	A particular shift a cop works. A day tour, night tour or midnight tour are the three basic tours a cop can work.
U.C.	Abbreviation for Undercover officer or type of assignment.
Volun-told	An assignment the boss tells you to do but may make it seem like you had a choice or volunteered to do the job.
Zip Gun	A homemade gun made from metal tubing and a spring/latch mechanism. Generally able to fire one small caliber round of ammunition at a time.
"Zips"	A cop that does absolutely zero in the eyes of his/her fellow cops. Usually a House Mouse but can also be a lazy patrol cop.

Authors Bio

Tony's police career started in 1989 when he joined the New York City Police Cadet Program as part of a college internship the New York City Police Department was conducting. In 1990, as part of the "Safe Streets, Safe City Act", then Mayor David Dinkins began hiring large numbers of cops to replenish the depleted force from years past in an attempt to get the rank and file over the 30,000 mark.

Eager to become a police officer, Tony dropped out of college and the intern program and entered the Police Academy in 1990 as a recruit in one of the largest classes in the history of the NYPD.

After completion of the Police Academy, Tony was assigned to the 28th Precinct in Harlem. After years on patrol, experiencing each tour of duty available, he went to the Community Policing Unit where he found his niche and excelled at his work, becoming one of the most active cops in the Precinct and getting involved in as many different aspects of police work the Precinct could offer.

As a result of his work ethic, arrest record and willingness to take on assignments, he was promoted to the rank of Detective in 1999. He remained in the 28th Precinct continuing the work at the precinct level doing the work he thoroughly enjoyed and taking on additional responsibilities and assignments.

Throughout the first ten years of his career, along with being promoted, he went back to college and finished his undergraduate degree in Criminal Justice and Criminal Law, earning a Bachelor of Science degree from John Jay College of Criminal Justice in NYC. He continued to go to school, enrolling in a Masters Program for Early Childhood and Elementary Education at The College of New Rochelle.

Tony continued to work in the 28th Precinct and took on even more assignments, constantly attempting to do the best he could, while using his experience to help both rookie and veteran cops who needed his help.

Having a desire to teach, Tony attended a Police Academy course for instruction and training and taught classes from time to time on various subject matters where he had become an expert, such as fencing operations and traffic courtroom testimony.

Although he taught veteran, in-service officers in the Academy, he found helping rookie police officers much more rewarding. In the last three years of his career he accepted a Precinct assignment as Senior Field Training

Officer where he was able to work side-by-side in a hands-on training program teaching and developing newly appointed police officers. In this assignment, he was given the freedom to teach these new recruits in both the classroom and on the street in the way he thought was best. Tony enjoyed these years of his career the best because he helped develop a lot of good young cops and made many great friendships while working closely with this group of newly appointed police officers.

In his twenty plus years as a cop and a detective, Tony never took a single sick day and always tried to do his best. His only goal was to be able to walk away with the respect and admiration of his peers and bosses. Tony always strived to give the job his all and wanted to go out on top, leaving everything he had on the street before he left the job. Tony retired in 2011 and left the job with over 1,100 arrests.

Tony is married, has three children and currently works part time. He now puts his efforts back into his family life, trying to make up for a lot of time lost, during the twenty plus years that he dedicated himself, serving the City, doing a job he truly loved.

70221211R00133

Made in the USA
Middletown, DE
12 April 2018